Jury Woman

Jury Woman

The story of the trial of Angela Y. Davis
—written by a member of the jury

Mary Timothy

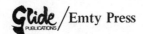 /Emty Press

Alternative cataloging-in-publication

Timothy, Mary.
    Jury woman; the story of the trial of Angela
Y. Davis—written by a member of the jury.

    Revision of the 1974 Emty Press edition.

    1. Davis, Angela Y., 1944— 2. Jackson,
George, L., 1941-1971. 3. Jackson, Jonathan.
4. Trials—California. 5. Jury reform. I. Title.
II. Title: The trial of Angela Y. Davis.

                        347.730753

Jury Woman was first published in a limited edition by Emty Press, Palo Alto, California. This edition is a copublishing venture of Glide Publications and Emty Press.

Order directly from:

Glide Publications
330 Ellis Street
San Francisco, California 94102

$4.95 paperback
Please add $.50 for postage and handling.

Back cover photograph: Nancy Wehner

Design and composition: Zoe Brown

Production: David Charlsen/Charlsen + Johansen & Others

All trial quotations are from the official court transcript of *People of the State of California v. Angela Y. Davis.*

To Margaret Crowley Middleton

Contents

Introduction

> Angela Davis is a woman; she is black; she has espoused an unpopular political cause. We believe that equal rights under the law must be guaranteed to every person—regardless of their race, creed or sex. Angela Davis is uniquely subject to possible discrimination in each one of those categories.
>
> Because of NOW's commitment to *equal rights for all,* we call on the courts of this country to guarantee Angela Davis a fair and just trial as is her right under the Constitution of the United States.

On January 16, 1971, the Board of Directors of the National Organization for Women, meeting in Houston, Texas, adopted the preceding statement by a unanimous vote. As National President of NOW at the time and a resident of San Francisco, I journeyed to the Marin County jail, endured the humiliating security checks required for all visitors, and finally came face to face with Angela Davis in a small anteroom. She was mildly curious, but gracefully appreciative, as she read NOW's full statement calling on the courts to assure her a fair trial. She—a Black woman and a Communist—must have been surprised to receive the unsolicited support of the "women's lib" organization usually—if not totally accurately—referred to as white, middleclass and conservative. And to receive the statement from the Black president of NOW must have been confusing! We did not talk about her case. I told her the statement had been proposed by the Atlanta NOW chapter and drafted by the Houston chapter; she talked about the sexist conditions in the jail—the double standard for male and female prisoners. And then the brief visit was over.

As I left the beautiful Frank Lloyd Wright-designed Marin County building, I remember having grave doubts that Ms. Davis would get a fair trial— in spite of NOW's statement of support! Where would the court find a jury of twelve people who had not been influenced by the public furor over Ms. Davis' Communist beliefs, for which she had been fired by the University of California? Where in the *state,* much less in the county which was the "scene of the crime," could she be assured of her constitutional "right to a speedy and public trial, by an impartial jury? " The possibilities seemed nil.

More than a year after my visit, Angela Davis finally went to trial in Santa Clara County, through a change of venue granted by the courts. When the newspaper accounts of the trial emphasized that *no* Blacks sat on the jury, the triple jeopardy of Angela's being Black, female and Communist seemed overwhelming barriers for that jury to hurdle. *Jury Woman* takes us into personal contact with one of those jurors, Mary Timothy, and the encounter suggests the importance of reform in the jury system. Though she never for a moment suggests it herself, Ms. Timothy was no run-of-the-mill juror. To paraphrase a well-known advertisement, "she cared enough to do her very best." And that's not easy!

The responsibilities *and* rights of a jury member should be a required course of study for all registered voters, but it isn't. A person selected to judge the guilt or innocence of an individual accused of a crime is performing one of the most important—and one of the most difficult—duties of citizenship, and yet, as Ms. Timothy points out in her account of her service on the Angela Davis jury, jurors are *not* prepared for their sensitive task. They are left to stumble through the legal and procedural maze of jury duty, with only minimal instruction by the court. Ms. Timothy, as a juror, was daring (she risked censure by taking notes); she was conscientious (she researched the duties of jurors at the Palo Alto library during a jury break); she was an educator (she shared her new-found knowledge with her co-jurors); she was analytical (she developed a chronology of the Angela Davis / Jonathan Jackson activities that persuaded her that the prosecution had not proved, beyond a reasonable doubt, the charges against Angela Davis); she showed leadership (when selected to head the jury, she had a plan of action which moved the jury logically and speedily to a decision).

Jury Woman should be must reading for all persons who register to vote and thereby (in many states) become eligible for jury duty; it should be must reading for people concerned with improving our system of justice. Ms. Timothy finds the flaws in the system and makes some thoughtful and reasonable recommendations for change. She also gives a highly personalized account of her own reactions to serving on one of the most publicized cases in recent years and gives us a compassionate juror's-eye view of the "players" in the courtroom drama that had worldwide significance.

And, in the end, we see very clearly the need to correct the flaws in the jury system—to ensure its impartiality, to draw from a broader base of the population in selecting jurors, to train prospective jurors, to equalize the sacrifice of jury duty by a more adequate compensation for jury service, and to protect the privacy of jurors. Those who attack the jury trial might well remember the admonition of Winston Churchill in assessing democracy as the "worst system, except for all the others."

Mary Timothy's book is a compelling look at a system described by William Blackstone two centuries ago as "the great glory of English law" and "the grand bulwark of every (citizen's) liberties." Jury power may be the last line of defense by the people in a society increasingly run by "the experts."

Aileen C. Hernandez
Former National President of NOW

San Francisco
August, 1975

The Jury

Do You Know the Way . . . ?

"John! Guess what? I've been called for the jury panel for the Angela Davis trial!"

My son looked at me in complete amazement. "I don't believe it. You?" He turned to his sister laughing. "Say, the system must be honest if Mom got called."

He was teasing me and I got defensive. "What do you mean by that? Don't you think I'd be a good juror?"

"I think you'd be a great juror. But you're so nonpolitical and uninvolved I don't think either side would want you. There's no reason for you to be on the panel . . . unless it were purely by chance."

Like many people, John had a cautious mistrust of our government processes but was enough of an idealist to be pleased when any part seemed to be functioning as it should.

On the other hand, I usually assume that people are honest and I tend to depend on the trustworthiness of institutions. I had never questioned the method of selecting jurors, nor would it ever have occurred to me that the process might be manipulated to give advantage to one side.

For the first time, I began to wonder. Even though the mechanics of selection were fair, the ultimate selection of the jurors could still be affected by subtle influences—and the composition of the jury might affect the outcome of the trial.

How did I happen to be called? I was a registered voter in Santa Clara County, State of California—it was that simple.

We had moved there in August, 1969, from the agricultural San Joaquin Valley. My husband had worked in the public school system as a teacher and administrator, studying law at night. After passing the bar examination, he practiced on a part-time basis. I returned to college about that time, taking an undergraduate pre-med course. I had hoped to get into medical school, despite the fact that I was a woman, over forty, and not a very good student.

After graduation I was lucky enough to get a job at Stanford University working in medical research. My husband retired from the public school system; we moved to Palo Alto, and he opened a law office. We registered to vote.

I was busy decorating the house in preparation for the Christmas holidays when I received in the mail a card from the Office of the Jury Commissioner, County of Santa Clara. The questionnaire on the card was similar to that on a job application—age, length of residence in county, occupation, employer, condition of hearing and eyesight, ability to read and write and understand English, the number of small children at home and the care provided them.

On the back of the card the questions were more specific and personal, asking about "mental or physical disability," "ill dependents," "conviction of a felony." The card also asked whether I had served as a grand or trial juror in the county during the last three years. Apparently, having served recently would make one unacceptable for the new list. And it asked, "If, under the law, you are entitled to an occupational exemption from jury duty, do you wish to claim it?"

I flipped the card back and forth trying to find a list of exempt occupations. They weren't identified. I was tempted

to ignore the card and toss it away with the junk mail, but I
quickly marked the proper squares, dropped it in the mailbox
and promptly forgot all about it.

About a month later I received in the mail a Jury Summons.
It sounded very definite and a little grim:

PLEASE NOTE

A juror shall not be excused by a court for slight or trivial causes, or for hardship or for inconvenience to said jur-
or's business, but only when material injury or destruction
to said juror's property or of property entrusted to said
juror is threatened or when juror's health or when the
health or proper care of said juror's own family or when
the sickness or death of a member of said juror's family
make it necessary for said juror to be excused.

I continued reading the card which notified me that I had
been regularly drawn for jury duty for the ensuing year, the
exact date and hour to be specified by further order of the court.

Just below the PLEASE NOTE paragraph, another in equally
bold-faced type explained that this summons could be used as
a parking permit at the lot across the street from the courthouse. It struck me as ironic that such a formal summons
would double as a parking permit.

Along with the summons, the Jury Commissioner sent a book-
let entitled *Juror's Handbook,* which gave a brief history of the
jury system and a description of how a jury is selected.

In this county of California the jury list is made up from the
voter registration sheets. The procedures, the people involved,
the terms used in a trial, and the duties of a juror were discussed.
It seemed to be an excellent pamphlet and I checked to see who
had written it. The judges of the Superior Court of Santa Clara
County had prepared it—surely they would be very knowledgeable
about what a person needed to know in order to serve on a jury.

The pamphlet concluded with the statement:

> Jury service is one of the most vital functions of a citizenship. It is the most important duty of a citizen of the United States, *next to fighting in the defense of one's country*. (emphasis mine)

That seemed to me a strange way of equating the value of jury duty, one which didn't fit too well with my own philosophy. I would have said that actively working for peace was the most important duty of a citizen. I must admit, however, I had never thought seriously about the importance of serving on a jury, although I knew it was an act of a good citizen—like voting, obeying laws, paying taxes. Whether one thought jury duty important or not, it was something that had to be done.

The average citizen seldom has the opportunity to participate at the decision-making level in any branch of our government. We can vote or sign petitions, but these acts are usually far removed from the final results. Whenever I had heard of friends being called for jury duty, I had always been a little envious, thinking they were getting a chance to experience something new and interesting—a deeper level of participation.

I had read about Angela Davis' being fired from UCLA in 1969 for being a Communist. My reaction at that time was one of mild amazement that Communist Party alliance would still be considered cause for dismissal from a university, but I accepted her firing with no more than a shake of my head.

When the courts ruled her membership in the Communist Party was not grounds for dismissing her, I read about it and was satisfied that the ruling made sense. But I was not personally concerned.

When she was fired for the second time on the pretext of "unprofessional conduct" because of speaking at rallies, I felt that the real reason still was her Communist affiliation. I was embarrassed as a citizen of California that this subterfuge was used, but the incident was not really important to me. I didn't feel personally involved.

But a similar incident had been very important to me when I was a student in college in 1939. An excellent teacher in social studies was fired from the junior college I was attending, not because he was a Communist, but because it was suspected that his wife was. Since she was employed by the federal government, the local town officials could not fire her. But they managed to have her husband dismissed in an attempt to drive the couple from the area.

Many of us students were very upset. We called for a mass meeting of the student body in the school auditorium, to be followed by a protest march down the main street to the center of town.

While we were getting organized and making placards and calling the press, another coalition was forming. The school president, the mayor and some of the parents were contacting each of the leaders individually. They warned us that we would not be allowed to continue in school anywhere in California and would be "blackballed" and unable to obtain employment anywhere in the state. Remember, we were still in the Depression. Most of the students involved were without any income, and were living at home with their families, who were making great sacrifices to send them to school.

The protest strike was broken and I got my introduction to power politics. When Angela Davis was fired for the second time, I was reminded of that situation thirty years before. But still I wasn't personally involved, and I didn't think it would affect my life.

I recall next reading about Angela Davis shortly after an escape attempt in Marin County in which a judge had been killed. Guns used in the escape attempt had been identified as belonging to her. She disappeared and was found a couple of months later in New York. Stories of her extradition to California were in all the papers.

I don't remember anything else until the announcement in the local paper that her trial had been transferred to Santa Clara

County. The location of the trial was discussed—would it be held in the county seat, San Jose, or in Palo Alto, where I lived?

My phone rang at work on Wednesday, February 23, 1972. A man's voice asked me to identify myself. "Are you Mary M. Timothy who lives at 840 Moreno Avenue in Palo Alto?"

I hesitated. A salesman? No, he sounded too official. Had I parked in a restricted area this morning?

I admitted that I was Mary Timothy and the voice informed me that I was to report to the Superior Court Building, Criminal Division, on Monday morning at 8:30 for jury duty. I could park across the street in a section of the parking lot reserved for jurors. I should leave my summons on the dashboard in plain sight, and I should also keep track of the mileage from home. I hung up the phone and stared at it. I had been too surprised to ask any questions. I looked at the notes I had made: "Monday morning. . . . Feb. 18th . . . 8:30 . . . Superior Court."

I had been summoned for jury duty!

"Do you know when the Davis trial is going to start? Is it Monday? I just got called for jury duty for Monday."

My co-worker didn't know; she thought it was an exciting possibility. But, she added, ". . . if it is, the Chief won't like it. That trial might last for months. He isn't going to be very happy about one of his staff being called away from work for a long period of time. What'll you do? Will you try to get out of serving?"

Get out of serving? The thought hadn't crossed my mind. Even if I didn't take the civic responsibility seriously myself, I was the mother of three children. What kind of an example would I be setting if I tried to wriggle out of jury duty? I just couldn't do that.

Yet she was right. It wasn't going to be easy to explain to the senior investigator of our National Institute of Health-sponsored research project that jury duty took precedence over my work.

I liked my job and didn't want to lose it. The work was

interesting and challenging, though some mornings I felt as though
I were one of the worker bees entering the hive as I approached
the Stanford Medical Center. But once inside, the routine of the
investigative procedures absorbed my attention.

A disadvantage of that absorption is that it tends to isolate
one. With so little contact with people outside of the Center, it
is difficult to maintain objectivity in evaluating the importance
of our work. Many of us become so involved in the details of the
work we are doing that the circles of our interests become pro-
gressively smaller and we lose touch with what is happening in
the rest of the world.

Well, I could not worry about my job. The summons probably
had nothing to do with the Angela Davis trial; if it did, the odds
were against my being picked for the jury. I decided to ignore
this issue at work and hope it would resolve itself.

No problem arose at home. Everyone in the family gave complete support. My husband, Art, being more informed than I,
wasn't too excited. He thought I would never be selected since,
almost axiomatically, wives and daughters of attorneys are excused by peremptory challenge.

"What do you mean? Do you mean trial lawyers assume that
attorneys' wives and daughters can't think for themselves? That's
awful!"

"Right or wrong, that's the way it usually works. If you're a
defense attorney, you don't want the wife of the D.A. sitting
on the jury—or the other way around."

Art was being pragmatic about the whole thing, but I wasn't
willing to accept this practice, which was something which could
affect me directly.

"Well, I just hope it comes up in the questioning. I'd like to
make a public statement about how I feel about that!"

I asked Art about another issue which might arise. I had decided years ago that I could never participate in any trial that
might have an execution as its ultimate end. The death penalty
had been declared unconstitutional in California—just one week
before. I needed to know whether any possibility existed that

the ruling would be overturned. If so, would it affect a trial already in progress?

He reassured me that it wasn't likely to happen and, even if it did, I could ask to discuss it with the judge if I were concerned about it.

What should I wear to court? Most California courts have no restrictions as to attire. A few years ago it would have been necessary to wear "proper" clothing for court—coats and ties for the men and dresses for the women. A person would have been thrown out of court for appearing in informal clothes and might have been cited for contempt. But all that had changed, so I needn't worry on that score. I just wanted to present myself to the court as I really was.

At work I wore pantsuits almost exclusively. Would pantsuits at a time like this really represent the "true" me? Though that was what I usually wore, I felt myself to be more a conservative-suit-and-low-heels type. I didn't want to go into court on Monday morning and have the attorneys look at me and miscategorize me.

What *was* my category, anyhow? I tried to think of what role I fit into in today's society.

I had a job, a husband and three children. John, twenty-seven, was a piano player; Ellen, twenty-four, was a graduate student; sixteen-year-old Laura was in high school and the only one still living at home.

Politically, I had been a Democrat since the summer of 1952, when Richard Nixon successfully took over the Republican Party of California in his maneuverings to obtain the vice-presidential nomination under Dwight Eisenhower. In recent years, as my distress over the war in Southeast Asia increased, I found I was aligning myself with the liberal wing of the Democratic Party.

Socially and morally, I was fairly conservative—by the standards of the day. I had been raised strictly in a middle-class, small-town environment as a Catholic and I accepted the mores of that time and place. I like people on a one-to-one basis; I do not like organizations and clubs. I am not a "joiner."

I was just becoming aware of the women's movement. I had not yet read *The Feminine Mystique,* by Betty Friedan. But I did have a copy of the preview issue of *Ms.* magazine and was very excited about some of the ideas expressed in it.

So, in an effort to stereotype myself, I decided I would wear a tailored cashmere suit and flat walking shoes.

That settled, Art had a suggestion. "You'd better take something to read. Like any other bureaucratic situation, there will be a lot of waiting around involved."

At the bookstore, as I looked at the titles of some of the new books, I found most of them politically oriented. I searched for something neutral and finally chose William Saroyan's *The Bicycle Rider in Beverly Hills,* and Sean O'Casey's *Drums Under the Window.* Saroyan wrote about people and places in California that I was familiar with; I looked forward to renewing my acquaintance with him. In the other book, O'Casey's opening paragraph read, "Pug-faced pleasant-hearted George Middleton . . . ." My mother was Irish and my father's name was George Middleton. The temptation to read what an Irish poet wrote about someone of that name was too great to resist.

Monday morning, with my big purse stuffed with food for lunch and the books and wearing my conservative suit, I got in the station wagon and headed for the Civic Center in San Jose —about fifteen miles to the south.

Half an hour later, when I found the parking lot across the street from the Superior Court Building and pulled in, all the slots reserved for jurors had been filled. Either I was late, or everyone else had arrived early. I headed for the front of the building. No one was waiting there and the door was locked. I stepped back and looked around. A sign on the door gave instructions to go around to the other side of the building. I walked quickly and found other people in a slow-moving line extending out and meandering through a courtyard. I joined the line after making sure that those in front of me had also received jury summonses.

I was glad I had worn walking shoes. Thirty or forty people were in front of me, the line moved very slowly. As I finally approached the entrance, I saw what was causing the delay. Each person was being subjected to a search.

As people entered, they were stopped, told to set packages and purses and the metal contents of all their pockets—including keys, coins and even foil-wrapped cigarette packs—into one of two plastic bins on a table to the right of the door. They were then instructed to step through a metal detector—a carpeted ramp through a flimsy metal archway. This archway emitted atonal beeps if any metal object was on the person—even metal arch supporters in shoes.

Two deputies with hand detectors conducted more careful searches when the arch rejected a person. Behind the table sat two sheriff's matrons who searched quickly through personal belongings and removed anything considered a possible weapon, such as a nail file or sewing scissors.

Some of the people made a joke of it, but most of us were irritated. Americans are not used to being subjected to search. I would have felt much better about it if we had been forewarned so I could have decided myself what I wished to bring for public scrutiny.

Only after passing through the arch without making it cry out were we admitted, allowed to collect our possessions from the plastic basins and directed up the stairs to the "Jury Assembly Room."

We entered a large meeting hall filled with rows and rows of folding chairs. Windows flanked the right-hand side and a windowed partition separated us from a similar room on the left side. The room was light and open.

Two television monitors stood near the windows and in the front of the room were a couple of desks. A deputy sheriff, festooned with badge, gun and walkie-talkie, sat behind one. The other was used by a middle-aged female bureaucrat who seemed to be in charge. I could see an adjoining room—smaller and unfurnished—through an archway behind the desks.

The chairs gradually filled as the prospective jurors slowly made their way through the search area. One hundred fifty people had been summoned. One hundred sixteen showed up. The others had been excused.

Upon entering, each person would look quickly around the room, choose an empty chair and establish personal territory by moving the chair a little to the right or left, jiggling it up and down, setting books or papers or purses on the floor beneath it. After settling into this tiny space, the person would turn and smile tentatively at neighboring people.

Strangely enough, these seats became as much ours as if we had been assigned them by someone in authority. On the second or third day, those who found their chairs filled before they arrived were obviously disturbed, some to the point of standing and staring down until the interloper moved.

Roll was called by the woman at the desk. She combined the officious behavior of a government bureaucrat with the ingratiating good manners of a middle-aged office worker as she instructed us to indicate our presence by giving the mileage from our homes to court.

Darn! I had forgotten to check the mileage. Everyone else seemed to have done it; the numbers were being called out— four, twenty-two, eight . . . . I decided to fake it. The names were listed at random, so I listened carefully for my own. When it was called, I guessed at the mileage. "Twenty miles," I called out loud and clear. (When I checked and found I was five miles over, I made the correction the next day—much to the clerk's annoyance.)

I looked around the room at the people. They appeared to me to be a fair cross section of the county. The people of this area are varied: university professors and migrant farm laborers, space and electronics engineers and cannery workers, industrial laborers and small businessmen. Racially, they are mixed, the vast majority being white, but with 0.4 percent American Indian, 18 percent Chicano, 1.8 percent Asian, and 1.7 percent black people.

I was surprised at the high percentage of young people in the room, until I realized that eighteen- to twenty-year-olds were being called for the first time. They were now legally adults and were registering to vote.

The male-female ratio seemed even. The group looked like a fair representation of citizens from which to draw the jurors for a trial.

After roll call was repeated four or five times to pick up the stragglers, we were informed that we were in fact the "lucky citizens" who had been drawn for the Angela Davis trial.

This announcement was a great equalizer. We turned to one another with subdued murmurs. I could hear: "My baby is only five weeks old . . . ." "Oh, God! Finals are next week . . . ." "I can't lose that much pay . . . ." "How long will it last?" "How long . . . How long . . . ?"

Recent similar trials had lasted for months. The jury on the Manson case had been sequestered for nine and a half months. The enormity of perhaps having to serve on a jury for months really shook us up. It's not too hard to serve for a couple of days or a week—but this trial might last for five or six months.

Still I felt there wasn't much chance I would be picked. With 116 people to choose from, the odds were at least 10:1 that I wouldn't be one of the final twelve.

The official explanations were continuing. Since the building had no courtroom large enough to accommodate such a large group, all court procedures would be brought to us by closed-circuit television. We were to comport ourselves as though we were actually in court.

The television sets were turned on. The room quieted down. Court was convened and we were greeted by Judge Richard Arnason.

We all sat looking intently at the screen. Was she there? Was that Angela Davis sitting over in the right-hand corner of the screen? The woman looked like her but we couldn't be sure. The picture was black and white, the lighting was only adequate.

The camera was located in the rear of the courtroom, so we could see most of the court but not the spectator section; no closeups were shown and no instant replays.

Judge Arnason instructed the clerk of the court to draw the first twelve names. The clerk was sitting directly in front of and below the judge. He had a squirrel cage on his table. He cranked the handle and rotated the cage, round and round and round, then opened the top and pulled out twelve names—one at a time. The first twelve people had been called. I wasn't one of them.

They got up from their seats, walked to the front of the room, identified themselves to a deputy, and then the whole group followed the officer out the back door—reappearing seconds later on the television screen. We watched them file into the jury box and take their seats.

All the prospective jurors were asked to stand—those in the jury box and those of us still up in the assembly room.

We rose, faced the television sets and raised our right hands while the clerk read the oath, swearing us in as the jury panel.

That was really a strange scene: a room full of people pledging to uphold the law of the land and the rules of the court— to a TV set.

Judge Arnason introduced Angela Davis (yes, that was she on the corner of the screen), her attorneys and the two prosecuting attorneys. We couldn't see their faces, but were to become familiar with their voices and mannerisms as we watched them on the tube.

The clerk of the court read the three counts of the indictment against Angela Y. Davis.

First count, Kidnapping—on or about August 7, 1970, at and in the County of Marin, State of California, the said defendant did forceably take Judge Harold Joseph Haley, Gary M. Thomas, Maria Graham, Joyce Redoni and Doris Wittner, and carry them from one place in Marin County to another place in Marin County, with the intent to hold said hostages for ransom, reward or extortion.

Second count, Murder—the said defendant did murder a human being, to wit: Judge Harold J. Haley.

Third count, Conspiracy—Angela Y. Davis is further accused of a conspiracy in that she and Jonathan Jackson, now deceased, did conspire, combine, confederate and agree together to willfully, knowingly commit the kidnapping and murder, and the escape of James McClain and other prisoners, and the rescue of the prisoners George Lester Jackson, Fleeta Drumgo and John Cluchette—"The Soledad Brothers"—from San Quentin.

There followed a listing of thirteen "overt acts," which included a rally in support of the Soledad Brothers, the purchase of guns and ammunition, visits to San Quentin with Jonathan Jackson (the seventeen-year-old brother of George Jackson), and her flight from the San Francisco airport on the afternoon of August 7, 1970.

The indictment was even more detailed than I have indicated. I couldn't absorb it all from that one reading. But I understood that three counts were held against the defendant: Kidnapping, Murder and Conspiracy.

Judge Arnason turned to the jury and explained that Angela Davis was charged with these three counts and that she had pleaded not guilty to those charges. By the rules of our courts, she was presumed to be innocent until the prosecution proved beyond reasonable doubt that she was guilty as charged. He defined "reasonable doubt" as not merely possible doubt, but as "no feeling of an abiding conviction to a moral certainty of the truth of the charge."

Albert Harris, Jr., the Assistant Attorney General of the State of California, the prosecutor of the case, then read a list of 104 witnesses he planned to call. If we knew any of the people on that list, we were to inform the judge. I didn't recognize any of the names.

Each of the twelve prospective jurors was asked to give a brief biographical sketch, including any friendships with law-enforcement people, any crimes committed against the juror and any previous jury service. When all twelve had introduced themselves thusly, Judge Arnason announced that each juror would now be interviewed singly. All but one of the jurors in the box would be taken to another room, the television sets would be turned off, and one juror at a time would be left for preliminary questioning.

The TV sets went blank. We started the first of a series of waits. The chairs became more and more uncomfortable; the air became hot and smoky; boredom set in. We started making little overtures of friendliness to the people around us.

I was sitting between a hospital nurse about forty years old, very neat, quiet and controlled; and a student at San Jose State University who had brought his books and was concerned about the amount of time he would lose from school.

In front of us was a small, quiet, well-dressed man reading a Spanish paperback version of *The Saffron Robe*.

As the tedium increased, the movement around the room increased. Some people seemed to adapt very easily to the confinement and the sitting. Others were restless and seemed to find it very difficult to sit all day.

By 3:30 that afternoon, we were all hot, tired and uncomfortable. All at once the television sets stuttered on. The jury box now had three empty seats.

We had sat there for a whole day and only three of the 116 veniremen had been questioned and dismissed. At this rate, a person could be left sitting up in the assembly room for weeks!

That's just what happened to me. For two weeks I sat and waited while others were called down, questioned and dismissed.

Two Weeks of Waiting

That first day had been a pretty fair introduction to what was to be the hardest part of being a juror in this long involved trial —the waiting.

Every morning for two weeks I drove to San Jose. The sense

of anticipation and excitement I had felt originally faded during those two weeks. All of the procedures became routine, even the daily indignity of being searched. I learned to carry nothing metal in my pockets and to wear no jewelry. I had my keys and coins in my hand as I hit the door, dropping them into the basins along with purse and books—all in one motion.

I climbed the stairs, stopped at the vending machine for a cup of coffee, went directly to "my" chair, greeted my neighbors and waited for roll call.

Once roll had been taken, those of us remaining in the assembly room were ignored by everyone—except for brief intervals when the TV came on and we could watch the questioning of someone in the jury box or when another name was plucked from the squirrel cage.

This trial was called the "trial of the century" and we had been selected from the hundreds of thousands of residents in the county. We had come to the courthouse full of excitement and ready for our moment of glory. Now we were stuck in a hall on uncomfortable folding chairs—and ignored. We felt no glory. We felt no excitement. We felt nothing but complete and utter boredom.

The lottery of the drawing for the next juror became terribly important. As the cage whirled, the suspense was intense—the announcement of the name was followed by low moans of disappointment, then words of encouragement for the holder of the lucky number.

One young woman, after reporting in the morning, slipped out to take care of personal business right after roll call. Her name was the next one called. When she couldn't be located, the judge issued a warrant for her arrest!

That incident impressed us all.

We had been told no excuses would be considered until we were actually in the jury box and could be questioned by the judge and attorneys. Even medical excuses would not be accepted unless they were supported by a letter from a doctor.

As the days passed and it became obvious that the wait before many of the veniremen were called down might be very long, the restrictions were eased. First the students heard a rumor that they could be excused if they brought letters from the heads of their departments. It was the last week before finals for the winter quarter. If the trial went on for six to eight months, they would lose a year's work if they served on the jury. While the lost time was important, a break in attendance at college would result in loss of financial aid for many of them, which was even more important.

No official notice was given, but the rumor spread. The next morning most of the young people were lined up at the front desk with letters in their hands. They were soon on their way back to school.

As the initial excitement gave way to the inevitable boredom, people found all sorts of compelling reasons why it would be impossible for them to serve. Medical excuses were coming in more and more frequently as time dragged on and the chairs got harder. All the aches and pains that had been ignored the first day now were discussed freely; the disabilities people had considered too minor to mention on the cards they filled out for the Jury Commissioner now assumed major importance. The flu bug hit; its victims joined the others in checking with their doctors.

The people in the room would be perfectly quiet as we sat waiting. Suddenly someone would stand up, walk to the front and confer with the woman at the desk. After a few sentences, the person would come back and sit tensely waiting until the next break—then head for the telephone. That might be the last we would see of the reluctant jury panel member.

The next group to leave were the workers. Those whose income depended on day-to-day employment were allowed to present evidence to show that remaining on the panel would cause them undue hardship. The self-employed and those who worked for small concerns would have suffered great financial loss if the trial lasted for many months.

Over forty people disappeared without ever being called down to court. The group remaining was far more homogeneous than the original 116. The students had gone, as had the workers, the poor, the old and the weak. Those remaining were largely middle-aged, middle-class people employed by the large industries of the area—industries large enough to absorb the financial loss of an employee's long absence.

Not all large companies, however, had a policy of continuing salary for employees while they served on juries. The Southern Pacific Railroad informed an employee of thirty years that he would be paid for two weeks, but no longer. Yet a local department store allowed a salesperson hired just two weeks before the trial to serve without loss of salary. No set pattern was clear, but it seemed to me that workers belonging to strong unions, such as the Retail Clerks Union, were guaranteed no loss of job, salary or seniority.

Economics had a great deal to do with the composition of the jury.

With this early exodus, most of the minorities also disappeared. The two black members had gone. One was selected in the first drawing and was down sitting in the jury box. The other, a well-dressed woman with children in school, was excused when one child got the flu. I had the feeling that she didn't want to be identified with the case—and was glad to have a legitimate excuse to leave.

Thirty more people were released after their preliminary questioning in these first two weeks. We didn't know why so many were being let off the jury since the television sets were turned off during this time.

I found out later that the individual private questioning dealt with the personal problems of the prospective jurors—their health or financial difficulties which might interfere with their ability to serve through a long and difficult trial.

It also dealt with the effects of pre-trial publicity and whether the juror could be fair and unbiased despite the press stories that Angela Davis was an avowed Communist, that she had been a member of the Black Panthers, that she had been active in prison reform, that she had been labeled a black militant—or that she was being persecuted as a political prisoner.

The reason for having the television sets turned off and the other jurors out of the courtroom was to prevent the spread of information, or misinformation, about the case.

I had never heard the term *voir dire* used before this trial. It is a French phrase meaning "to truly say," but in a trial it has come to mean the questioning of a witness or juror under oath, in order to qualify that person for serving. Our *voir dire* was conducted in two parts: the preliminary section which had been done privately, and then the more intensive questioning by both the defense attorney and the prosecutor. The television sets were turned on for this second section, and the twelve jurors who had survived the first round were all back in the box.

I listened intently to the interrogation, knowing I was likely to be asked the same or similar questions if I were called down. In my mind I attempted to answer the questions with greater sophistication than the poor souls in the box.

The defense attorney always questioned first. Four attorneys served for the defense—five, if you counted Ms. Davis, who had been authorized to act as her own attorney. Leo Branton, Jr., and Howard Moore, Jr., did most of the questioning, but occasionally Doris Walker conducted the *voir dire*. Margaret Burnham sat quietly listening and watching. Branton was the star of the show, the colorful personality, the "chess player." I felt he always knew where he was going and why and how—keeping track of the time (ending his interrogation of a juror just two minutes before twelve, for instance), cooperating completely with the judge, treating everyone (including Prosecutor Harris) with great courtesy. He was completely charming.

Even more important to me as a prospective juror, the questions he asked were formed so that they were easy to understand and could be answered directly.

The attorneys for both sides were involved in two interlocking explorations during the *voir dire*. It was terribly important for them to discover the prejudices and preconceptions that might influence a prospective juror. At the same time they were educating us about their respective theories of the case.

The defense emphasized first of all that Angela Davis was black and that black witnesses would testify. This aspect was repeated time and time again. It was brought out, I thought, so that the jurors would not be uneasy when people were labeled black or not black. By establishing their blackness, the attorneys made it less mysterious.

The attorneys did the same thing with the Communist aspect. By emphasizing it, reiterating it, talking about it explicitly, making the jurors answer questions about it, the attorneys were making sure no latent fears existed that might influence a juror's verdict.

It was interesting to watch how people responded to these questions. Publicly admitting racial prejudice is no longer socially acceptable, so racism was not acknowledged by any juror. They all claimed they could be fair and unbiased, even though Angela Davis was black.

However, the Communist aspect was another matter. Many of those questioned professed to be so disturbed by the threat of communism, they felt they could not sit on a jury in which this was involved. They remained adamant even though the prosecuting attorney (but not the defense) reassured them that the defendant's political philosophy was not on trial in this court—it was not an issue in the case.

Occasionally it was obvious that the person truly was very disturbed about this aspect of the trial, but many panelists, it seemed to me, were using this very safe method to remove themselves effectively from a situation they wanted to get out of. It was one sure way of getting off the jury and no social stigma would be attached to it. After all, who could criticize someone for having such strong anti-Communist feelings?

For example, one prospective juror very readily stated that he would not be able to disassociate the fact that Angela Davis was a Communist from the other aspects of the trial and therefore he could not be a fair juror. Under questioning from the prosecution, he retracted that statement, and then added that he was really concerned about his job situation. Even though his employer, Hewlett-Packard Corporation, would pay his salary while he was serving, he felt that he would return after the trial to " . . . not the same job—but to a position of less pay, less responsibility."

He was not alone in that fear.

The defense also brought out that Ms. Davis had a good education, that she was young and attractive—and that these facts should not be held against her. This cautioning was done in the form of questions: "Would you hold it against her that she is young and black and speaks two languages, has her Master's Degree and almost her PhD, and has taught at the university?"

They talked about the Soledad Brothers. I hadn't known just who they were or how they were supposed to tie into this case. But the defense, by asking the jurors what we knew about them, was able to inform us about the Soledad Brothers.

Three inmates of a prison located in the town of Soledad, south of San Jose, had been accused of killing a guard. Their trial had been transferred to San Francisco and they were moved to San Quentin prison in the summer of 1970. Their names were George Jackson, Fleeta Drumgo and John Cluchette. It had been George Jackson's young brother, Jonathan, who brought guns into the Marin County courtroom where James McClain, another San Quentin inmate, was on trial. This escape attempt was the one that Angela Davis was charged with conspiring to commit. It had resulted in the death of Judge Haley, James McClain, William Christmas (another inmate) and Jonathan Jackson.

Jurors were asked what they knew about Jonathan Jackson, the seventeen-year-old boy who had brought the guns into the courtroom. And whenever a prospective juror had children about that age, he or she was asked if the fact that Ms. Davis was Jonathan's friend and teacher could be accepted—and then was asked, "Did your children ever do something that you didn't approve of, even without your knowledge?"

By planting this interpretation of the relationship of Jonathan Jackson and Angela Davis, it would be easier for the attorneys to show that she wasn't responsible for the actions of a seventeen-year-old.

The attorneys even talked about hairstyles. They questioned people as to whether the Afro-natural hairstyle was repulsive to them, and if it would cause loss of objectivity in judging a person.

They discussed (always in the form of questions) the use of the term "pigs" for policemen, and noted that historically the term had been used since the days of the French Revolution.

They asked about the jurors' experience with guns—whether we had owned guns, if we kept guns around the house. They even asked one juror if she would be terrified if the jury were taken out into a field and a sawed-off shotgun were fired in demonstration.

The prosecution questioning was not nearly as extensive as that by the defense. They seemed almost bored with the whole procedure—not very interested in determining our prejudices and preconceptions. I eventually realized that their only purpose in questioning people was to bring out in public the things the prosecution already knew, so when it came time to dismiss a juror the reason for the release would be apparent.

For example, the prosecutor questioned one man rather pointedly about whether or not he had ever been convicted of a felony. He replied that he had not, " . . . unless you consider a drunk driving conviction a felony." Obviously, this offense was what the prosecutor had been leading up to.

Prosecutor Harris did his share of educating us too. He asked most of us if we could understand the concept of "reasonable doubt" as it would differ from a vague general doubt, since doubt exists in everyone's mind about everything; no absolutes exist.

The prosecutor discussed the weight that should be given to circumstantial evidence and how it was as valid a way of presenting evidence as direct testimony. He talked a lot about conspiracy as a crime and asked us whether we could accept the fact that a person need not actually have been present, or the one who pulled the trigger, to be equally guilty of murder.

At the end of the interrogation of each juror, the attorneys would state that this juror was "passed for cause." At this signal, the questioning was over.

Each side was also allowed twenty peremptory challenges. This meant they could dismiss a juror without giving any reason. They took turns and the prosecution had the first challenge. Mr. Harris stood and said, "The prosecution asks for the dismissal of Juror Number 1, Mrs. Ruth—with thanks."

The judge turned to Juror Number 1 and said, "You are excused, Mrs. Ruth." She got up and walked out of the courtroom.

The move by Prosecutor Harris wasn't unexpected. Mrs. Ruth was a woman who, despite the fact she said she had never heard of Angela Davis before the trial, seemed to be very pro-defense. I had a lot of doubts about the sincerity of her attitudes. While I was listening to her *voir dire,* I felt she was either faking it, hoping that by being so pro-defense she was surely setting herself up to be challenged by the prosecution, or was sincere but so foolish she didn't realize the effect of her answers. Either way, I worried about her being on the jury, and was not surprised when she was dismissed.

Another name was called immediately, another prospective juror came down and filled the vacant chair, and the questioning of this juror proceeded as before.

The prosecutor also challenged a woman who was working as a bookkeeper of a large concern. This young woman said that she felt that Angela Davis' firing from UCLA was "hasty." She also remarked that she felt when Ms. Davis disappeared, the flight was caused by fear. These two demonstrations of sympathy were enough to cause the prosecution to be suspicious of her objectivity, and she was peremptorily challenged.

The third challenge by Prosecutor Harris was made to Mrs. Janie Hemphill, the lone black person of the jury. Mr. Harris has been accused of blatant racism because he did not allow the only available black juror to remain. I would like to speak a word in his defense. I felt he had no recourse. He was the Assistant Attorney General of the State of California and the chief prosecutor in a case that had been labeled the "case of the century." President Richard M. Nixon had congratulated J. Edgar Hoover on the capture of Angela Davis in New York. Mr. Harris' responsibility was to prosecute the case. If he had left Mrs. Hemphill on that jury, he would have been accused by the press of not faithfully representing the prosecution, and criticized for accepting a juror who might be biased.

Mrs. Hemphill had started working on her own when she was twelve years old, picking cotton. She had many jobs over the years—baby sitting, domestic, short order cook, dishwasher, bookkeeper. She was married and had three children and her husband worked in construction.

She and her husband had been in conflict with law-enforcement authorities. The Hemphills had started up a "liquor club" and were struggling to make it a success. It was a weekend-to-weekend operation. They were raided by the police one weekend, her husband was arrested, and they were shut down on suspicion of running a gambling place—and that broke them. They didn't have enough money to reopen the next weekend.

During her *voir dire,* she had shown herself to be a strong, calm, independent woman with a lot of insight. She did not permit the intensive questioning by the prosecutor to provoke her into any display of anger.

"I am not offended, if you are asking me if I was offended [when served with the gambling citation], because right now it has nothing to do with our lives . . . ." When asked if she felt she could still be a fair juror she said, "I have had, for so many years, to blot out so many things—and I have tended to, for so long—that I could . . . actually blot this part out because there's a lot of things that I've had to blot out in my life."

Mr. Harris was too good an attorney not to realize all the repercussions which would come from his act. But he was in an untenable position. He was damned if he did and damned if he didn't.

He could have challenged Janie Hemphill after just a cursory interrogation, and allowed himself to be accused of racism—as he was bound to be anyway. But he chose to question her about her entanglement with the police and embarrass her, in order to justify dismissing her.

Defense Attorney Moore objected strenuously to this line of interrogation, stating that when a similar circumstance had risen before, the questioning had been done privately in the judge's chambers.

Mr. Harris replied that he had no objections to continuing with Mrs. Hemphill in the judge's chambers if that was what was wanted.

Attorney Branton asked to be heard. "I resent in the deepest way possible what Mr. Harris is doing here . . . I think it's unforgivable the way he has attempted to embarrass Mrs. Hemphill in the manner that he has. To me as a lawyer and as a human being, I disassociate from it entirely . . . this is a sign of the very kind of white racism that we have been dealing with in this case . . . I resent it very deeply. As long as it's out in open court, I suggest that we stay here and deal with it in open court."

When Mr. Harris announced, "The People will excuse and thank Juror Number 9, Mrs. Hemphill," murmurs arose among her fellows in the jury box, and hisses from the spectator section.

She had been spending her days with the other jurors for two weeks. Friendships were formed. Sympathy and support for her position had grown. We all knew she was going to be excused. She knew it. But there was nothing any of us could do.

No matter how the courts explain the theory behind it and how rational that theory is, to be excused from jury duty because one or the other of the attorneys thinks you might be biased or unfair is insulting. There is no getting around it. It is a blow to one's self-esteem. We were all embarrassed and saddened that Mrs. Janie Hemphill had to suffer another insult.

The defense used their first two challenges to dismiss two men. Both of them expressed fairly strong anti-Communist sentiments. Neither of them had close associations with black people. One felt that he would want Angela Davis to "explain her position."

The other thought that a gift from his church to the Angela Davis Defense Fund would have been better spent some other way—such as for missionary work.

On Monday morning, March 13, 1972, we had just gotten settled in the jury assembly room when the lottery resumed. The defense dismissed one of their challenges; the squirrel cage was spun. My name was drawn. Even after all that time of waiting and watching, I started to shake.

I followed the deputy through the empty anteroom, waited while he unlocked the door. We went down the back stairs, out a door which was locked behind us by a deputy who was standing guard. We were in an open area, a courtyard in a "U" of the building. The fourth side was enclosed by a ten-foot-high cyclone security fence covered with heavy canvas tarps. Another deputy was stationed at a padlocked gate in the fence.

We passed a row of telephones with names over them— N.Y. TIMES, SAN JOSE MERCURY, NBC, S.F. CHRONICLE, UNITED PRESS —which were attached to the outside wall of a temporary type of building which appeared to have been stuck into the courtyard.

This building contained kleig lights, cameras, plastic bins, fingerprinting paraphernalia, metal detectors, cordoned-off areas. Suddenly it dawned on me that this building was the search area for spectators who wished to attend the trial. The deputies on duty smiled at us as we passed through and entered the hall leading to the courtroom.

Two more deputies opened the door and stepped aside to let me enter the courtroom. I walked down the center aisle through the spectator section, stumbled over a box of chalk and pencils on the floor in front of an artist sitting in the front row.

When I reached my chair I sat down quickly. My legs were trembling so much I was afraid they would give out at any moment. I was handed a microphone and gripped it tightly. It was slippery. I looked at my hands. The sweat was pouring out. I wondered if anyone had ever been electrocuted from holding a microphone with sweaty palms. I tried to hold it by my fingertips to keep it from getting too wet.

After a greeting by Judge Arnason, and my brief introductory statement, Mr. Howard Moore, Jr., rose to interrogate me for the defense. I looked around. Everyone in the courtroom was looking at me—and they were all smiling. I started to relax a little, but I was still wary.

Two weeks ago I wouldn't have been so tense, but I had been listening to the intensive questioning to which some of the jurors had been subjected, and I was no longer confident I could answer the questions freely and openly without getting myself entangled in rhetoric and displaying the vestiges of my racist background. I knew that I was not a conscious, overt racist, but I also knew that I was not always the most sensitive and aware person in the world.

I had decided to take my husband's advice: "Don't talk. Just answer the questions. Answer them briefly and to the point, and don't go into long explanations."

It was easy. I wasn't asked any questions about my relations with minorities—not even if the neighborhood in which I lived was integrated or if the schools my children attended were racially mixed.

I was asked about my family and my job. I was asked if our son, John, had served in the armed forces. He hadn't. He had been a conscientious objector.

From the tenor of the questioning of other jurors, I had expected this fact to come out, and so was prepared for it. John had been actively involved in the anti-war movement for at least ten years.

As his political philosophy developed, I had been sympathetic but not always supportive. I accepted the fact that he was sincerely involved in anti-war activities but I didn't agree that his stance was correct. But because of his involvement, I did more reading and thinking than I would have otherwise done. I decided that the war in Vietnam was a grave mistake. I supported the anti-war movement—but only by talking, and signing petitions and voting for anti-war candidates.

As Prosecutor Harris was asking me about my son, I mentioned his name—John. Harris repeated it, asking if his name was "John

Timothy." I answered that it was, and out of the corner of my
eye I saw the prosecutor's assistant grab his pen and write it
down. I got the impression they had not checked up on John.
Well, if they sent his name out on the teletypes, they would discover that he had been arrested last spring in a demonstration
in Berkeley. As a result of mistaken identification by a police
officer, he was charged with assaulting a police officer with a
deadly weapon—a felony. Eventually the charges were reduced
to a misdemeanor and he was still on probation when I was being interrogated in the jury box—but until I saw the prosecutor
write his name down on a pad, it hadn't even occurred to me
that anyone would consider the incident important.

I hadn't been asked anything about my attitudes toward
minorities, but there were some questions relating to communism
—would I allow it to interfere with my thinking?

I had been asked about my knowledge of guns, and whether
or not we owned any. My husband still had a shotgun and a .22
rifle. I had given my own shotgun away a few years before when
it became apparent that no one in the family would ever hunt
game again. Prosecutor Harris asked me what model my gun had
been; when I answered that it had been a .20-gauge pump, which
was plugged to hold a maximum of three shells at a time, he
seemed satisfied that I knew about guns.

When the questioning was completed, and I was passed for cause
by the attorneys for both sides, I handed the microphone back to
the bailiff and took a deep breath. I tried to wipe the palms of my
hands on a piece of tissue unobtrusively. I thought about all the
things I had said, and decided I hadn't made a fool of myself. That
was a big relief.

Then I started thinking about the implications of John's involvement with the law-enforcement officers. As soon as the prosecution
got the data—which would be as soon as they made inquiry on the
teletype—they would suspect that I might question the accuracy of
police officers' eyewitness identifications.

That, plus the fact that John had been a C.O., plus the fact that my husband was an attorney, would surely be enough to cause the prosecution to challenge me.

I didn't think any of those things would affect my own personal integrity, but I could see how others might be convinced it would.

My interrogation was over. I couldn't do anything now. I might just as well sit back and enjoy the rest of the day's proceedings.

While I was waiting for the next venireman to be brought down from the assembly room, I looked around at the physical setup of the courtroom, and the people in it.

The big double doors at the rear, guarded by deputies, formed the entrance from the hall and opened onto a center aisle leading through the spectator section. This section consisted of five rows of seven seats on either side of the aisle. Every chair was filled. The front two or three rows were reserved for members of the press, including a half dozen artists with their big drawing pads and boxes of pencils and chalk. No cameras were allowed in court, and so the only pictorial record of the trial was made by these artists.

This section was separated from the court proper by a heavy oak balustrade, the gate of which was toward the left side of the room. A uniformed sheriff's deputy sat at a table to the left of that entrance into the court. His duty was to summon the witnesses. He had a telephone and a walkie-talkie, and he was wearing a gun.

Along the front of the balustrade was a row of chairs. A sheriff's matron sat to the right of the entrance; further down the row sat a young black woman who looked very much like Angela Davis. Most of us jurors assumed it was Ms. Davis' sister (after we decided that she wasn't Angela Davis herself), they looked so much alike. Later we heard that this woman was a good friend, Kendra Alexander, who was working as a defense investigator.

The floor of the court was full of tables. To the right of center was the double L-shaped table of the defense team. Attorney Margaret Burnham sat facing the spectator section at the top of the "L"—a small, casually dressed black woman with a round face and a short natural hairstyle, she seemed too young to be an attorney. She watched and listened and took notes. She seldom smiled and I never heard her speak.

Down the side of the table sat Howard Moore, Jr., the attorney who had interrogated me, and Angela Davis—quiet, serious, but with a quick smile for anyone whose eye she caught. She looked frail, ill (prison pallor?), her shoulders wrapped in a purple shawl against the chill of the courtroom.

Along the base, with their backs to the spectators, sat attorneys Doris Walker and Leo Branton, Jr. Ms. Walker, middle-aged with sharp features and short-cropped grey hair, had interrogated a few of the jurors. She didn't question easily—she used a lot of "ahs" and "let me rephrase that." She passed notes back and forth and seemed to keep on top of everything.

Prosecutor Albert Harris, Jr., and his assistant, Clifford Thompson, Jr., were at a table left of center. Mr. Thompson was a young man—a blend of greys—whose appearance and mannerisms seemed more suited to a law library than to the courtroom of a murder trial.

In front of them was another wide table on which exhibits were to be placed. Between the judge's bench and this exhibit table were two straight-backed chairs and two small stands for the reporters' shorthand typewriters.

Along the front wall, in the center, was the raised dais of the judge's bench. To the right and a step or two lower was the chair and table for his bailiff. To the left and down a couple of steps was the witness stand.

Against the left wall was the jury box. It looked just like all the jury boxes in the movies, with two rows of seats behind a heavy oak front. We in the jury were a step above the spectators, the defendant, the attorneys and the clerk—but a step below the witness and the bailiff—and far below His Honor, the Judge.

Superior Judge Richard E. Arnason was not a local judge. He came to the trial from another of the Bay Area counties, having been appointed to the Davis case after a series of judges had been disqualified. It was he who had decided the trial should be held in Santa Clara County.

I wondered about his politics and if he would be able to keep

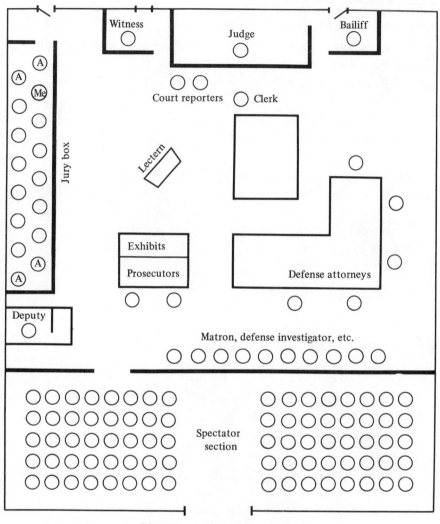

Witness

Judge

Bailiff

Court reporters   Clerk

Jury box

Lectern

Exhibits

Prosecutors

Defense attorneys

Deputy

Matron, defense investigator, etc.

Spectator section

Sketch of the Courtroom

from interjecting his own prejudices into the case. I watched him closely the rest of the day. He sat relaxed in his chair, his speech was calm and unhurried. I didn't think he would be pressured into making hasty, ill-considered decisions. I left court that day feeling that we probably had an excellent judge working on the case.

Doors on each side of the bench led back into the bowels of

the courthouse. Through these doors, the attorneys, the court personnel and Angela Davis entered each court session. A door directly
behind the witness stand—heavily locked, with a small wire-reinforced
window—looked as though it might lead to some kind of cell.

Flags were draped behind the judge's bench, a large calendar hung
above the double doors leading outside—and high on the back wall
was the small unmoving eye of the television camera. It was completely unobtrusive. We soon forgot it was there.

That evening when the family heard the news that I had been called
down they asked me how I had done. I told them I thought I would
be off the jury the next day. We were having company for dinner
the next evening, and I told Art not to worry about the meal—I
would be home early in the afternoon to put the roast in the oven.

Twelve—Good and True

After almost an hour's delay the next morning, court convened.
Judge Arnason called on Mr. Branton. It was the defense's turn
to challenge. But neither Mr. Branton nor Mr. Moore rose to
speak. It was Angela Davis.

"We have long contended, Judge Arnason, that it would be
virtually impossible for me to receive a fair trial in Santa Clara
County. As you know, we have made a number of change-of-
venue motions challenging the ruling that the case be tried in
this county." (What was she getting at? Were they going to move
the trial to another county? What would happen to the jury then?)

"As I look at the present jury, I see that the women and men
do reflect the composition of this county. There are no black
people sitting on the jury." (Right—and there are no others
up in the assembly room—should that be grounds for asking to
have the trial changed?)

"Although I cannot say that this is a jury of my peers, I can say that after much discussion we have reached the conclusion that the women and men sitting on the jury will put forth their best efforts to give me a fair trial.

"I do not think that further delay in the jury selection process will affect in any way the composition of the jury, and because we have confidence in the women and men presently sitting in the box, I am happy to say that we presently accept this jury."

(What? Wait a minute! She couldn't mean that. She couldn't possibly accept a jury with the daughter of a sheriff's captain on it, as well as an Annapolis graduate who said at one point in his *voir dire* that he didn't think he could be objective about Communists. What's going on?)

Prosecutor Harris rose and also accepted the jury. I couldn't believe it! I had been sure I would be released. I stared at the prosecution attorneys. They were sitting there smiling at the jury.

I felt almost betrayed.

The clerk of the court asked us to stand and raise our right hand and he administered the oath. We murmured, "I do," and sat down. Court proceedings continued without a pause. Four alternate jurors must be selected, and names were being drawn.

We were the jury, we twelve. I turned around in my chair and looked down the two rows to remind myself who remained.

In a sense, the jury was, as Ms. Davis had said, a representative one. But it was representative of the large middle class of the county. The poor and the rich, the laborers and the executives, the farmers and the industrialists—none of these groups were represented.

We were eight women, four men—the youngest twenty-two years old, the oldest sixty-seven—and most of us were employed by large industries or businesses: Sears, Bullocks, IBM, Memorex, Stanford, San Francisco airport. One was retired after working for the Veterans Administration, and two were housewives.

The religious affiliations were varied—Catholic, Episcopalian,

Jewish—and only three or four were active; most of the rest of us no longer attended religious services.

. Nine members of the group were married, and all but one of those had children. One bachelor sat on the jury, one woman who never married and one divorcee.

Only a few were native Californians—the rest were from Connecticut, Montana, Kansas, Mexico, Michigan . . . .

Politically, the members of the jury seemed to be equally varied in their philosophy. Most of us were not politically active, but some were very involved in local politics.

Bookkeeper, engineer, accountant, salesperson, flight controller, data processor, medical researcher, picture framer, housewives, retired librarian, accounts collector—eight of the twelve had graduated from colleges or universities, and the others had all had some work in college. (In the conspiracy trial of Dr. Spock in 1968, though, only one juror was a college graduate.)

When we were dismissed for lunch, we hurried up to "our" assembly room and gathered in small groups, telling each other how surprised we were to be selected. The prosecution had seventeen challenges left, and the defense had eighteen—we had thought they would all be used and none of us would be left on the jury.

We were all excited, and interested in each others' stories. We knew we would be spending a lot of time together and we wanted to get acquainted. We started calling each other by first names and talked about bringing books and magazines to share with each other.

One of the first people I had become acquainted with up in the jury assembly room had been Luis. I was so happy he was going to be one of the jurors. He had been sitting in front of me reading a book in Spanish. On the second day we waited, he brought in a chess set and we started a tournament in our area of the room. Each day as the other veniremen disappeared, Luis and I sat together and talked. He had been born in Mexico and had come to San Jose when he was eighteen years old. He started to work for his uncle as a dishwasher, then joined the Army hoping to learn English and a trade while he served. Unfortunately the Army neither taught him the language nor trained him in a marketable skill. After he returned to San Jose, he went to night school and had held a variety of jobs. He was now a data processor for IBM, and was studying abstract art at night. He was married and had two sons in school. He was a very shy, quiet, gentle man.

Ruth, Roz and I quickly discovered that we all lived in the same section of Palo Alto. Roz was the head of the household, with three children. She was a part-time picture framer, and had taught school in Kansas. She had been active in the civil rights movement in the 60's and now was interested in the women's liberation movement. She was an intense, emotionally responsive individual who had made a great statement during her *voir dire.*

She was asked by Prosecutor Harris to consider that all the evidence was in. "Do you think that it would be easier to find Angela Davis not guilty, than guilty?"

Roz replied, "It would certainly be easier to."

Mr. Harris, not realizing that he had phrased the question wrongly, stopped for a moment, then said, "Easier?"

"Do you mean emotionally?" she asked.

Harris was still confused. "Yes."

"Yes."

He had to try again. "Do you think, then, you would have— even if the evidence satisfied you intellectually beyond a reasonable doubt—you would have difficulty emotionally in finding Angela Davis guilty?"

"Emotionally, I would find it difficult to find anyone guilty." She stated very simply what was in the minds of all of us. I felt like adding my own "Amen!"

Ruth was a slim attractive woman who worked as a sales representative for a department store. Her husband was an unemployed electronics engineer; this area had many, many unemployed electronics engineers since the government cutbacks. She and her husband had a nine-year-old daughter. Ruth was a graduate of Michigan State with a degree in business. She had read most of the best-sellers, both fiction and nonfiction, and was also interested in the women's liberation movement.

Besides me, two of the other women were named Mary. This caused a little confusion at times. Mary B. was raised in San Francisco. She had worked as a bookkeeper for a real estate developer until about a year before, when she quit in order to take care of her terminally ill mother. She was still finding it difficult to adjust to her mother's death. Mary had children in their late teens and early twenties. Both her sons had served in the Navy. She was very much involved with her home and family and brought knitting and crocheting to the jury assembly room.

Mary T. sat next to me in the jury box. She had been born in California and had lived most of her life in this area. She was married, had children and was now a housewife although in the past she had worked as a bookkeeper. She belonged to the Episcopalian Church. Her father had been a captain in the sheriff's department of this county. She was very proud of her father. When I listened to her *voir dire,* I had been impressed by the way she always had the perfect answer to all the questions. She seemed to be very confident that she would be an excellent juror.

The oldest juror to be selected for the original panel of twelve was Winona, a retired librarian. She had never married and was very involved in the lives of her nieces and nephews and their children. She had apparently enjoyed her work and she still kept up with innovations in library organization. She took long walks, read children's books and took the family children on vacations. When she was asked during her *voir dire* if she knew that Angela Y. Davis had made herself unavailable after the escape attempt, she had replied, "It seemed the reasonable thing to do."

Stef was the youngest juror, twenty-two years old. She worked in the accounts collection department of Sears. She was a very well-organized young woman who enjoyed her work. She seldom read or watched television. She seemed to have boundless energy and a need to keep busy–a happy extrovert who met life head-on and made friends with everyone.

Anne was a quiet woman–young, married, with two small children. She showed her willingness to be on the jury when she said that she would have no difficulty providing care for her children if she were selected. Anne had attended segregated schools in the Deep South, but when she was asked during her *voir dire* about her views on black militancy, she said she felt it was a "means used by blacks to raise themselves up from the bottom," and that she felt it was not the wrong thing to do. She also had read parts of *If They Come in the Morning,* by Angela Davis (New York: The Third Press, 1971).

The juror who was sure he would be challenged next by the defense was Jim. He was an alert young man who had gone up from the ranks to the Naval Academy, had been graduated from Annapolis and become a Navy pilot. He then flew commercial planes for a while and now was a controller for the San Francisco airport. He was very much aware of racial discrimination in the Navy and in commercial aviation. He had black friends. Jim was married and had two small children and attended church regularly. When he was being questioned by Mr. Branton, he admitted that he might find it difficult to be objective when dealing with Communists. Mr. Branton immediately asked that Jim be dismissed for cause. Judge Arnason took over the questioning and, by rephrasing it, made it possible for Jim to reply that yes, indeed, he could be a fair juror. So he was left on the jury.

Ralph had spent his early years in Montana on a Blackfoot Indian reservation where his mother taught school. He had served a couple of years in the Navy, stationed in Italy. He graduated from the University of Montana and was now working as an electrical engineer. Married, he had "darlin' daughters" in school and seemed to be a very happy man. He wore sport shirts and rode a motorcycle—and carried a book by Alan Watts. He was an ex-Catholic, as I was. Ralph was politically the most active of all the jurors, working primarily on a state initiative to protect our environment. He was against the war and supported Shirley Chisholm for president.

I noticed Nick the first day we were assembled for possible jury duty. I thought he might be a plainclothes police officer assigned to observe us. He was a stocky, balding man who kept his remaining hair cut very short. He dressed very conservatively. But it wasn't his looks as much as his behavior that set him apart. He came in late, swung a chair around and tipped it against the side wall, unfolded a newspaper and sat leaning against the wall, watching all the people over the top of the paper. I was really surprised when he was called down to the jury box.

Nick's parents had emigrated from Sicily to Connecticut. He had graduated from college, taught a year or so, then went to work learning accounting. He was now working for Memorex, a large electronics firm. He was a bachelor who lived with his sister and her family. He was a practicing Catholic. His hobby was sports and he coached a Little League ball team. He didn't often join in the conversations.

Both the prosecution and the defense had stated repeatedly that what they were looking for were twelve people who would listen to the evidence with open minds and arrive at a fair verdict. We had been chosen—the twelve people who had been questioned, whose activities had been checked, and who had been judged to be fair, unbiased and unprejudiced.

It seemed to me to be a balanced jury—only time would tell if we were fair.

The seating of the alternate jurors was much more rapid than that of the original twelve, but it was no less important. The second day of this section of the trial, the juror sitting next to me,

Juror Number 8 (Mary T.), turned to me while we were waiting for the judge to enter court after a short break, and asked if my family supported me—if my children were "on my side." When I answered that I thought they were, she went on to say that all her family except one supported her—and she didn't know what was wrong with her relationship to that one child. I smiled in sympathy and waited for her to continue. She didn't.

After court convened, four alternates were quickly accepted —and then Judge Arnason announced that Juror Number 8 had asked to be excused from jury duty for personal reasons, and her place would be taken by the first alternate juror.

Mary T. stood up and left the courtroom with no explanation —no one knew what had happened, why she had been dismissed. We had no further contact with her.

The alternate juror who moved over to the seat next to me, taking her place as a juror, was a twenty-year-old secretary, Michelle, who became the first juror under twenty-one to serve in California under the new law which made eighteen-to-twenty-year-olds legal adults.

The judge reopened the selection process for the group of alternate jurors and the questioning and challenging continued for the rest of the week.

—A large motherly woman, an American Indian, told how she was involved in her work with the activities at the Indian Center. She was excused by the prosecution.

—An office worker from Stanford said she couldn't be a fair juror, because she associated Angela Davis with student riots and she was frightened. The judge dismissed her for cause.

—A young man admitted that he knew a couple of police officers casually. It turned out that he lived across the hall of an apartment house from an officer who had been involved in shooting an unarmed black research worker. Two officers, off duty, stopped to offer assistance to a fellow officer who was citing a man for an illegal U-turn about 2:30 in the morning. An argument began and the black man started running into his apartment building, calling for help—when he was shot in the back. This killing had aroused the town and many news stories had appeared in the papers at that time. I couldn't recall what the final outcome had been. The defense excused this juror.

—A young woman who had spent two years as a missionary for the Mormon Church was questioned by Leo Branton. He interrogated her long and carefully. At no time was the woman embarrassed or insulted. Mr. Branton was very gentle but very persistent as he gradually drew out her inherently racist religious beliefs. (Since blacks were all descendants from Cain, they could never become bishops in the Church—and if only one out of a hundred or thousand of your ancestors was black, then you would still carry the "Mark of Cain.") She was obviously very sincere and very sure that her beliefs would not interfere with her ability to be fair.

As she continued and explained the concept of "revelations" in her religion, Mr. Branton asked if God were to come to her in a revelation saying that Angela Davis was guilty, then she would have to judge Ms. Davis guilty no matter what evidence had been presented in court, wouldn't she? The woman admitted that she would. The defense excused this juror.

While this woman had been answering questions and explaining her beliefs, I could see how honest and sincere she was in denying any prejudice against blacks—but to another person, such as myself, without those religious beliefs, it was so apparent that she really had no concept of the meaning of the word "prejudice."

I wondered if statements I might make could also be recognized as racist by someone more enlightened than I.

During the *voir dire* of the jurors, Mr. Harris had questioned many of us about our ability to distinguish between Angela Davis, the defendant, and Angela Davis, acting as attorney. He wanted to impress us with the fact that statements she might make while acting as an attorney would not be under oath, so could not be taken as evidence. I could see that it would be confusing, perhaps, but it would depend on just how important a role she were to play in the trial.

Her acceptance of the jury was the first occasion we jurors had to hear her speak, but what she was saying at that time was such a shock to me, I really didn't pay too much attention to the person who said it, to Angela Davis.

The next day, we were given another opportunity to observe her as a person, rather than as the nebulous entity called "the defendant." She conducted the *voir dire* examination of one of the prospective alternate jurors. One of the regular defense attorneys had done the preliminary interrogation the day before and no indications had arisen that this man might be an unfriendly juror.

The questioning started out rather formally, but as she began probing into his attitudes toward the struggles of blacks, he started to open up and respond more freely. They joined in what was tantamount to a dialogue. She seemed to forget her prepared list of questions as she became involved in his attempts to articulate concepts that were only half-formed.

The two of them seemed to ignore the rest of the people in the courtroom, all of whom were listening attentively.

At one point, when the thrust of the questioning dealt with white racism, the juror suggested that possibly Ms. Davis was a "black racist," as contrasted to white racists. She stopped, and said in a kind of wondering amazement, "I've never been called racist before!"

Another time, he protested that he was trying to be honest, but that he didn't really want to be on the jury—he didn't want to be there. Ms. Davis replied wryly that she didn't want to be there either.

He finally admitted that he felt he might even be prejudiced in favor of Ms. Davis now—but he wasn't sure he could accept the testimony of any other Communist without prejudice. He was dismissed for cause. I was sorry to see him leave; I felt that he had reached the point of being truly honest with himself in his thinking, and that type of person was needed on a jury.

I was far more interested in Angela Davis herself than I was in watching the duel between her and the prospective alternate. She was wearing an inexpensive blue suit, the sleeves of which were too short for her long slender arms. My daughters and I have the same problem in buying clothes off the rack. Our arms are always too long.

Angela Davis was a celebrity. I had heard that stars of the entertainment industry were performing in big shows for her defense fund. Someone had put up $100,000 for her bail. But the clothes she and her friends wore and the car they drove away from court (a beat-up old Mustang) were not the clothes and car of a Hollywood-type celebrity.

She was interested and friendly in her approach to the juror. It was hard to believe that she was dealing with someone who might convict her of murder. She seemed more intensely interested in their mutual communication than in her own danger.

The final seats were filled by Friday. The man who was selected as first alternate, and who would become a regular juror if anything happened to another of us, had been born in Denmark. He was a retired executive of a food processing plant. Bob provided the court with one of the few moments of real humor.

Mr. Branton was questioning him about his contacts with black people. Asked if he knew any, Bob, speaking with a slight Scandinavian accent, replied that he had worked with many in South Africa when his company had sent him to supervise the installation of machinery there. Mr. Branton reminded him that South Africa had one of the most rigid systems of segregation. Bob agreed, mentioned that it was called "apartheid," and said he did not approve of it. He went on to say that he belonged to a social club of immigrants—formed to give each other assistance in living in the United States. He said some black men were members of the club. Bob went on to explain that these people were not technically immigrants since they were from the South, " . . . unless you think that Georgia is a foreign country."

The room exploded with laughter.

The evening of the day the jury was accepted by Angela Davis and Prosecutor Harris, a guest at our home picked up the phone to make an important call. The phone was dead. We kept trying to call out for more than half an hour, without success. This was very unusual—in fact, none of us could recall it having happened before in the three years we had lived in this house. Finally, as we were about to give up, the dial tone came on and the call was made.

We joked about the possibility that our phone was being tapped. It probably was just coincidence, but we did have a lot of trouble with our phone for the next few months—strange noises, whirring sounds and clicks, and periods when the phone went dead again.

Since we had nothing to hide, it didn't bother me. My sixteen-year-old daughter would start her conversations with her friends, "OK, you FBI guys, get off the line, I'm going to talk to my friend about boys now—so hang up!"

I wasn't the only juror who suspected that the phone was tapped. Roz called me up about a week later and said that she was having trouble; what should she do?

We decided that discussing what we should do about it while we were talking on the phone wasn't too smart, so we both hung up right away.

Later, after the members of the jury got to know each other better, I found out that many of them had similar experiences, and accepted the fact that it was a good possibility that we were under surveillance.

The possibility that our phone was tapped was only one of the pressures I began to feel—most of them were not significant by themselves, but the cumulative effect made me apprehensive and unsure of myself and my ability to perform adequately as a juror.

The importance of the trial, and the interest in its outcome as evidenced by the masses of reporters and photographers, was always in my mind.

I was very worried about my job—irrationally, maybe, but my work was very important to me. I didn't want my relations with the people I worked for and with spoiled by the final outcome of the trial, whichever way it went. I wanted to come back when the trial was over and take up where I had left off—even though I knew that would be impossible. Changes would be made while I was gone. My status in the close-knit group would be different.

And I had close friends who were black. Would a conviction at the trial's end cause me to lose their trust? Would I become another "white oppressor?" I didn't know, and I worried.

My father and brothers, I was sure, would already be convinced of the guilt of Angela Davis because of their political and social beliefs—but I was also sure they would have confidence in my integrity. But I wondered why I didn't hear from them when the California newspapers carried the story of my being on the jury.

I felt pressures even at home—the sharing of the day's activities and adventures became impossible for me, since we jurors were constantly being reminded not to discuss the trial with anyone. I couldn't even join my husband in watching the 11:00 o'clock news, or listening to the radio. Our daughter, Ellen, called home to tell us that she was getting divorced. Because of the trial, I couldn't take a few days off to go to her and offer my support and assistance if she needed it.

I felt no threat from the Davis supporters. I saw them only for the few seconds as we entered the courtroom or left it. They looked up at the jurors with hope, not with threats.

The sheriff's department officers assigned to protect us (Protect us from what? Surely not from the supporters of Angela Davis—we, the jury, were their only hope for gaining her freedom) were all pleasant, courteous, attractive young men and women—probably as nice a group of law-enforcement officers as could ever be found. They were all fairly excited about being a part of this historic trial, and about being the center of attention.

But they were always with us. They met us at the door in the morning. They escorted us from the jury assembly room and down to the court, where we were met by a couple more of them standing in the doorway. Their presence was almost palpable as they stood in the back of the room—always watching. Even when they were out of sight, the constant rackety-clacking of their walkie-talkies reminded us of their presence.

There were just too many of them. And by playing their role of "protectors," they built up their own fears and made us uneasy. Rationally, intellectually, I could find no reason for their presence and for the elaborate security precautions of the link fences and the locked doors and the searches. They seemed such a waste. They were an expression of the fear that the events in Marin County would be repeated, and that an attempt would be made to effect an escape of Angela Davis. It became obvious that all the law-enforcement people thought she was guilty as hell, and that they needed to be on constant guard to keep her friends from shooting up the place.

This attitude continued even after the reason for it was no longer valid—a week before the trial started, Angela Davis was freed on bail. She and her attorneys left the courtroom through one door, we the jurors left through another. We all came out in front of the courthouse and walked toward our cars to go to lunch. Once we were away from the immediate vicinity of the Civic Center, none of us were being guarded.

Over and over we had been told that the trial would probably last four to six months, perhaps longer. We jurors prepared for a long hot summer. The folding chairs in the assembly room had been replaced by comfortable upholstered chairs and matching couches, plenty of Formica-topped tables, ashtrays. A small anteroom was similarly furnished, and was to be maintained for our exclusive use. We rearranged the furniture and brought pillows for the couches. One of the jurors brought in a large coffeepot and we each brought our own coffee and tea. Every morning someone brought fruit or donuts or coffee cake—the men as well as the women.

After a few days, we decided to chip in and buy a small refrigerator to keep our lunches and drinks in.

Games were brought, and books and magazines. A book on astrology gave us all a chance to talk about ourselves and our families as we matched our characteristics with the signs of the zodiac.

I brought in my first copy of *Ms.* magazine, and some of the articles in it were the subject of great discussions. As a result, we all became much more aware of manifestations of male chauvinism, none of which were tolerated in the jury assembly room.

We were a very pampered group of people. Everything possible was done to make us comfortable. Once the final selection was made and the trial got under way, the security precautions as far as we were concerned were eased. We were allowed to enter the building without a search. It was a little embarrassing to walk past a line of people waiting to be checked, smile hello at the matron and deputy, and walk on in.

We were physically pampered, but emotionally pressured.

The Trial

The Trial Begins

March 27th. The trial was to start this morning. I woke early
and lay in bed quietly waiting for the alarm to go off, thinking
about the day ahead.

When I had finished my shower and had dressed for the day,
I went into the kitchen. Art had the coffee ready and had cut
all the references to the trial out of the morning's *San Francisco
Chronicle.*

Perhaps I should explain. Since we had been instructed not
to read any newspaper accounts of the trial, nor to listen to the
radio or television news, my husband and I had decided that the
easiest and safest method was to have a member of the family
go through the papers carefully and clip out all references to the
trial before I was allowed to see them. Every morning and evening during the trial, the related items were cut out, dated, filed
daily in a manila envelope and saved for me to read after the
trial was over. This procedure allowed me to keep up with the
rest of the world events without having my reactions influenced
by the reported events of the trial.

Most of the trial stories were on the front pages and continued on page three, or the back page of the same section. It was
doubly irritating to have great gaping holes in the front page,

and then to turn the page and find the stories on the back of the page missing or so chopped up that they had no continuity.

I like a neat newspaper, and I like to read it in the order it is made up, section by section. Our older daughter, Ellen, had worked for a few months as a reporter, and from her experience I had come to realize that a newspaper is in fact a complete unit; the design is not haphazard, but is organized to give the maximum readability. Reading a paper after it had been hacked to pieces made the daily ritual of coffee-and-the-morning-paper less than satisfying.

This morning I was too excited to do more than glance at the headlines. The tension was building up. I was ready to get started. Today was like the first day on a new job. I thought I could handle it, but I didn't know just what to expect, or what was going to be expected of me.

Since three of us on the jury lived within a few blocks of each other in Palo Alto, we decided to form a car pool and save a little on the expense of driving the thirty miles daily. To a small extent, we might also help to alleviate the smog which was becoming more and more severe as the spring continued without a sign of rain.

Ruth was ready when I pulled up in front of her house and tapped the horn. She and I tried to relieve our nervousness by the usual small talk of strangers who find themselves forced into close contact, as I turned the car around and headed toward Roz's house. We made little apologies for our clothes, the car, the difficulties of getting ready for this day's work.

Roz was waiting outside her home, leaning against her red Datsun station wagon in the morning sunshine, watching the neighborhood children going into the school across the street. She climbed into the back seat and the small talk began again.

This was to be the first day of our great adventure and we were very uncertain. We tried to reassure ourselves by asking questions of each other and found that we were all equally uninformed. The attempts at conversation faded as we drove along.

Each of us lived what seemed to be two separate and completely unique lives. On weekends and in the evenings we were typical middle-class women, concerned with our families, homes and jobs. We blended into our environment and were indistinguishable from all the other women in our community. Each morning of the trial, as we approached the turnoff to San Jose that led to the Civic Center, we grew quiet and prepared for the other life we were now living—that of a juror.

Each day I became tense, alert, and always a little uneasy about arriving late. One of my peculiarities is that my stomach starts churning if I think I am going to be late to work, to meetings, to shows.

Today, we pulled into the parking lot across the street from the courthouse and found a space in the front row. The court for our trial was convening at an earlier hour than the other courts, so the spaces reserved for jurors were available to us each morning.

We hesitated a little before getting out of the car. The courtyard between the Superior and the Municipal Court Buildings was filled with television and press people. We were surprised. The public interest in the trial had waned, once the twelve jurors had been accepted. The press had not scrutinized and reported on the alternates so carefully and completely. Also, since the defense attorneys had already covered the points they wished to emphasize to the jury during the questioning of the regular panel, they seemed to go more directly to the point of bias and prejudice, and so were no longer generating front-page stories. We had become accustomed to finding the courtroom only partly filled with spectators and had gradually lost our feelings of self-importance.

So today we composed our faces into our "jurors' masks," gathered up our belongings, got out of the car and walked across the street along the sidewalk through the courtyard without glancing to the left or right. We needn't have bothered; they ignored us. They were waiting for more interesting participants —Ms. Davis or the attorneys.

We passed through the metal detectors and on up the stairs

to the jury assembly room. This morning we kept close together, ready to start work, too excited to sit down and read a book or write a letter.

Court was due to convene at 9:00 o'clock but it was well past 10:00 before the door to the stairwell opened and Norm, one of the deputies assigned to escort the jury to and from court, entered in full uniform, gun on hip, radio in hand. By then we had passed through the stage of eager anticipation and had reached the stage of irritation with the law's delay.

He greeted us and started counting heads by pointing the antenna of his walkie-talkie at each of us, checking off the sixteen jurors. The time had come to go to court. A few of us made mad dashes through the large assembly room, out the door for a quick visit to the rest rooms. Then we were lined up and started down the stairs, women first, followed by the men. Bringing up the rear was Norm, with his walkie-talkie sputtering all the way.

We walked single file up the center aisle and stepped into the jury box, taking our assigned seats. Things were serious this morning. The spectators and press were quiet. The court was empty. We waited. One of the court reporters came in and sat down in front of her recording typewriter, pulled the stand between her knees, poised her fingers above the keys, looked up at no one and smiled. She was ready.

Two women alternated in taking the official transcripts of the trial. One recorded for ten to fifteen minutes at a time; then the other came into the court from the door between the jury box and the witness stand, took the other chair, pulled up her stand, turned to the first reporter, smiled, nodded, and took over the recording. For a moment their hands moved in unison, then the first reporter stopped, reached around to the back of her machine, tore off her strip of paper, folded it and, clutching it in her hand, hurried out the door to type up this section of the transcript so it would be available for the use of the court. Their fingers flicked quickly over the keys and they seldom asked for a word or name to be repeated. Their eyes were blank and their ears pricked; the sounds of the courtroom seemed to flow directly through their ears down to the fingers, into the machine and out onto the strips of paper. When either of them was requested to read back a question or section of the transcript from her notes, she read in a crisp, staccato, machine-like manner as though the system had merely been reversed.

Art Vanick, Clerk of the Superior Court, came in next and took his place at the large table in front of the judge's bench. The squirrel cage was no longer on his table. Instead, it held sheaves of papers and stacks of folders. He shuffled through them, arranged them into neat piles; then he, too, looked up and smiled. He was ready.

We waited.

The door opened again and the two prosecution attorneys, the four defense attorneys, Ms. Davis and her companion, and the sheriff's matron came through—a stream of well-dressed, attractive people. It appeared that the men had all gotten haircuts during the week the court was in recess. Mr. Harris' white shirt gleamed against his neat, dark grey businessman's suit.

They took their seats with no conversation, settled their papers, and all turned (almost in unison) to look at the jury, as though they suddenly wondered if we were in fact the same twelve and four that they had accepted last week.

The bailiff peeked out of the door by the jury box, saw that all were present, pulled his head back in, closed the door and appeared almost immediately at the door on the other side of the judge's bench. He stepped forward and announced, "Remain seated. Come to order. Superior Court of the State of California, in and for the County of Santa Clara, is now in session. The Honorable Richard E. Arnason, Superior Court Judge, presiding."

From behind him, in strode the judge, the hem of his robe gathered in his right hand. He sat, dropped his robe, turned in his chair and surveyed the scene:

"Good morning, ladies and gentlemen. Good morning, counsel, ladies and gentlemen of the jury.

"The record may reflect the presence of Ms. Davis together

with counsel. The People are represented by Mr. Harris and Mr. Thompson. The jury and the alternate jurors are in their assigned places."

Judge Arnason went on to apologize for the delay, stating that counsel had matters that they needed to discuss with the Court, and that the public and the jurors might find this to be disconcerting, but, unfortunately, such discussion was a part of the judicial proceedings.

He then made a formal statement as to what we could expect in the course of the trial in the way of procedures:

> This is a criminal case, commenced by the People of the State of California, which I may sometimes refer to as the prosecution and sometimes as the People, against Miss Angela Y. Davis. The case is based on an indictment which has previously been read to you and which counsel have stipulated does not have to be reread at this time.
>
> You should distinctly understand that the indictment is simply a charge and that it is not in any sense evidence of the allegations it contains. The defendant has pleaded not guilty to the indictment.
>
> The People, therefore, have the burden of proving each of the essential elements of the indictment beyond a reasonable doubt. The purpose of the trial is to determine whether the People have met this burden.
>
> Now, this is the order in which the trial will proceed: first, the parties have the opportunity to make an opening statement . . . . What is said in the opening statement is not evidence. The statements simply serve the purpose of an introduction to the evidence which the party making the statement intends to produce.
>
> Second, the People will introduce evidence in support of the charges contained in the indictment.
>
> Third, after the People have presented its evidence the defendant may present evidence but is not obliged to do so. The burden is always on the People to prove every

element of the offense charged beyond a reasonable doubt. The law never imposes on the defendant in a criminal case the burden of calling any witnesses or introducing any evidence.

Fourth, at the conclusion of the evidence, each party has the opportunity to present oral argument or comment in support of the case. What is said in the closing argument is not evidence, just as what is said in the opening statement is not evidence. The arguments are designed to present to you the contentions of the parties as to what the evidence has shown and what inferences may be drawn from the evidence. The People have the right to open and close the argument.

Fifth, I will instruct you on the applicable law, and you will then retire to consider your verdict. Your verdict must be unanimous on each count. Your purpose as jurors is to find and determine the facts. Under our system of criminal procedure, you are the sole judge of the facts.

If at any time I should make any comment regarding the facts you are at liberty to disregard it. It is especially important that you perform your duty of determining the facts diligently and conscientiously, for ordinarily there is no means of correcting an erroneous determination of the facts by the jury . . . .

You must not consider anything you may have read or heard about the case outside of the courtroom, whether before or during the trial.

In considering the weight and value of the testimony of any witness, you may take into consideration the appearance, attitudes and behavior of the witness, the interest of the witness in the outcome of the case, if any, the relation of the witness to any party in the action, the inclination of the witness to speak truthfully or not, the probability or improbability of the witness's statements and all other facts and circumstances

in evidence. Thus, you may give the testimony of any
witness such weight and value as you believe the testimony of the witness is entitled to receive . . . .
     Until this case is submitted to you, you must not
discuss it with anyone, even with your fellow jurors.
After it is submitted to you, you must discuss it only in
the Jury Room with your fellow jurors . . . .

Judge Arnason set aside his notes, looked over at the jury and
said, "At this time, ladies and gentlemen of the jury, Mr. Harris
will present his opening statement."

Albert Harris, Jr., was the Assistant Attorney General of the State
of California. He was not an elected official. He was a career lawyer in the Attorney General's Office, and his duties had been
largely of an investigative nature.

He gave the appearance of being short, but he was probably
around five feet, eight inches or five feet, ten inches, barrel
chested, with short arms and stubby fingers on thick heavy hands.
His complexion was florid and his hair grey, streaked with silver,
curling crisply. His neck was short and thick and his white button-
down collars crumpled under his chin and jowls.

He had a short nose, a wide mouth, and lines around his eyes
that showed he smiled often and spent some time in the sun.

He wore conservative dark suits, white shirts and moderately
wide, moderately flashy ties.

His voice was low, his speech clear and unhurried. He stam-
mered occasionally. When he did stumble or had difficulty
phrasing a question, he looked over at one or the other of the
jurors, blushed, grinned sheepishly and almost seemed to be
ready to dig his bare toe into the sand of the schoolyard and
say, "Oh, shucks."

This "I'm-just-a-simple-country-boy" approach was very effective, whether it was natural or contrived. The jurors as a group
felt no animosity toward him. We wanted to help him resolve
his dilemmas.

He had a habit of removing a folded white handkerchief from the right back pocket of his pants, opening it one fold, swabbing his forehead with it, carefully wiping the tips of his fingers on both hands, refolding it and replacing it in his pocket. He seemed to do this when the pressure was great—particularly when he was reading aloud.

This morning his manner was almost "folksy" as he set up a standing podium in the center of the court, moved it here, then over a foot, then back six inches, then turned it this way and that. He twisted around and apologized to the defense for having to turn his back to them.

Open floor space in the court was limited. The two reporters had chairs and typing stands. The court clerk had a large table for all his papers and exhibits. The defense team had a double table in an L-shape and the prosecution had a smaller table. Only narrow pathways remained for any movement on the floor of the court.

And now a podium had been added.

Mr. Harris then started bringing out large pictures and charts which he placed on a raised, movable three-foot by five-foot easel. Each of these was covered with an overshield of heavy plastic film which caught and reflected the lights, making it difficult to see through the glare. Much fussing around went on while the stand was being placed, the glare was being discussed; finally the plastic film was folded back over the top of the stand leaving the picture exposed. These sheets of plastic over each of the prosecution's exhibits remained a problem throughout the trial. I never understood why no one took a pair of scissors and cut the darn things off. I wondered if it involved some abstruse legal precept that prevented their changing any exhibit that had already been introduced. Or did they merely wish to preserve the pristine condition of the paper charts and pictures? Perhaps they just didn't think of it.

A picture of the Marin County Civic Center showed the two wings of the building, and a beautiful aerial photo showed the building nestled in the green foothills, seemingly miles from any city. This building was designed by Frank Lloyd Wright. All its lines are curved and its color is blue and tan so it blends in with the rolling hills and the clear blue sky of the countryside north of San Francisco. The curved lines of the building are continued within. All the benches, tables and seating areas are curved in semi-circular lines.

A chart showed the courtroom in Marin where the crime took place; another showed the corridor out in front of the courtrooms with the elevators, stairwell, phone booths, planters. A cutaway showed the North Arch and the building entrances; an overhead chart pictured the building, roadways and parking lots.

Mr. Harris took quite a bit of time explaining and describing the physical setup of the Marin Civic Center and the Courtroom Number 2. We jurors listened attentively, even after it became obvious that the charts were doing a better job of communication than any verbal description.

Mr. Harris then spent the rest of the morning giving his version of the escape attempt, with a great deal of repetition and backtracking. First he told the story, basing it on the indictment. He went through the indictment, paraphrasing it step by step. He stated that evidence would be presented to substantiate the charges. He said that no evidence would be presented involving the exercising by the defendant of her right to free speech and assembly. He stated that we would be convinced that this was not a trial of political or racial persecution.

The next section of his opening statement dealt with the actual physical act of the escape attempt, the taking of the hostages and the shootings. Little mention was made of Ms. Davis in this section, other than statements that the guns and ammunition used had been purchased by her and that her name was in some books used by Jonathan Jackson to cover up the guns in a briefcase.

The afternoon session was devoted to delineating Angela Davis' involvement with the elements of the crime through her association with Jonathan Jackson.

I had never heard or read a complete story of the events of

the escape attempt, and I was very interested in hearing the details. I had a lot of questions in my mind, so, even though I knew that this was not evidence, I listened closely.

This then is the story told by the prosecuting attorney, Albert Harris, Jr.

On Friday, August 7, 1970, Judge Harold Haley was on the bench in Courtroom Number 2. The trial in progress was that of a San Quentin convict, James McClain, who had been accused of assaulting a prison guard. San Quentin prison is in Marin County and any crimes committed in the prison are tried in the Marin County Courthouse.

The trial had started on Monday, August 3. McClain was acting as his own attorney and was opposed by the Assistant District Attorney of Marin County, Gary Thomas. The court reporter was taking down the statements made. The jury of ten women and two men were in their seats. Ruchell Magee, another convict and a witness for the defense, was on the witness stand. The bailiff was present but not armed. No spectators were present.

Jonathan Jackson entered the courtroom about a quarter to 11:00, wearing a trench coat and carrying a blue briefcase. He sat in the spectator's section for a few moments, then stood up. The court reporter typed out: "A VOICE FROM THE AUDIENCE: 'All right, gentlemen, just hold it right there!'"

Jonathan Jackson was barely seventeen years old. He had another year remaining to go at Blair High School in Pasadena, California. He was the younger brother of George Jackson, one of the three convicts known as the Soledad Brothers, who were at that time just a few miles away in San Quentin awaiting trial for killing a prison guard at another California prison, Soledad.

Jonathan had a .380 Browning automatic in his hand. (This gun had been bought by Angela Davis two years earlier.) He handed this gun to James McClain and pulled from beneath his coat a .30-caliber carbine rifle with an extendible stock. (This gun was purchased by Angela Davis in April, 1969.)

Jonathan emptied the bulging briefcase. It contained a

.12-gauge, single-shot, sawed-off shotgun, a roll of adhesive tape, a roll of wire, and six paperback books—*The Politics of Violence, Violence and Social Change,* three books in French and another. (These books had Angela Davis' name on the inside covers.)

James McClain took charge. He took the tape and fastened the sawed-off shotgun to Judge Haley's neck. (This gun was purchased by Angela Davis two days before in San Francisco.)

Ruchell Magee was released from his chains—chains around his waist to which his handcuffs were fastened—the usual chains that prisoners wear when they leave the prison for a court appearance. McClain handed him the Browning automatic.

McClain ordered the judge to phone the sheriff and tell him that the courtroom had been taken over and for him to call off his "pigs" or there would be deaths.

William Christmas, another convict called to be a witness for the trial, had been waiting outside in the corridor. He was brought in. This completed the group—the seventeen-year-old Jonathan Jackson, and the three convicts, James McClain, Ruchell Magee and William Christmas.

Three women jurors were selected for hostages. They were wired together around their waists with the wire brought into the courtroom by Jonathan. As the group prepared to leave, McClain decided to include Gary Thomas, the Assistant D.A., as another hostage. He was wired to the front of the line of hostages. William Christmas took charge of this group. In his left hand he had three highway flares taped together to look like dynamite. He draped his left arm around the neck of the last juror in the group, with the "dynamite" tucked under her chin. He had in his right hand a .375-magnum revolver taken from a deputy.

McClain was in charge of Judge Haley. He kept his hand on the trigger of the sawed-off shotgun taped to the judge's neck. These two groups, plus Magee with the Browning automatic and Jonathan with the carbine, came out of the courtroom and into the corridor which led to the elevators.

A number of law-enforcement men were present in the corridor.

The convicts took what guns they wanted from them. On the way out, they met a newspaper photographer and posed for pictures. As they started to get on the elevator, McClain told this photographer, "Tell them that we want the Soledad Brothers released by 12:00 o'clock!"

The escape group went down the elevators, out to the parking lot and got into a rented yellow Hertz van. With Jonathan Jackson driving, they started out of the lot, through the South Arch and onto the exit road leading to the highway.

The van was met by San Quentin guards who, having received the report of an escape attempt, set up a roadblock.

A seventeen-second fusillade of gunfire erupted. When the doors of the van were opened, Judge Haley was dead, with his face blown apart; Gary Thomas was wounded in the spine, crippled for life; one of the women jurors was severely wounded; Jonathan Jackson was dead; James McClain was dead; William Christmas was dead; and Ruchell Magee was wounded.

That described the kidnapping and murder. Those charges were the first two counts of the indictment. It was not claimed that Angela Davis was present or had actively participated in this act. It was claimed that she did aid and abet Jonathan Jackson in the commission of the two crimes and that she did conspire together with Jonathan Jackson. While the escape attempt was going on, Ms. Davis was waiting at the San Francisco airport.

At the end of this segment of his presentation, Mr. Harris informed the judge that it would be a convenient time for a break. Judge Arnason dismissed court for the noon recess.

Recessed for lunch! Lunch? What were we supposed to do after a session like that? Leave all our sense of shock and outrage in the courtroom and go off to restaurants and cafeterias and eat our usual luncheon fare? Apparently that was just what was going to happen.

I had brought a sandwich, some cheese and an apple for lunch. I had planned to sit in the sun and read a little. But I was too stirred up to sit quietly and read. I put the brown bag back on the shelf and joined a group going over to the large impersonal cafeteria which was on the seventh floor of one of the Civic Center administration buildings nearby. The clattering noises and constant movement and chattering of the government employees provided the break that we needed.

The courtroom had been a little chilly that morning, and most of us had left our sweaters up in the assembly room. So when we started back down the stairs for the afternoon session, we made sure that we had our wraps. But they weren't necessary. The sun was shining on the high narrow windows, and the room was light and warm—almost too warm.

Angela Davis' involvement with George and Jonathan Jackson, which led to her being charged with conspiracy, was the theme of the final segment of Albert Harris' presentation. He stated that the evidence would show that she rendered assistance with criminal intent, with knowledge of the purpose of Jonathan Jackson; that Jonathan Jackson aided and abetted Ruchell Magee and William Christmas in bringing about the death of Judge Haley; that it was a willful, premeditated and deliberate killing; and that it was the natural and probable consequence of what the defendant did in rendering assistance with criminal intent to Jonathan Jackson.

Mr. Harris then explained that since most of the principals were dead, except Ruchell Magee who was awaiting trial, the evidence must of necessity be circumstantial evidence. He defined the classic elements of circumstantial evidence as four: motive, means, opportunity and knowledge of guilt.

MOTIVE: Mr. Harris stated, " . . . her own words will reveal that beneath the cool academic veneer is a woman fully capable of being moved to violence by passion. The evidence will show that her basic motive was not to free political prisoners, but to free the one prisoner that she loved. The basic motive for the crime was the same motive underlying hundreds of criminal cases across the United States every day. That motive was not abstract. It was not founded basically on any need, real or imagined, for prison reform. It was not founded on a desire for social justice. It was founded simply on the passion that she felt for George Jackson, and the evidence of that motive will not be circumstantial. You won't have to make any inferences. It will rest on the defendant's own words."

After this introduction, Mr. Harris went on to explain that in February of 1970 in Monterey County an indictment was filed by the grand jury of that county charging George Jackson and two other prisoners with killing a guard at Soledad prison. These three inmates became widely known as the Soledad Brothers.

Early in May, Angela Davis applied to prison authorities for mail and visiting privileges with George Jackson but was turned down. When George Jackson appeared in court in Salinas, the county seat, she was present at the proceedings.

According to Mr. Harris, Angela Davis was writing letters to George Jackson during the month of June, and during this same period of time was purchasing fifty rounds of .380 ammunition and fifty rounds of .30-caliber M-1 ammunition.

In the middle of July she traveled to San Francisco and appeared in Superior Court with George Jackson's attorney with a request that she be appointed an investigator for his case. This request was denied.

"The most open disclosure of Angela Davis' feeling however, is in a number of letters that we will offer into evidence . . . that were written by her while she was confined in the Marin County jail awaiting trial . . . George Jackson was confined a few miles away in San Quentin state prison and Miss Davis was confined in the Marin County jail.

"There will be evidence that on July 8, 1971, a meeting was arranged between the defendant and George Jackson at the Marin County jail. They met together with their attorneys in the messhall at the county jail. They went to a holding cell on the court floor adjacent to a courtroom over the lunch hour, and then they returned to the messhall.

"The evidence will show that the defendant and George Jackson used this meeting, their only physical meeting that I know of, as an opportunity for a close, passionate and physical involvement." Mr. Harris went on to tell how a series of letters from Angela Davis to George Jackson was found in his cell one month later after he died in San Quentin, " . . . and the defendant considered herself married to George Jackson."

These letters would be the evidence that would show why it was possible for Angela Davis, a professor at UCLA, to become involved and to commit the crimes that she was charged with.

This, then, was the motive—uncontrolled passion.

MEANS: According to Prosecutor Harris, evidence would be presented to show that as early as May 30, 1970, the defendant and Jonathan Jackson went to the Western Surplus store along with the mother of the Jacksons, and that Mrs. Jackson purchased fifty rounds of .30-caliber Winchester ammunition. This same kind of ammunition was later found in an attaché case in the yellow Hertz van.

On July 6th, Ms. Davis purchased 100 rounds of .30-caliber ammunition, 150 rounds of .30-caliber and 100 rounds of 9-mm. ammunition. On the next day she bought more ammunition and more again twelve days later.

On July 25, 1970—thirteen days before August 7th, she exchanged a faulty carbine for one that worked, and bought two banana clips (attachable chambers to hold bullets) and another 200 rounds of ammunition. The carbine bought on this day was also found in the yellow van.

On August 5th, in San Francisco, just two days before the commission of the crimes, Angela Davis and Jonathan Jackson bought a .12-gauge shotgun and a box of twenty-five rounds of shotgun shells. This gun was the sawed-off shotgun that was taped to Judge Haley's neck.

On August 4th, Angela Davis cashed a check for $100 in Oakland; on August 5th, she purchased the shotgun; on August 6th, Jonathan Jackson used two twenty-dollar bills to rent the Hertz van.

Mr. Harris stated that evidence would be presented that Angela Davis spent much of the day of August 6th in that very Hertz van.

OPPORTUNITY: Evidence would be presented showing that the defendant and Jonathan Jackson were together in a variety of places and at a variety of times during the weeks preceding August 7th, with increasing tempo as that date grew near, according to Albert Harris.

"What were they doing together? If they did, if the defendant and Jonathan Jackson did associate together frequently in those days and weeks just before August 7th, then you will know that she had the opportunity to aid and abet Jonathan Jackson, to render assistance to him, to know of his purpose, to share his criminal intent, to furnish the means for the commission of the crime and to conspire with it."

He reviewed the data that he had already discussed and continued with additional details. By the end of June the defendant was so closely associated with the Jackson family that they traveled together to San Jose for a meeting related to the campaign to free George Jackson. She was close enough to Jonathan so that he added a postscript to a letter that she wrote to George.

By early July, according to Mr. Harris, she and Jonathan were at the Western Surplus store buying the ammunition mentioned before.

On July 17th—just three weeks before August 7th—the defendant left the apartment where she had been living for some time and moved into a new apartment. Jonathan Jackson helped her move into the apartment. Evidence would be presented to show that they shared living quarters in that apartment.

Jonathan then went to northern California. He visited his brother in San Quentin on three consecutive days. He returned to Los Angeles, and was with Angela Davis when she cashed a check on July 29, 1970; again, on the next day, they were at another bank and cashed a check for $200.

That same night, the night of July 30th, the defendant and

Jonathan Jackson were stopped at the California-Mexico border
as they were returning from a trip into Mexico. The next night
the Los Angeles police department picked up Jonathan while
he was "hot-wiring" Ms. Davis' car—a Rambler station wagon.
She came down tc the police station and identified him and
they left together.

On Sunday, August 2, 1970, the central office of the Soledad
Defense Committee, to be known as the Soledad House, was
opened in San Francisco. Jonathan Jackson was there. Angela
Davis was still in Los Angeles.

"The final critical week commenced on Monday, August the
3rd," said Mr. Harris. "This was the day that James McClain
went to trial in Marin County. On the same day, Jonathan Jackson, together with his mother and a friend, Joan Hammer, went
out to visit George Jackson at San Quentin. And that night the
defendant left the Los Angeles airport and came to San Francisco. She was not to leave the San Francisco Bay Area again
until August 7th had become a bloody page in our history.

"On Tuesday, August 4, 1970 . . . Your Honor, would this
be a convenient moment to break?" Mr. Harris had looked up
from his pages of notes. The jury was dozing off. He had lost
his audience.

Incredible! In the middle of the "trial of the century," with
the Assistant Attorney General making his opening address,
going right down the line, step by step, in very minute, very
precise details purporting to show the involvement of Ms. Davis
in this shocking crime, almost everyone in the courtroom was
two-thirds asleep!

The room was comfortably warm, and very quiet except for
Mr. Harris' sonorous monotone. I had actually nodded off for
a second or two. I don't think I lost a word or phrase, but
seemed to hear it all as though it were coming from a great
distance.

I had straightened up in my chair, opened my eyes wide,
blinked hard, and looked around the room. Judge Arnason's
eyes were slowly opening and closing. The defense team was

very still. Mr. Branton was staring off into space. Those jurors that I could see were struggling to stay awake. It was at that moment that Mr. Harris asked for a recess.

Judge Arnason was instantly alert. He agreed to the recess and suggested that the usual admonition to the jury need not be given, if that were satisfactory with counsel. Mr. Harris nodded. Mr. Branton still stared off into space. The judge waited a moment, and said, "Mr. Branton, are you satisfied that I don't have to give the admonition?" Mr. Branton jumped, turned quickly to the bench and agreed, smiling.

This scene was so unbelievable that it was almost funny. At another time and place we would have laughed about it. Today it was cause for amazement.

We jurors hurried upstairs to the vending machines to get cold drinks to wake us up. The break seemed all too short, and we made little pacts with each other to poke one another if we noticed anyone going to sleep.

Mr. Harris went on to finish his opening statement in less than an hour. He continued chronologically, showing Angela Davis' close involvement with Jonathan Jackson as the details of the plot were worked out.

Tuesday morning Angela Davis cashed a check for $100 in an Oakland bank. That afternoon, she and Jonathan went to San Quentin prison, arriving too late to visit his brother. Jonathan signed the visitor's register at the main gate with his own name, and just below that the name "Diane Robinson." But Angela Davis was the woman with him.

Later that day Jonathan borrowed a Volkswagen from a friend in San Jose. He promised to return it the next day, but he never did return it. It was found two weeks later at the San Francisco airport parking lot.

The next day he was again at San Quentin. He visited his brother for two hours. Angela Davis stayed in the waiting room. Later that day the two of them went to the Eagle Loan Office on Third Street in San Francisco, where the defendant purchased a shotgun and a box of Remington shotgun shells. A box of Remington shells with one shell missing was found in the yellow van.

Evidence would be introduced to show that the link of communication between Jonathan and James McClain was Jonathan's brother, George.

Prosecutor Harris then recounted his version of the happenings of the day before the escape attempt. Early in the morning Jonathan Jackson rented the Hertz van in San Francisco. At 10:30 o'clock he entered the courtroom of the McClain trial, wearing the coat and carrying the briefcase, just as he was to do the next day.

A few moments later, he walked into a Mobil service station across the street from the Civic Center. He was accompanied by a tall, young, black woman. Four men at the filling station saw her. She was Angela Davis. Jonathan needed help getting the yellow van started. A station attendant, the son of the owner of the business, took the two of them over to the parking lot behind the Civic Center and pushed the van to start it.

By 11:15 they were at San Quentin again; Jonathan went in while Angela waited out in the parking lot in the van. At 3:00 o'clock, Jonathan, again wearing a coat and carrying the bulging blue briefcase, arrived at the courtroom, only to find that the McClain trial in Courtroom Number 2 had recessed early that day.

That night, at about 7:45, Jonathan Jackson registered at the Holland Motel in San Francisco. He was accompanied by another person and he rented a room for one night.

The next day at about 11:00 o'clock, the escape attempt took place.

These events were related by Mr. Harris to demonstrate his third point—opportunity.

KNOWLEDGE OF GUILT: Mr. Harris stated that " . . . flight may manifest guilt."

At 2:00 p.m. on August 7th, the defendant presented herself

at the PSA ticket counter in San Francisco airport. She was very rushed and hurried, and she bought a ticket to Los Angeles. On August 14, 1970, one week later, a warrant was issued for her arrest. She was not found for two months. When she was found in New York, she was wearing a wig, she had changed her style of glasses, and she was carrying identification cards which purportedly identified her as Lorraine Robinson or Lorraine Poindexter.

Mr. Harris concluded. "We think that after you have heard the evidence, your insight into what the defendant did will be as keen as the vision of those who saw through her disguise in New York City. We think that the evidence, when all is said and done here, will show you why the crimes in Marin County were committed. We think the evidence will show you that they were committed because of the commitment of Angela Davis to George Jackson. We will show, I think, that the two people who cared most for George Jackson in the entire world participated in those steps . . . . We are satisfied that when you have heard all of the evidence that is presented by both sides in the case, you will be convinced of the guilt of Angela Davis. Thank you."

Court was dismissed for the day. After the usual admonitions by Judge Arnason, we jurors filed out of the courtroom and back up the stairs to the assembly room. We quickly and quietly gathered up our belongings and started out to our cars, without any conversation, hardly even a "goodnight!" or a "see you tomorrow!"

We were stunned. The prosecution's case seemed incredibly complete. As Mr. Harris had itemized the events implicating Ms. Davis, one could almost hear the previously open minds of the jurors click shut. I firmly believe that if the jury had to make its decision at that precise moment, the vote would have been 12 to 0 for conviction. Every one of us would have voted "GUILTY!"

Ruth, Roz and I got into the car and rode the fifteen miles home without saying a single word to each other. As I let

each of them out, we said, "Same time?," and "Same time."
That was all.

I was exhausted. It was still early in the afternoon and my
husband and daughter weren't home. I went into the bedroom,
closed the door to separate myself from my elderly mother-in-
law and her nurse companion. I stretched out on the bed. I
needed to sort out my thoughts and emotions.

Until today I had felt aloof, an observer at this drama. I had
been allowed to play a minor role for a few minutes two weeks
before, and had been accepted for a later appearance. I had
then been allowed to sit in a front row seat while many of the
first-act characters were introduced. The subplots of racial prejudice, political oppression, prison reform and the role of wom-
en had all been touched upon earlier. Suddenly the main plot
was being presented, and the fact that this trial was no stage
drama was brought home to me abruptly and definitely.

Now I was confused and uncertain. My thoughts were jump-
ing from one remembered item to another with no continuity.
Fortunately, nature took over and I fell asleep soundly, as though
drugged. I didn't waken until Laura burst in to tell me all the
news of her day at school. I was back to my normal life. As
the routine of the home took over, I was able to set aside the
trial and let it rest until I had a quiet time in the late evening
to recall the day.

I had decided to spend some time each evening talking into
a tape recorder. I knew that talking about the trial would help
me sort out my thinking, and the court instructions prevented
my talking to any person. The recording of my impressions was
a tremendous help psychologically; I was able to review the day
and think about my reactions to it.

During the prosecution's opening statement, the defense attorneys and Ms. Davis had listened carefully. They had taken notes.
Their faces had remained impassive. They did not interrupt Mr.
Harris with distracting tactics. They allowed us to give him our un-
divided attention. I couldn't tell if it was fear that kept them so
still; I wondered if they had expected to hear so damning a story.

Judge Arnason's introduction to the trial had been very reassuring. It gave us the basic rules of the game. Unfortunately, his statement that the prosecution would make an opening address had in no way prepared us for the actual event.

I knew, of course, that the opening statements were not evidence and were not to be considered in the decision as to guilt or innocence, but this was the first time I had heard the prosecution's case in its entirety and it was very believable—terribly confusing, but believable.

The confusion I felt was in the numbers and kinds of guns, the dates the ammunition had been purchased, the names of all those involved. We had been told that 104 prosecution witnesses would appear. I would never be able to remember them all. I wondered if it would be acceptable for a juror to take notes during the trial. Was this something that every good citizen should know? I had never seen it done on any *Perry Mason* show. What would happen if I took a pad and pen into court? Would the judge turn on me, and embarrass me in front of the world's press corps?

I decided I was going to have to chance it. I found a calendar-type notebook and two ball-point pens that were still working and dropped them into my purse. That gave me a start on tomorrow.

But tonight I was still very frightened. If the statements made by Mr. Harris were valid, and if evidence was presented to support them, it seemed quite likely that I was going to have to be one of a group of people to condemn a fellow human to a lifetime of imprisonment.

Fortunately, no decisions had to be made tonight—and the defense would have their chance to refute the story in the morning.

Just before I dropped off to sleep that night, I thought of something in Mr. Harris' opening address that had not rung true. When he had been relating the events of the escape attempt and the involvement of Jonathan Jackson, his phrasing had been very positive.

But in his final summarizing of the involvement of Angela
Davis in the conspiracy, he repeated the phrase, "I think . . . ,"
over and over. He said, "I think we will show . . . ," and "We
think the evidence will show . . . ."

Perhaps Mr. Harris was not as confident as he seemed.

The next morning when we got to the Civic Center, even more
people were in the area around the Superior Court Building
than the day before. The press was out in full force and what
seemed to be an inordinate number of policemen were standing around.

Additionally, a hundred or more people in the courtyard stood
in groups of two or three, or alone. Somehow they looked out
of place. I was not able to categorize them. They didn't look
like the typical "Free Angela" supporters, who were usually
young, casually dressed in work clothes, moving about and talking; neither did they look as though they could all be employees of the Civic Center.

I noticed very little movement in the crowd. Everyone seemed
to be waiting. As we got out of the car and looked around, we
saw Angela Davis starting into the crosswalk from the parking
lot, heading toward the courtyard. That must be the reason for
the crowds. Did all those people waiting there know something
that we didn't? Perhaps it had been announced that she would
make a major statement.

Ruth, Roz and I decided to jaywalk, cut across the street in
the middle of the block and go directly to the side door of the
building to avoid any confrontation. Captain Johnson, the sheriff's officer in charge of our security, had told us that if we were
to enter that door we wouldn't have to wait in line to pass through
the metal detectors. Just as we reached the walk, two calm,
friendly officers stepped in front of us and said we couldn't go
down that way. We smiled and said smugly, "We are on the
Davis jury, and . . . ."

"Sorry, just go on around to the other side of the building."
Obviously, he wasn't impressed. We did as we were told,

irritated because we were being delayed and might not have time for a cup of coffee before being called down to court.

We hurried past the strangers in the courtyard, noticed the press surrounding Ms. Davis, and headed toward the steps of the building entrance. The doors were closed. A deputy stood in front of them with arms folded across his chest, his feet widespread and firmly planted.

We saw others of our jury standing nearby and we joined them. Not one person in the whole area seemed the least bit excited—just patiently waiting. Waiting for what?

"Hey, what's happening?"

No one seemed certain. Ralph said a jailbreak was going on at the county jail; the rumor going through the crowd was that two or three prisoners were holding two hostages on the second floor. The county jail was in this complex of Civic Center buildings, immediately to the south of the Superior Court Building. None of us had ever been around behind the courthouse so we didn't know if these two buildings were connected in any way.

About half of our jury group had arrived early and had entered before the doors were locked; they were probably up on the second floor. We were concerned. We started checking to see who was up there.

Just at that moment a deputy came out of the double doors, stepped forward onto the wide concrete balustrade and called out, "Attention, please! All those called for jury duty for Courtrooms Number 2, 3, 4 and 5 are excused for the present. You are asked to go home and to return at 1:30 this afternoon."

"What about the jurors for Courtroom Number 1, the Davis trial?" I asked.

He checked a slip of paper in his hand and said that no mention was made of Courtroom Number 1—only 2, 3, 4 and 5 were excused.

So we stood there a little forlornly, while almost everyone else left the area. The courtyard seemed almost empty. The police were still standing around and the press people were still clustered around Ms. Davis, whose group had expanded with the arrival of her attorneys.

This north side of the building was shaded and still a little chilly. We decided to go across the yard to the Municipal Building and get a cup of vending machine coffee. The steps over there were warm and sunny. We stopped. This seemed like a good place to sit and wait and watch. We were out of the way and could see much of what was going on. We seven jurors and one alternate stayed close together and kept a little apart from the few other people standing and looking out across the courtyard.

We could see the officers with rifles on the roofs of buildings. We talked about the possibility of tear gas being dropped from the helicopter.

It wouldn't have been my first exposure to tear gas. I had been on the University of California campus in Berkeley just the year before during the Cambodia crisis.

As the helicopter circled over the buildings at San Jose, I felt like a veteran telling recruits what steps to take to protect their eyes and lungs. We talked a little about the students and then about the people in Vietnam and tried to imagine their terror as they watched similar helicopters fly over. Impossible. Real terror had never been a part of my life.

Actually, this whole scene seemed unreal. It wasn't nearly as tense and exciting as crime shows on television. With the exception of the helicopter, there was very little activity. No police cars were racing up with red lights flashing and sirens screaming, their tires screeching as they pulled to a stop. No bells were clanging nor were buzzers going off. No one was running. No one was yelling.

We had no feeling that we were ever in any actual danger. We were just waiting.

The international press corps and the local reporters who regularly attended the trial had been admitted earlier to the security area behind the courthouse. The gate had been locked behind them. They were now back at the wire mesh security fence, clamoring to get out. A big story was breaking and they were being kept from it. The gate was finally opened and they left in a scurry, heading for the jail. One of them circled by us. We asked if he knew anything, but the only additional rumor that he could give us was that one of the prisoners supposedly had a knife. He hurried on. We waited.

Angela Davis and her entourage of attorneys and press started from the front of the buildings and headed down the sidewalk in front of us. One of the TV cameramen, with his heavy camera balanced on his shoulder, walked backward, focusing on Ms. Davis' face. Just as the group got opposite us, he backed directly into a concrete planter filled with greenery. He took a perfect pratfall, holding his camera up to protect it. We all broke into spontaneous laughter and applause, led by Angela Davis and Leo Branton.

They went on through the gate into the security area and disappeared around the back of the courthouse. The helicopter was still circling, but except for the noise it made, we now ignored it. The officers were still on the roof, not moving. Most of the spectators had gone on over toward the county jail. We were left pretty much by ourselves. We waited.

John, the young alternate juror, decided to follow the crowd and see what was going on. The rest of us, who were regular jurors, decided that it was not worth the risk. Something might happen that would cause us to be dismissed from the jury or cause a mistrial. He went running off. We waited.

Art Vanick, the clerk of the court, came out through the security gate, looked around, saw us sitting there and hurried over. He asked, "What in the world are you doing here? Weren't you sent home?"

He seemed uncertain as to just what should be done with us, but knew we shouldn't be left sitting on those steps. So we followed him around the building and entered the courthouse by the back door. He led us to a small windowless room. I looked around. It held a long table with twelve chairs around it. It had a blackboard, ashtrays, two doors leading to diminutive rest rooms, and a cupboard with an open door showing a disarray of papers and notebooks. Nothing else. This obviously was a jury deliberating room. It was designed to provide the minimum of distractions. This room or one just like it would probably be the site where we would decide the case.

In a few minutes the other jurors, those who had been up in the jury assembly room all this time, were escorted in to stay with us. We were relieved to see them. We exchanged greetings and questions. They knew even less about what was happening than we did. Apparently no one had paid any attention to them while they waited up on the second floor, and they were getting very worried about us!

We looked at each other smiling, asking questions, showing our concern for each other. Yesterday afternoon we had left the courtroom as individuals. Now we were happy to be back together as a group; only John was missing.

The bailiff opened the door and asked us to follow him. He led us through a maze of halls and we abruptly entered the courtroom through the door between the jury box and the witness stand. No spectators were in the courtroom, and no members of the press. I recall only one deputy. The attorneys and Ms. Davis were present, and the court reporter and the clerk. Judge Arnason entered, and told the jury that because of what had happened (and he didn't say what had happened!) he was going to dismiss court for the day and we were to return in the morning at the regular time. He emphasized that we were not to read the papers or listen to the radio, or watch television on any subject pertaining to today's activities in San Jose, and we were not to discuss this incident with anyone. We were to leave the court, collect our belongings, go get into our cars and leave the area immediately. Court was dismissed.

We did as we were told. As we passed out of the courtroom we went through the corridor that fronted the court. It was filled with the morning spectators, people who had gotten down to the gates at 6:30 a.m. in order to be sure of getting into court. As we passed by, they looked at us with questions in their eyes. I wondered if they had any inkling as to what was going on. Most of them had been isolated in that corridor since early morning. I doubted if they knew anything that had happened. They must have been thinking that this was a very peculiar way to run a trial.

I didn't think it was relevant to the Davis trial that an escape was attempted from the county jail just as the trial started to get under way. Neither side could hope to profit by instigating such an event. If only one juror were to become frightened and worry that his or her own life might be in danger, it could really hurt the defense.

The fact that prisoners do attempt to escape, without the attempt having been a Communist plot or the result of violent sexual passion, surely could not help the prosecution.

So Judge Arnason's admonition not to read about this day's events seemed a little unreasonable. For the first time I felt some real conflict with his instructions. I had been willing to refrain from reading about the trial itself, but these new instructions seemed extreme.

I was perfectly capable of deciding for myself what I should refrain from reading. The arbitrary assumption that I and my fellow jurors were not able to maintain our intellectual integrity if we were exposed to inflammatory statements in the press was almost insulting. Where did the courts think we had been for the first twenty, thirty or even fifty years of our lives?

Presumably jurors are selected because they are believed to be honest, fair-minded, normal human beings with enough intelligence to understand the legal aspects of the trial and to determine the validity of the evidence. They are not picked from the nunnery, or from some remote mountain tribe that has never been exposed to living in our society.

Supposedly the prosecution is looking for a juror who is not automatically anti-establishment and who will listen to the prosecution's evidence with an open mind and view that evidence favorably.

Supposedly the defense attorney is looking for a juror who, despite having read the daily papers, has not already come to the conclusion that the defendant is automatically guilty merely because of having been charged with a crime.

Both are looking for "honest, fair-minded, intelligent" citizens. These classic statements made by members of the legal profession are reiterated again and again.

But what happens the minute the jury is sworn in? These twelve citizens suddenly become suspect of all sorts of personality defects and character weaknesses. People who have been reading the newspapers for twenty years and have managed to retain some semblance of sanity must now have their reading material restricted, lest their minds become confused and no longer able to distinguish between evidence presented on the witness stand and the interpretation of that evidence in the daily papers.

The restrictions placed on the Davis jury were much less extreme than those placed on the jurors in other recent trials such as the Manson case in which the juries were sequestered for the entire trial. To me this confinement is inexcusable and a travesty of the constitutional rights of both the accused and the jurors.

The accused has a right to trial by a jury of peers. While this term is certainly arguable, it has come to mean twelve people selected randomly from the population where the crime was committed, who are then screened for bias and incompetence. If these people are then protected from direct, deliberate attempts to influence their judgment—that should be all that is needed. If I were the accused, I would much prefer that those considering my case be allowed to maintain their normal lives as much as possible. I think I would question the independence and common sense and even the motives of an individual who would accept being locked up for months without protest.

Certainly the rights of the citizen who is selected for jury duty and then sequestered are being denied. Someone who has committed no crime, who is not even accused of committing a crime, is taken from home, job and family, and deprived of choice of reading material, of privacy, of freedom of movement and of association with friends. This dutiful citizen is under police guard at all times. The only possible rationale for this confinement would be to protect a juror from direct physical assault.

Each person has his or her own way of relieving tension. Some work in the garden, some exercise in the gym, some have a cocktail, some jog, some sleep. Whatever the method, it is important each juror be allowed to follow his or her own pattern of behavior. Otherwise the delays of the court procedures assume too much importance. Any legal maneuvering that prolongs the ordeal from which there is no release cannot help but affect the jury.

I believe that this type of influence could have more effect on the judgment of the jurors than any reading of papers or listening to the radio or television.

When I went to the grocery store that afternoon, I saw the headline: ESCAPE ATTEMPT—ONE KILLED. I turned my eyes away, but the headline remained in my thoughts as I finished buying the food for dinner, as I drove home, and as I went about preparing the meal.

Having seen the headline, the answer to one question became very important to me. Had the person who had been killed been a police officer, one of the hostages, one of the prisoners or an innocent bystander? The information was important to me as a citizen and a person—not as a juror. We had been told to refrain from discussing this "incident" with anybody, yet something had happened in the community and I could not merely dismiss it from my mind. I decided my thinking about the trial would not be disturbed if I asked the one question, "Who was killed?"

It had been one of the prisoners. I heard, read or discussed no more about the incident. The answer did not affect my thinking about Angela Davis and her guilt or innocence, nor would it have if a policeman or a hostage had been the one killed. The death was a tragedy. It was a tragedy that was a part of the world we were living in.

After the trial, I read that three desperate men, one a murderer captured after having escaped from San Quentin, had taken a deputy public defender and a medical secretary as hostages.

They used twelve-inch knives as weapons. They demanded that an automobile be made available and that they be allowed to escape or the hostages would be killed. Negotiations were carried on for an hour and a half. But when it became apparent the prisoners were going to make good their threats, a deputy killed the ringleader with a single shot. The other two then surrendered and the hostages were unharmed. No reason was given for their escape attempt and none seemed necessary.

It was almost ten o'clock when court convened the next morning. While the judge and the attorneys had been deciding how best to handle the possible effects of the previous day's events, we jurors sat upstairs and drank coffee and ate donuts—and waited.

After the usual routine opening of court, Judge Arnason turned to the jury and said that he would now ask the bailiff to escort all of the jurors and alternates except Juror Number 1 into the jury room, and we would then be asked some questions individually. We filed out of the court, leaving Ralph sitting alone and defenseless in the upper-right-hand corner of the jury box.

We were led back behind the courtroom into the same small windowless room we had been in the day before. Obviously, the questions were going to be about the effect the escape attempt had on us.

When Ralph came back into the room, he said he had been instructed not to discuss the questioning with the rest of us, and so we exchanged little conversation as we waited. The questioning took only a few moments. As one returned to the room, the next went back to the jury box accompanied by the bailiff.

While we waited those who smoked lit their cigarettes. The room began to get stuffy. We had no place to look, except at each other or the bare walls. The room seemed to get smaller and smaller as we sat there.

I hadn't thought it was important enough to mention during the *voir dire,* but I would never voluntarily stay in a small confined space. I do not like elevators or closets. My uneasiness couldn't be classified as claustrophobia. I am just happiest out-doors—on top of a mountain or at the beach. Small windowless rooms bother me.

Claustrophobia in a juror could cause quite a problem during deliberations. I wondered if any of my fellow jurors would be bothered by it. I looked around at the others. No one seemed uneasy or looking for a way to get out.

One event occupied our thoughts for a while. As we sat in the chairs around the table, we noticed next to one of the ash-trays an envelope lying on the table, face down. After a while, Nick reached out casually, turned it over and read the address. He quickly dropped it on the table face down and pulled his hand back. He sat looking at it. Another juror watching him asked, "What's the letter?"

He answered, "Take a look."

The letter was addressed to Angela Davis! Well! Now what to do? We were faced with our first real group decision. We all agreed that the letter had been on the table when we came into the room. We also agreed that it might look strange if, after the jury left the room, a sheriff's deputy found a letter addressed to Angela Davis lying on the table. Suppose it was an unsigned letter of support or of hate. That would surely be possible grounds for a mistrial.

We, the jury, decided to hand it to the bailiff the next time he entered the room, and to make a full explanation to him at that time, with all of us present and concurring.

Great! We did this. The solution worked. We felt very good; we had acted together to solve our problem. After that, going into the court alone and being questioned by the judge as to where we were and what we had seen the day before seemed less difficult.

After each of us had been questioned and had given assur-ances that we would still be able to function as fair and im-partial jurors, we were returned to the jury box as a group and Judge Arnason repeated the admonition he had given to us on the first day we came to court as prospective jurors:

You are admonished it is your duty not to converse
among yourselves or anyone else on any subject connected with the trial, or to form or express any opinion
thereon until the case is finally submitted to you.

You are further admonished that there may appear
in the newspapers or on the radio or television reports
concerning this case, and you may be tempted to read,
listen to or watch them. Please do not do so. Due process of law requires that the evidence to be considered
by you in reaching your verdict must meet certain
standards. For example, a witness may testify about
events he himself has seen or heard, but not about
matters of which he was told by others. Also, witnesses
must be sworn to tell the truth and must be subject to
cross-examination. News reports about the case are not
subject to these standards and if you read, listen to, or
watch these reports, you may be exposed to misleading
information which unduly favors one side and to which
the other side is unable to respond.

In fairness to both sides, therefore, it is essential
that you comply with the instructions.

Judge Arnason went on to include specifically the events of
the jailbreak attempt of the day before. He assured us that those
events had no relevance in this trial whatsoever. No connection
existed between the events of the day before and the issues involved in this case.

I understood. The San Jose jailbreak attempt had nothing to
do with the Davis trial. Right! But we jurors were not to read
or talk about the jailbreak. Why not?

Judge Arnason turned from the jury and directed his attention
to the court. "At this time, ladies and gentlemen, we will now
proceed with the opening statement by the defense . . . ."

Angela Y. Davis rose quietly from her chair and walked to the podium. She set her notes on the stand, looked up at us pleasantly. She waited a few seconds for the room to settle down and then began her "lecture." She was well prepared. She spoke easily and directly, referring to her notes on occasion, but giving the impression that they were merely available to remind her of items too important to chance forgetting.

I had been amazed that Angela Davis had been called in all the papers the "beautiful" young black woman. Seeing her in court the first time, on the day of my *voir dire,* I wondered that anyone would call her beautiful. She was tall, yes, but she sat hunched over her notebooks, with a shawl around her shoulders. Her face was impassive. Her Afro hairstyle and large glasses covered the upper part of her face and in the early days of the trial she seldom smiled.

The day that she had questioned one of the alternate jurors, she had seemed very young, physically very delicate and a little shy and unsure of herself in the role of inquisitor. My impression at that time was that she felt it wasn't really quite in the best of taste to question a person publicly about personal philosophy and beliefs. She was charming and personable, but still not beautiful.

As she made the opening statement for her defense, she stood tall and confident. She was at ease in her area of excellence. Ms. Davis, lecturer in philosophy, suddenly emerged and in that role she reviewed the thesis of Albert Harris as though she were in a classroom. She reviewed it with consummate skill and utter scorn. He did not get a passing grade from this teacher! One almost expected her, as she finished, to toss his paper back on his table and suggest he rewrite the whole thing, and "for God's sake, start with a more logical hypothesis, before giving it to me to read again!"

She took the prosecution's opening statement and went through it step by step, pointing out what she considered to be inconsistencies, false logic and great gaps in the evidence he planned to present—"gaps you jurors are going to have the burden of filling with surmise and conjecture."

She stated that the defense would present evidence to support alternative theories to the implications Mr. Harris had made from the evidence.

Three aspects of the case seemed to me to be of utmost importance, after having listened to the prosecution's opening statement: 1) Angela Davis' ownership of the guns and purchasing of ammunition; 2) her close association with Jonathan Jackson; and 3) her activities during the few days preceding the escape attempt.

These three aspects were discussed by Angela Davis. She told of growing up in Birmingham, Alabama, and of living in an area called "Dynamite Hill," so called because of the frequent attacks by racists. She told how her own father went out at night with other neighborhood men on armed patrol of their neighborhood. Owning guns and knowing how to use them had been a part of her childhood. She mentioned that the four little girls who had been killed in the bombing of a church in Birmingham had been friends of her family.

When she came to California and was involved in radical movements, she often found herself the target of extremist individuals in the community. So, again, obtaining means of self-protection became imperative. She stated that the evidence would demonstrate that the situation in this regard became particularly tense after her position at UCLA in the Department of Philosophy was threatened by the regents of the university. Testimony would be given as to hundreds and thousands of threats on her life.

She said she felt there was good reason to need some sort of protection, if she intended to live out her years.

Another point that Ms. Davis made was that she purchased guns and ammunition for her friends as well as for herself simply because she worked and, having money, bought weapons just as she would pay rent or medical expenses for her friends when they were unable to do so. The purchase of those weapons was related to her fears for her own life and for the lives of those around her.

The ammunition was purchased because she felt, as most

people feel, that the owner of a gun should become familiar with it and learn to use it effectively. In doing so, Ms. Davis said that she became interested in target shooting as a sport. When engaging in target practice, using up large numbers of shells is very easy.

As she was talking about the ammunition, I realized that the prosecution never talked about bullets or shells, but always referred to "rounds of ammunition." To someone not familiar with the terminology, a "round" sounds like a series of bullets, perhaps a cartridge full, or a clip of twenty to thirty shells, or even the belt of bullets that are used in machine guns.

In fact, a "round" is a single bullet. The words "a shell" or "a bullet" do not have nearly as formidable a sound as has the term a "round of ammunition." (We talked about this during jury deliberations, and some of the jurors were not aware of this distinction.)

In discussing her close association with Jonathan Jackson, Angela Davis reminded us that the first overt act of the conspiracy count in the indictment issued by the grand jury consisted of a description of a rally in which she participated. This rally was not for George Jackson alone, but for John Cluchette and Fleeta Drumgo as well. She stated that she was "exercising constitutionally guaranteed rights—rights guaranteed to me by the First Amendment . . . ," when she participated in this rally.

She said that the evidence would show that she had been involved in the movement to free the Soledad Brothers long before she had any personal contact with George Jackson. The prosecutor, however, had transformed the character of the case, by substituting sexual passion for political conviction as the motive. He would now have the jury believe that she was a person who would commit the crimes of murder, kidnapping and conspiracy, motivated by pure passion.

"Members of the jury, this is utterly fantastic. It is utterly absurd. Yet it is understandable that Mr. Harris would like to take advantage of the fact that I am a woman, for in this society women are supposed to act only in accordance with the dictates of their emotions and passions. I might say that this is clearly a symptom of the male chauvinism that prevails in our society."

Male chauvinism? I would never have thought of that! But once said, it became obvious. Of course the prosecution would find it far more reasonable that a woman, a black woman, would act from sexual passion rather than political motivation. They would also assume that the jury would accept that motive more easily.

I looked over at Albert Harris. He was looking down at his hands. His lips were pressed tightly together. His neck was slightly red.

Mr. Harris had already interrupted the opening address of the defense with objections on two occasions. Very early in the statement, he made the point that an opening statement should be confined to descriptions of the evidence to be presented. Ms. Davis answered that she was merely making an introduction that would allow the jurors to understand the need for such evidence. Judge Arnason allowed her to continue.

Harris stopped her again with the same objection just a few sentences before the male chauvinist remark, saying, "Your Honor, excuse me. But isn't the opening statement to outline the evidence that the defense is going to present and not to comment on what the prosecution may or may not present? There is a time for that at the end of the trial. It is called argument."

His manner was patronizing, and Ms. Davis fought back. "I would appreciate it, Judge Arnason, if you would ask the prosecutor not to interrupt me during the deliverance of the opening statement. We patiently sat through four hours of the prosecution's opening statement. And although we felt that many times he said things that were not appropriate for an opening statement, we did not make one objection. I would appreciate it if he would do the same for us."

Judge Arnason answered slowly, "Well, that's a good argument for the equal dignity rule, I suppose . . . I am going to allow you to continue."

After that ruling, Mr. Harris sat down, picked up a stack of papers and straightened them by tapping them again and again against the top of the table. He leaned over and whispered something to his associate, Clifford Thompson. He shuffled through his papers. He snapped his attaché case open and put the papers inside. He snapped the attaché case closed, and shoved it to the front of his table. He hitched his chair roughly across the floor as he settled back.

The disturbance that he made distracted my attention from Ms. Davis. Was this a deliberate ploy to counteract the effect of the judge's ruling, an effort to rattle Ms. Davis, or just a display of poor sportsmanship?

Meanwhile, Angela Davis continued, giving no indication that she was bothered. She stated that, long before she became involved in the Soledad Brothers' defense, she had had a history of involvement in efforts to assist in freeing people accused of criminal activity—Huey Newton, the twenty-one Panthers arrested in New York, Ericka Huggins and Bobby Seale, the eighteen members of the Black Panther Party in Los Angeles, the Soledad 7 who had been charged with a crime similar to that for which the Soledad Brothers were charged.

"In all of my activities, including my activities to free the Soledad Brothers, my goal has been to aid in the creation of a movement, a movement encompassing millions of people, indeed, the majority of people in the United States, a movement which might ultimately result in a more humane socialist society."

All of these cases had resulted in acquittals or dismissal of charges!

Amazing! I hadn't realized that!

Ms. Davis stated that evidence would show that her efforts to free George Jackson always expressed themselves within the context of a movement to free all the Soledad Brothers and to free all women and men who are unjustly imprisoned. It would be confirmed on the witness stand that all of her activities were open and legal.

" . . . We organized demonstrations, rallies, leafleting campaigns and various other informational and educational activities. You will learn that before any of us had any personal contact with any of the Soledad Brothers, we on the defense committee felt that these three black men charged with killing a prison guard were being persecuted not because they had committed any crime, but because of their militant political stance and because of their efforts to improve the character of prison life from within. . . . [Therefore] we knew that our most effective approach had to be that of informing and educating the public about the case . . . ."

According to Angela Davis, during the entire time she was involved in the movement to free the Soledad Brothers, she was the object of an extensive spy campaign. Numerous reports were made to various police agencies. The prosecutor himself had police reports on rallies and films of demonstrations. He had evidence gathered by an entire network of police spies, and spies from the Department of Corrections on the content of her political efforts to free George Jackson, Fleeta Drumgo and John Cluchette. But the jury would not see this evidence, because, if we did, it would show us the process whereby an innocent person can be set up and accused of outrageous crimes.

" . . . My activities toward the freedom of the Soledad Brothers and the freedom of George Jackson in particular, far from being evidence of my guilt, are on the contrary evidence of my innocence . . . . Members of the jury, we were correct in our understanding of the Soledad Brothers' case, for Monday morning as you sat here listening to the prosecution's opening statement and as you heard that I was not interested in furthering the movement to free the Soledad Brothers, the ultimate fruits of our labor were attained, for twelve women and men who for a period of many, many months had listened to all the evidence that the prosecution could muster against the Soledad Brothers, ended in the courtroom in San Francisco and pronounced the two surviving Soledad Brothers not guilty. And if George Jackson had not been struck down by a San Quentin prison guard in August of last year, he too would have been freed in that way from that unjust prosecution."

Ms. Davis told how her activities led to friendships with members of Fleeta Drumgo's family and with members of John Cluchette's family and with George Jackson's family—Mr. and Mrs. Jackson and their daughters, Penny and Frances, and their son, Jonathan. On many occasions she went to rallies with one or the other or all of them.

After the controversy at UCLA constant threats were made on her life. For her to travel any distance alone was not safe, without the company of others. For that reason she often traveled together with Jonathan Jackson, as well as others.

She then went on to talk about Jonathan, and the angry frustrations and concerns of a young man who had no memories of his older brother except those which had been obscured by prison bars. Jonathan was a child of seven when his brother was first taken to prison, and for ten long years he accompanied various members of his family to various prisons throughout the State of California to visit with his brother. These visits must have left an indelible impression on him about what a prisoner's life was like; though he was only seventeen years old, he must have been extremely and intimately sensitive to the plight, the frustrations, the feeling of depression and futility that men like James McClain and Ruchell Magee and William Christmas must have felt.

"Jonathan Jackson and I were friends, but my friendship with him is absolutely no basis for contending that I played some role in the events of August 7, 1970."

Concerning the eyewitness testimony that would be used to place her close to the activities of that week, she asked us to examine that testimony very carefully and critically. She reminded us that judicial history is replete with instances where people such as her have been convicted on the basis of mistaken identification, particularly where identification of black people is made by white people.

Mr. Harris had said that flight was evidence of guilt, and that she had made clear in no uncertain terms her belief in her own guilt by fleeing from the State of California, beginning on the day of the commission of the crime.

Ms. Davis said that it would become abundantly clear that she bought a ticket with her own check and conducted herself as any other person who would have been catching that flight at that time. The prosecution was attempting, she said, to transmute normal, everyday human conduct, such as going to catch a plane, into evidence of guilt.

She said that only after she felt that her own safety was in danger had she departed from the State of California, and that evidence would show that she had good reason to fear police violence, should she voluntarily submit to the authorities. She feared the prospect of many, many months of incarceration without bail, the prospect of a trial before an all-white jury, and of other obstacles which would stand in her way. She said that evidence would show that, particularly in the black and Chicano communities, people have great fear that once one is accused of a crime, one may find it extremely difficult to overcome the many obstacles that stand in the way of protecting one's innocence. The processes, such communities believed, would not be fair.

"This is a sick kind of game which the prosecutor has been playing. He has invented a scheme, a diagram, a conspiracy and then he fits his conspirator, his criminal into that picture . . . . He must shape his circumstantial case out of the ordinary circumstances of everyday life. And he leaves it to you, the jury, to supply the missing link which converts ordinary activity into criminal conduct."

Examples of implications made by the prosecution about which the jury would have to guess, speculate, conjecture or surmise were given. "Take for example the fact that I moved in July of 1970. Can you fathom what this has to do with the conspiracy? I don't think that the prosecutor ever told you on Monday what that fact had to do with my participation in the conspiracy. But you are left to wonder and to guess and to speculate. He says that she moved. Therefore, it must have been in connection with some conspiracy, he asks you to think.

"The prosecutor says that Jonathan Jackson lived in my apartment for three weeks. The evidence will demonstrate that this was not true. Yet, clearly, this was said because you are being asked implicitly to speculate that we were living there together in an apartment in order to participate in a conspiracy.

"He says that the evidence will show that I cashed a check for $100 on August 4th. He tells you about the $100; then in his very next breath he says, 'Jonathan Jackson rented a van on August 6th and paid for it with $40, with two $20 bills.' And you are the ones supposed to put these two facts together, facts totally unrelated to one another. You are supposed to guess that I had something to do with the rental of the van. I cashed a check for $100 in Oakland. Jonathan Jackson, two days later, rents a van and pays for it with $40. Ergo, I rented the van.

"But is there any way you can really hook up these two facts —the cashing of a check by me and the rental of a van by another and find criminal intent without making a wild guess?"

Three more aspects of the case about which Angela Davis said that we jurors would have great gaps to fill were striking enough so that I realized how credulous I had been. They broke the continuity of Mr. Harris' very involved story.

One was the fact that Jonathan Jackson registered at a motel the night before the shoot-out, and asked for a room for two. We were to infer that if a second person checked in, it must have been Angela Davis. No evidence of that would be given; we would have to guess, to speculate.

Next, from the fact that she openly bought guns later used in the escape attempt, we were to infer that she knowingly supplied Jonathan Jackson with the guns for use on August 7th. No evidence would be introduced to that effect, only speculation and conjecture.

Again, from the fact that she, Angela Davis, caught a plane at the San Francisco airport to go to Los Angeles on the same day as the alleged crimes, we were to make another guess, and believe either that she was waiting at the airport for the arrival of the van or for a telephone call, or that this journey was a flight—a flight that showed knowledge of guilt.

Each of these issues had seemed to me to be of great importance. Angela Davis had given me alternatives to consider. I was a long way from accepting all or even part of them, but I did feel that they were valid alternatives, and the evidence that was to be presented during the trial must be weighed with both the prosecution and defense theories in mind.

Angela Davis concluded her opening statement, "My political commitment, my political experience has always manifested itself in what I am capable of doing—that is, writing, speaking and organizing around the plight of all oppressed people, around political prisoners, the Soledad Brothers specifically, and thereby in my own way helping to promote an effective movement for progressive social change . . . a movement capable of creating a climate of public opinion in which, for instance, the death penalty could be declared unconstitutional . . . a movement capable of creating a climate of public opinion in which juries could acquit prisoners of politically inspired charges, an event we witnessed day before yesterday with the acquittal of the two surviving Soledad Brothers . . . .

" . . . We have the utmost confidence that your verdict will be the only verdict that the evidence and justice demand in this case . . . not guilty."

She looked at us, smiled briefly and gathered up her papers.

During the questioning of the jurors, as the selection process was going on, the prosecution had asked each of us if we would be able to distinguish between "Angela Davis, attorney" and "Angela Davis, defendant"—pointing out that we were to consider as evidence only those statements made under oath. They seemed very concerned about this issue, and I thought justly so. No statement made by Ms. Davis in her opening address was to be taken as fact. She was not testifying from the witness stand.

However, a far more important happening took place while

Angela Davis was acting as her own attorney during her opening statement, as well as during her earlier examination of a prospective alternate juror. She established her identity with us. Instead of looking across the room at an enigmatic figure representing black militant communism, we were given a chance to discover her as a fellow human being.

Perhaps this recognition could have been accomplished by having her testify on her own behalf during the defense at the end of the trial, but by then it might have been too late. We jurors would have listened to all the testimony by the prosecution witnesses without being able to relate it to the person involved. Early participation by the defendant is very important.

The original intent of those framers of our Constitution and Bill of Rights in guaranteeing trial by jury was to see to it that those who were to judge would know the accused or his family—or at least be familiar with his background and economic status. Today, living in an urban society, we are strangers. If an individual juror's attitudes and prejudices aren't thoroughly explored, the selection of the jury would be based on the attorneys' (both the defense and the prosecution) stereotypes of people, such as "young people are liberals," "blacks will not convict other blacks," "construction workers are for 'law and order.'"

This stereotyping is patently unfair to both sides. It is also unfair to the citizen who has willingly given time to assist in the judicial process. We are individuals and should be selected on that basis.

The other side of the coin is equally valid. The jury is asked to decide on the guilt or innocence of a person accused of a crime. We, the jury, are told that we are not to judge the person, but only the facts of the case. That instruction is very reassuring at the start of a trial, but it soon becomes obvious that no real analysis of these "facts" can be made without interpreting them in relation to the people involved. Since we do not know the defendant, we are forced to make decisions based on what we have heard or read about different types of people, or on personal knowledge of other individuals—which may or may not be valid.

Anything that allows the jury to look on the defendant as an individual rather than as a stereotype of his particular political, ethnic, social, or economic group is important to the defendant and to the jury.

We were not allowed to go home after the defense opening statement, to think about the implications and digest the information. After a brief recess, the first of the prosecution witnesses was called and the next part of the trial began.

The Case against Angela Davis

All of the people who had been selected as witnesses for either the prosecution or defense were excluded from the courtroom until they were called to testify. They were not allowed to sit in the spectator section and watch the proceedings. The purpose of this restriction was to prevent a witness from being influenced by another's testimony. In *Perry Mason,* the camera can zoom in and register the reactions of the other witnesses as they hear the testimony from the stand. How else would the audience know the guilty party as the plot unfolds? We were not given that added help.

Each witness was brought in through the center door of the courtroom, down the center aisle, past the spectator section, across the floor of the court in front of the jury box. When that point was reached, the clerk called out the person's name. Each one would stop and turn quickly, a little confused, wondering why the name had been called—probably assuming he or she had done something wrong. The clerk ordered, "Raise your right hand!" and the oath was administered rapidly, routinely.

The witness would turn back, take the two steps up and sit in the witness stand—a heavy oak chair with a curved back and solid arm rests. The table top was slanted slightly and had a narrow ledge to keep the varicolored marking pencils and a pointer from rolling off. A small microphone on a long swivel arm extended from the side of the table.

Often a witness would try to adjust the chair by sliding it closer to the table. After a couple of hard jerks the person would realize it was bolted to the floor. A large iron ring was bolted to the floor behind the chair, and another into the back of the chair itself.

When I first saw them, I wondered: Why all the hardware? The metal looked new and shiny—probably part of the insane security for this trial. Who had they planned to chain to the chair and bolt to the floor? Perhaps the surviving Soledad Brothers were expected as witnesses. Maybe Ruchell Magee—but no, I wouldn't think his attorney would let him testify; he had his own trial to worry about. Had they been planning to chain Angela Davis to the chair?

How could the Court expect a juror to receive the testimony of a person manacled and chained with the same acceptance as the testimony of an ordinary citizen?

Those of us at the end of the jury box could see the witnesses from head to toe. We could watch their hands twist in their laps, their feet tap and turn and dance as they were being questioned. The other jurors, all of the spectators, the attorneys and the court personnel were prevented from seeing anything below the chest level by the solid front of the witness stand. I truly had the "best seat in the house."

Mrs. Maria Elena Graham was a middle-aged, round-faced dark-haired woman who looked as though she might be of Southern European descent. A year and seven months ago she had been

selected as a juror in Courtroom Number 2, Marin County Courthouse, for the trial of San Quentin convict James McClain. She
was Juror Number 12. The trial had started on Monday, August 4,
1970, and on Friday, August 7th, at about eleven o'clock the
escape attempt started. Mrs. Graham had been one of the three
jurors taken hostage and she had been wounded in the shoot-out.

She was the first witness in the trial and she was very nervous,
very frightened. Her hands kept clutching her stomach, as if to
stop its hurting. My impression was that a sharp pain, like an
ulcer, was being aggravated by the tension, and kneading it with
her hands was soothing. She took long deep breaths after answering questions. She was working very hard at keeping her composure.

Mrs. Graham was a very important witness. She described the
Marin courtroom and the positions of the people in it; and she
told the events that took place from the time Jonathan Jackson
came into the courtroom until she was pulled from the van with
a bullet wound in her arm. The brachial artery had been severed,
and she was bleeding profusely.

Now she was back in a courtroom, this time as a witness, and
she was obviously upset. Today was a very difficult day for
Mrs. Graham, and it was a very difficult day for me. An ordinary middle-aged woman had been a juror and by chance had
become involved in a continuing series of traumatic events. I felt
a great sympathy for her. If I had lived in Marin County and she
had lived in Santa Clara, our roles might have been interchanged
and I would have been sitting there!

Mr. Harris, in his questioning of her, made no attempt to calm
her or help her control her emotions. She answered his questions
carefully, telling us again the same story that the prosecutor had
recounted in his opening address. Details were added that made
the action in the courtroom real and vital.

She told how Ruchell Magee demanded that the shackles be
removed from his body and how Gary Thomas warned the jurors
to keep calm and not do anything foolish. She described how
McClain picked which jurors to take as hostages and how, when
one of the other convicts started to tie the hostages together by

looping wire around their necks, McClain made him stop, saying that it would be painful and that he should tie it around their waists.

She told of the nine people climbing into the van which had only one seat, the driver's seat. The rest of them sat on the floor, crowded together. The wires were removed as they got into the van. She told of the noise and confusion of the shoot-out, and of seeing the judge with his face half blown off and his teeth hanging out.

During her testimony news pictures of the day's action were brought out. The pictures were blown up to about three feet by four feet and were very clear and beautifully done. Identifying anyone in these pictures would be no problem. Most of them looked as though they were posed, or at least as if the subjects were perfectly willing to stand still for a moment while the pictures were being taken. We saw photographs of the three jurors and the Assistant D.A. wired together; another of Judge Haley in his judicial robes—taped to his neck was the sawed-off shotgun, with McClain's hand on the trigger; and a picture with a clear front-face view of Jonathan Jackson—young, scared, but under control. His eyes were wide and alert, his mouth open, and he had a carbine cradled in his arms.

Three guns were brought out—a sawed-off shotgun, a handgun and the carbine with the collapsible stock—and Mrs. Graham identified them as being the same or similar to guns used in the escape.

The guns and the pictures had a very traumatic effect on Mrs. Graham. She had difficulty continuing her testimony and had to ask for a glass of water, which was brought to her by the bailiff.

The most important testimony that Mrs. Graham gave, as far as I was concerned, related to the demand for the release of the Soledad Brothers by James McClain while he was talking to the sheriff's department on the phone in the courtroom. This demand was repeated by Jonathan Jackson in the courtroom, in the elevator, and even while they were walking out through the parking lot to the van. She said that she heard it repeatedly.

If that were true, it lent validity to the motive of the crime being the freeing of the Soledad Brothers, and most particularly George Jackson.

When Albert Harris finished his direct examination, the defense asked if the cross-examination, which would be fairly long, would be postponed until morning, since they would not be able to finish it that afternoon.

We went home—again exhausted. Again too much had happened for me to assimilate.

That night I had the first of a series of recurring nightmares. These dreams woke me up every night for the next week or ten days.

I dreamed that I was sitting in a darkened movie theater. Most of the seats were filled, but I was sitting by myself near the aisle on the left-hand side about two-thirds of the way down. The only light in the room came from the single ray from the projector in the back wall. Suddenly the movie was interrupted by the sounds of yelling and gunfire. I was confused as to whether it was part of the show, and I turned to look toward the back of the theater. The large double doors were flung open and in the light coming through those doors I could see figures running and flashes from guns. The noise of the guns and the screams from the audience all mingled and reached a crescendo—and I woke up!

I lay there for a while—terrified—waiting for my heart to slow down a little, afraid to go back to sleep.

The next day, Thursday, was the day I really became a juror. I was introduced to the art of cross-examination.

When court started, Mr. Harris asked to be allowed to continue his direct questioning of Mrs. Graham for a few moments. She had said during her testimony the day before that the bailiff in the courtroom had been disarmed. When Mr. Harris reminded her that she had made that statement, she said that it was an error. The bailiff had not been armed in the first place, and so could not be disarmed.

This point had been emphasized in Mr. Harris' opening address. No guns had been allowed in the courtrooms in Marin County, therefore there had been no way to resist an act of violence. The witness had carelessly stated something that was obviously in error and I hadn't even noticed! I was going to have to get to work. I couldn't just sit there and listen politely to the stories of the witnesses. I was going to have to question and analyze and worry about each statement.

The bailiff's being "disarmed" was not the only thing that I missed in the testimony of this witness, but fortunately the courts do not have to depend on the analytical ability of the jurors. The responsibility for analysis lies with the adversary attorney.

The cross-examination was handled by Howard Moore, Jr. Apparently the defense attorneys had available to them all the written statements made to the prosecution by their witnesses —such as the initial statements right after the crime, and the testimony given at the grand jury inquiry. Many of them were in the person's own handwriting; others were typed and signed.

Mrs. Graham's right arm had been wounded so her original statement was in the form of notes taken by an official while she was still in the hospital. Nowhere in this statement had any mention been made of a demand for the release of the Soledad Brothers made in the courtroom. Again a year later, at another interview, even though she said the demand was made by Jonathan Jackson out in the hallway, no mention was made of McClain's saying, "Free the Soledad Brothers" in the courtroom when he was talking on the phone to the Marin County sheriff's department.

This point was extremely important. If "Free the Soledad Brothers" were yelled by Jonathan Jackson in the halls, or were said spontaneously by McClain to the photographer as they were preparing to go down the elevator, it might have no real relevance to the motive. However, if it were part of McClain's statement to the sheriff at the very moment the taking of hostages was being announced to the authorities, it had to be considered a little differently. It became a condition for the safety of the hostages and a part of the whole plan of action, rather than a request or a statement or a scream of militant rhetoric. The use of the phrase would indicate a more involved plot—not just a simple escape attempt.

Mr. Moore kept after the witness, asking her to read again and again the statements she had made immediately after the crime, and those she had made eight months after the crime. He was forcing her to remember that she had not mentioned anything about McClain's demanding the release of the Soledad Brothers.

When she had accepted that point, she said that she just remembered it *now* and that details were coming back to her. Mr. Moore then moved on to the recent interview, a pretrial orientation interview she had had with Mr. Harris. He asked her just what the prosecutor had said to her that made it possible for her to "remember" this statement now?

She first denied vehemently that Mr. Harris had suggested anything to her, stating that he had merely told her to tell the truth. As Mr. Moore continued probing I heard her denials being voiced in a much less confident manner. She said that she didn't want to believe that Harris' asking her whether the statement had been made in the courtroom caused her to think now that she remembered it from the events of two years ago. "I hate to admit that I could be so easily influenced by anyone. I like to think I have a mind of my own and . . . this would be defeating my own intelligence."

Mr. Moore replied gently that whether or not she had control of her mind was not at issue here; what was at issue was the truth of what really happened in the courtroom that day.

Mrs. Graham finally admitted that very probably she had been influenced by the questioning, and that her recall of events would be much more likely to be accurate shortly after the events happened.

The next item of her testimony to be discussed was the statement that she made about recognizing as a sawed-off shotgun the gun taped to Judge Haley's neck. This woman was not familiar with guns, she did not shoot guns; she had not recognized the carbine as a rifle—she called it a machine gun. Yet she said that she knew that the gun in question was a sawed-off shotgun.

As Mr. Moore asked her about it, I turned to look at the gun. My reaction when it had been brought out the day before and shown to her had been, "So that's what a sawed-off shotgun looks like!" I doubt very much if a person not familiar with such a weapon would recognize it immediately. He or she would more likely look at it and wonder what that strange-looking gun was. I thought it looked like a homemade gun. When I was a kid, my brothers and I fastened pieces of wood and pipe together and made "guns" that shot large rubber bands cut from inner tubes. Those play guns were about the size of this weapon whose stock was sawed off about four or five inches from the hammer and whose barrel was about a foot long. The ends of the wooden stock and grip were roughly cut and unfinished. The metal barrel had jagged saw marks. The gun still had strips of adhesive tape on it. The tape was torn and stained— stained with dirt and blood.

Could she have seen news programs or read in the paper that it was a sawed-off shotgun, and that was why she "remembered" having been able to recognize it immediately for what it was? The answer to that query was definite. She had recognized it the first time she saw it!

Again, she was being very positive about what she remembered, but it didn't seem reasonable to me.

All right! I was learning.

Howard Moore, Jr., is a large man, about forty years old, tall, with broad shoulders. I first saw him on the screen of the closed-circuit television, and later that same day from a distance across the large courtyard. The first thing I noticed about him was his distinctive modified Afro hairstyle—thinning and short on top, wide and thick on the sides. The long oval of his face was accentuated by a short blunt goatee. In the courtroom, sitting behind the defense table, his dark, very bright, intense eyes dominated his face. He wore bright shirts and ties, and a red handkerchief in the pocket of his coat. He moved around the courtroom gracefully but, as many large men do, he held his arms close to his body as though he were afraid of bumping into things. The room seemed just a shade too small for him. He balanced on his toes, leaning forward slightly, which made him look as though he was always hurrying, even when he was standing still.

When he opened his cross-examination of Mrs. Graham, she tensed visibly and reached for the paper cup of water. Mr. Moore gave her a few moments to calm down, introduced himself and told her that his purpose was not to upset her, but rather to bring out certain aspects of the case which he thought were significant. He added, "If at any time you feel that you are going to cry or something, or that it becomes unbearable for you, would you indicate to the judge so we could have a small recess so you could regain your composure?"

She nodded but did not relax. Her manner was wary and just a little antagonistic.

Toward the end of the morning session, Mr. Moore started questioning her about what had happened in the van, where she sat, what happened when the firing started, what Gary Thomas had done, and who had helped her out of the van.

She said that she had had difficulty maintaining her balance when the van jerked to a halt. In attempting to get a full description of that scene, Mr. Moore sat down on the floor of the courtroom with his legs stretched out and his back pressed against the front of the jury box. He asked her if that was about how she had been sitting. Mrs. Graham leaned forward, helpful and relaxed. For the first time she seemed to feel safe, not threatened. The change in the woman was fantastic. She was able to handle the rest of her testimony with confidence.

When she left the courtroom she seemed to feel she had acquitted herself well. I watched her walk out, and then turned my head to look at Howard Moore, Jr. He was back sitting at the defense table looking over at us in the jury box, with a half-smile. He had done his job. He had shown the jury the unreliability of long-term memory. He had also introduced the possibility of questionable methods being used by the prosecutor in eliciting testimony.

The second witness was another of the Marin jurors. Mrs. Norene Morris was a very different kind of witness—careful and restrained. When she had started to read the newspaper accounts of the escape attempt, she had found the stories to be so distorted she decided to refrain from reading or listening to any news until after she had made her own written report of the events. While testifying in court, she was very careful never to make a statement that called for an assumption on her part. She felt free to admit that she didn't remember, and when she was questioned about statements she had made in her original handwritten report, she said that if she had written it, then that was how she remembered it at that time; she felt her recollection would have been much more accurate then than it was now.

Two points made by Mrs. Morris struck me as being important. She said that when McClain went up to Judge Haley with the sawed-off shotgun, he called down to Jonathan Jackson for "the tape" and Jonathan replied, "I didn't bring it!" However, a roll of adhesive tape was picked out of the pile of things dumped onto the floor from Jonathan's bulging briefcase. It was tossed up to McClain, who used it to tape the gun to the judge's neck.

McClain's asking for a specific item indicated to me that he and Jonathan had planned the escape together. McClain knew what was going on.

The second point that I felt was important was something that *didn't* happen. She said that she did not hear McClain or anyone else mention the Soledad Brothers while they were in the courtroom. This contradicted the statements made by the previous witness and lent strength to the idea that Mrs. Graham "remembered" too much.

As Albert Harris completed his direct examination of Mrs. Morris, he asked her to identify the people in some of the pictures—the same pictures that we had seen the day before. The final picture was the one of Judge Haley in his robes with the sawed-off shotgun taped to his neck, walking down the corridor with James McClain. She turned in the witness chair, took a quick look—and broke down, her shoulders shaking, her hand to her mouth. She was barely able to say the names, "Judge Haley and James McClain." Apparently the judge, who from his picture looked like a very kindly, grandfatherly type of man, was very well liked and respected. Mrs. Morris was shocked by the picture, the use of which was so unmistakably contrived by the prosecutor to get just that effect that it offended me. He had manipulated and used this woman by tricking her into displaying her deep emotions, just so that we jurors would become emotionally involved. My response was indeed emotional, but it was anger at the means he used rather than compassion for the witness.

I hadn't expected such a scene and wasn't prepared to deal with it. I would have to be more wary and guard against too much empathy with the witnesses.

Leo Branton, who cross-examined this witness, took a few minutes to reassure her that he was not going to frighten her. Then he complimented her on the candor and the honesty with which she had written her original statement, and also how she had answered the questions from the prosecutor. He asked about details of her original statement concerning the things she heard said in the courtroom, emphasizing that no report of the Soledad Brothers had ever been mentioned; nor had she recognized the sawed-off shotgun when it first appeared. She had said that it looked like a "piece of wood with metal on it."

Through Branton's questioning, another differing view of the events of the day was brought out. Mrs. Morris seemed to feel great sorrow for what had happened and showed sympathy and understanding toward James McClain. She mentioned the reassurances he gave the hostages, saying that he didn't want them to be frightened, that his own mother had come to court the first day of the trial and had been so frightened she had not been able to return. But someone [I didn't catch the name] had destroyed a report so he had no chance in court; he wasn't guilty and he had to be free.

When one of the other convicts suggested taking a baby which had been brought in with its parents, McClain refused to allow him to take the baby as hostage, or an older woman, or another woman juror who was shaking with fear. Again, when William Christmas started to tie the hostages together with wire around their necks, McClain had told him to stop, saying, "Cut that out! Haven't you had enough of that? We are not animals. We won't act like them!"

One more witness appeared before court adjourned for the day—another woman, again a juror from the Marin courtroom, and also a hostage. She remembered nothing that was said after Jonathan Jackson stood up and said (according to her), "Freeze!"

She seemed to recall most of the essential details of the events of the day and they were similar to those of the previous witnesses. The defense attorney asked her if she had heard any mention of Soledad Brothers in the courtroom. She replied that she hadn't, since she remembered nothing that was said in the courtroom and, although she was tied to Mrs. Graham, she did not recall hearing such a statement in the hall, or when the group was getting into the elevator.

So we ended the day with one woman stating positively that she remembered a demand for freeing the Soledad Brothers, one woman who did not hear such a demand, and the third one who could not recall hearing anything. It looked like a standoff, but taking into account the stability of the witnesses, my feeling was that no such statement had been made in the courtroom. Without further supportive statements I would have to ignore that aspect of the testimony of the first witness. The reliability of her remembered testimony was very doubtful.

The statements of the three women bore one marked similarity. They each, when asked to describe Jonathan Jackson, said that he was young, tall, slender, wore a light raincoat, had an Afro . . . then they stopped. Mr. Harris had to ask, "Was he black?"

They then said, "yes,"—and went on with the description. A few years ago the first thing they would have mentioned when describing Jonathan Jackson was that he was "colored" or "a Negro." Maybe we are learning and times are a-changin'.

Our son, John, and his friend, Nancy, came to Sunday dinner that weekend. It was the first time we had visited since I had been picked for the jury so we had lots to talk about that afternoon—not about the trial itself, but about the changes it had made in our lives. I was so full of my great adventure it wasn't until late in the evening that we started talking about their activities at the Dance Palace in Point Reyes Station.

As they were telling some of the amusing things that had happened, they mentioned that they had been "rousted" by the FBI.

About ten days before, as Nancy was loading her car with the week's laundry to take to the laundromat, a car pulled up to the side of the building, parking right in front of her. All four doors opened at once and six men in dark suits, white shirts and ties burst out. One came over to her while the others walked quickly around to the other sides of the building. She knew immediately that they were from the FBI—no one in Point Reyes Station wears a coat and tie—and bursting from the car like that was right out of a movie scenario.

The one who approached her identified himself and said that they had information that a draft evader, whose name they gave, was living there, and could they search the house? Knowing that no one by that name had lived there for the past few months since they had moved in, permission to look for him was given.

John said they went through the rooms quickly, looking into closets and under beds—all the large obvious hiding places. They did not look into drawers or cabinets for small items. When they started asking the names of all the people living there, they were refused the information, since that question seemed an unnecessary invasion of privacy. So all six agents piled back into the car and left, heading toward San Francisco.

The young people were laughing about it as they told the story. They were amused by the inefficiency of the FBI, saying that anyone in the tiny town would have told them who was living in the building. They didn't have to make such a big deal of it.

I didn't think the incident was very amusing and I didn't think the FBI was that inefficient. I asked them the date this search had taken place. It was March 23, 1972—just nine days after I was accepted on the jury of the Angela Davis trial, ten days after I told the Assistant Attorney General where my son John lived and worked. John and Nancy had never been bothered before (and have not been bothered since). The event seemed too much of a coincidence. Why would the agents decide to make a raid just then to pick up a draft resister who hadn't been around for months, if ever, and at a time when the war was "winding down"? It seemed highly unlikely to me that six agents would be sent on such an excursion without better evidence that their man was there.

I felt then and I feel now that the FBI did not make their raid to look for a draft dodger. That was merely the excuse. Rather, the agents arrived primarily to check out the "hippie commune" in which the son of one of the jurors was living. They probably suspected it of being a hotbed of radical militancy, and perhaps even directly involved in the Marin County escape attempt.

I felt, secondly, that they were sending me a message. They were telling me that my children were vulnerable.

I became very angry and planned to inform Judge Arnason in the morning of what had happened and to tell him that I wanted whoever was responsible to know that I had gotten the message, and that if another such incident occurred, I would go directly to the press.

The rest of the family persuaded me that I was probably being a little paranoid about the whole thing—it was most likely just a coincidence. If I were to make an issue of it, I would be basing my accusations on mere guesswork.

I finally agreed to do nothing about it, but only after I got everyone's assurance that any further episodes would be reported immediately. Paranoid or not, I wanted the children aware of possible problems they might have to deal with because of my new involvement. I phoned our daughter, Ellen, in the northern part of the state where she was attending school and suggested she be careful about her activities and associates for the next few months. This call served a double purpose: it would alert her—and if our phone was being tapped, it would let the authorities know I had gotten the message.

I didn't brood about this episode. In fact, I don't think it affected me at all, except that occasionally I looked closely at any person sitting quietly in a parked car in my neighborhood.

Back to the trial! We started the second week with the appearance on the stand of James Kean, photographer for the San Rafael newspaper—a man of about fifty-five to sixty years, very thin, rather handsome, mustachioed. He looked like a type-cast movie version of a British writer, or the owner of a shoppe in an art colony. He had been out on the freeway when he heard on his police monitor that an escape attempt was going on at the Civic Center. He had hurried there and was present as the convicts and the hostages came out of the courtroom. He was told to take all the pictures he wanted, that, "We are the new revolutionaries!"

So Mr. Kean took photographs. He took photographs of the action in the hall; from the balcony he took pictures of the escape group out in the parking lot, and getting into the van; after the shooting stopped, he took pictures of the resulting chaos. It seemed to me that the only evidence needed to prove the kidnapping and murder was the series of photographs taken by Mr. Kean. They left little question as to what had happened.

After identifying the pictures he had taken, he told about the events at the elevator door. He said that McClain without any prompting said to him, "Tell them we want the Soledad Brothers freed by twelve o'clock." Kean asked if he meant twelve today, or twelve midnight. McClain answered, "Twelve today!"

As they left, going down the elevator, Mr. Kean wrote down the words "Soledad Brothers" on a notepad.

The shoot-out followed and after taking the pictures of the van and the area around the van, he went back to the newspaper to develop them. He did not mention the Soledad Brothers statement to anyone until he was being interviewed by a reporter for his paper.

In cross-examining him about this statement, Mr. Branton called out loud and clear, *"Free the Soledad Brothers!"* and asked if this was not what Kean had heard—a political statement?

The shout rang through the courtroom. Although Mr. Kean maintained that he thought it was a demand directed at him, I would remember Mr. Branton's resounding call whenever the Soledad Brothers were mentioned.

I was interested in the time involved in the sequence of events. Kean said that he had heard of the break on his radio at about 10:45; that he drove in to the Civic Center from the freeway, parked his car, picked out which cameras to take, walked about a block to the Civic Center entrance, took an elevator up to the second floor, and arrived in the corridor about the same time as the prisoners and their hostages came out of the courtroom.

He then had time to take thirty to forty pictures as the participants milled around before going down the elevator to the parking lot. It seemed to me that a lot of confusion and no sense of haste or urgency was shown in the pictures. This impression was borne out by the length of time involved in each step of the escape. I would have thought that such a situation would have been without delays—things would have gone "click-click-click" so they could get away before the police had a chance to regroup and set up a defense. This casual attitude added to the unreality of the scene.

One of the prosecution witnesses did quote Jonathan Jackson as saying, "Hurry up, we only have five minutes." Five minutes for what? Were they supposed to be somewhere at a particular time? He didn't say, "Hurry up, we are running late," or "We are taking too much time to get out of here!" No, he said, "We only have five minutes." Perhaps they did have a time schedule, which would all come clear with later testimony.

A stream of law-enforcement officers followed. Between April 4th and April 20th we heard testimony from twenty city, county and state employees, the parade only momentarily interrupted by a couple of gun salesmen and another photographer. The officers were used to substantiate the story already told, and to identify their guns. No detail of the escape attempt and shoot-out seemed too small or too unimportant to be excluded. Each officer told just where he was standing and where he went from there, and what he heard and saw.

Once the fundamentals had been testified to by the hostages and the news photographer, and documented with his photos, it seemed to me to be so unnecessary to continue repeating the story. Each time it was told it lost a little of its impact. What started to come through was the inefficiency of the law-enforcement personnel—sincere but inept.

None of the officers wore their uniforms when they testified. I wondered why not. Since all were prosecution witnesses, it must have been done at the prosecutor's request. Did he feel that we jurors would tend to believe their testimony more readily if they were not in uniform? Or perhaps this procedure was not exclusive for this trial, and law officers always wear "civies" when appearing in court. Most of them seemed a little uncomfortable in their coats and ties, as though they had grown a little bigger and heavier on the job. I got to be fairly proficient in identifying the type of work they did by looking at their shoes as they came walking in. The men in the sheriff's department usually wore boots, the San Quentin correction officers wore high-top shoes with steel-reinforced toes, and the local police usually came in wearing straight, heavy, black walking shoes.

Most of the men tried very hard to tell their stories with honesty, and to answer the questions as directly as possible. The usual procedure was to ask the witness his name, his employment, and whether he remembered August 7, 1970—then a series of questions: Are you shown in this picture? Does this chart represent the area where you were? Would you please pick up one of the marking pencils and write your initials on the chart at that spot? Would you please write large enough so that it can be seen by the court?

Putting initials on a chart or picture presented a big problem for many of them. It usually took a few moments of short questions and answers to get a fairly legible and accurate set on the paper. Then the witness would be questioned specifically to allow for any small addition to the story he might have to offer, such as what he heard said or saw happen. Poor Prosecutor Harris had an awful time trying to communicate with the witnesses and to have them make the statements he wanted. They never volunteered anything. He would say, "Do you remember . . . ?" and the witness would say, "Yes." "Well, ah . . . was there somebody else there?" "Yes." "Well, ah . . . ah . . . could you describe them?" Then the witness would flounder even more. Mr. Harris never showed any irritation toward the witness. His face would get a little red, and his eyebrows would raise, but his voice remained calm and unhurried.

I decided that if ever I wanted to lead a life of crime, I would head for Marin County.

One of the many instances that convinced me of the logic of this plan was the testimony of Officer Hughes. T. V. (Ted) Hughes had been a deputy sheriff for Marin County for twenty-five years. He was standing around in the hall outside the courtrooms when the escapees and hostages came out. His service revolver, a .357 magnum loaded with .38-caliber military rounds (this information later became important in showing which gun shot whom) was taken from him by Jonathan Jackson. It was an older gun with a distinctive style of sight. Ted Hughes went down to the van as soon as the shooting stopped. He saw a fellow officer standing behind the van, holding a revolver in his left hand. It looked like his gun. Hughes took it and opened the cylinder to look at the serial number. Sure enough, it was his gun, so he put it in his holster. At the end of his shift, at four o'clock in the afternoon, he went home and put the holster and gun on a shelf in his room. He didn't look at it again until the next morning as he was getting ready to go back to work. At that time he opened the cylinder and checked to see if it was loaded. Lo and behold! All six bullets had been fired!

Incredible! A trained police officer, whose gun was taken from him by someone involved in a violent crime which he witnessed didn't even think to check if it had been fired, or to leave it to be impounded for evidence. If I had read about it, I would never have believed it. No writer of detective stories would dare to have a character behave like that. However, sitting in the jury box, watching this very sincere, bumbling middle-aged man tell what had happened, I felt it must be the literal truth.

Ted Hughes had also heard the demand for the release of other prisoners as the group was getting on the elevator. When Mr. Branton asked him to repeat it just as he heard it, saying the same words, and in the same tone of voice and just as loudly as he remembered it, T. V. (Ted) Hughes called out loudly, *"Power to the people! Free our brothers in Folsom!"*

Mr. Branton said, "Thank you. I have no further questions."

The problem of handling the guns after the shoot-out had been more than these men could cope with. They lifted rifles, hand-guns and shotguns out of the van, handed them to other officers, who placed them on the road or on the backs of cars or who walked around carrying them, trying to give them to someone in charge. No one seemed to have been concerned about preserving fingerprints or checking whether or not these guns had been fired.

A San Quentin officer had been out on the rifle range giving shooting instruction to some new guards. With him were four officers and one free man. (When asked to define what he meant by "free" man, he replied that it is any person who is neither a prisoner nor a guard.) When the call came in about the trouble at Marin Civic Center, he took the recruits and the guns over to help stop the escape. As soon as they arrived, he parked the car to form a road block, he passed out the guns, and then stationed himself behind a car parked near the South Arch of the building. He said the yellow Hertz rent-a-van approached, the driver saw the road block and stopped. The driver and passenger were scanning the area with their eyes when they spotted him crouched behind the car. They were about thirty feet away, just across the street. A revolver was fired at him by one or possibly both of the men.

The San Quentin correction officer described in a cold, flat, hard voice how he returned the fire with his .30-.30 pump-action rifle, shooting first the driver, who "flew back," then the passenger, who also "flew out of sight." When a black man in a green sport coat raised up from the back of the van, the officer fired at him; he "bounced down and reappeared immediately." The officer fired a second time and the man stayed down.

Then a white gentleman in a grey suit raised up and said, "Stop firing, I am hit!"

So the officer stopped firing.

A picture of a beach "fun house" shooting gallery with the painted sitting ducks flashed across my mind. His recital was so ruthlessly cold-blooded it didn't seem human.

I wondered, did he stop because of what had been called out, or because it was a white gentleman who called?

The correction officer prevented the escape. But what a terrible price!

On the third floor of the Civic Center, a state employee had been interviewing an applicant for a job. He had been taping the interview. At least one bullet came crashing through the window of his third-story office, and when the shooting was over he had a recording of the entire episode.

We heard it played in the courtroom.

The sequence of shots took seventeen seconds.

The judge was killed with a bullet in his chest and a shotgun blast in his face; the seventeen-year-old youth who was driving the van was dead with a bullet through his lungs; two of the three convicts were dead and the other severely wounded; the Assistant District Attorney was crippled for life with his spinal cord severed; and one of the women hostages was wounded with an artery cut in her right arm. All in seventeen seconds—and it sounded like popcorn popping!

One of the San Quentin officers who had been involved in the shooting explained that the policy of the prison was never to let hostages interfere with the capturing of prisoners. This policy was well known, and it applied to themselves as well as other people. In cross-examining this prison guard, the defense asked him for a fuller explanation.

Defense: "That means whether they are holding one judge or five judges?"

Officer: "Yes."

"Or one woman or twenty women?"

"Yes."

"Or one child or twenty children?"

"Yes."

"That the policy of the San Quentin guards and correctional officers is that, at all costs, they must prevent the escape? Is that right?"

"That also includes the officers that work in the institution, sir."

"In other words, it is more important to prevent the escape than to save human life. Is that correct?"

"Yes, sir."

Another of the officers testified he had been near his car over at the other roadway, the one leading into the North Arch. This spot was two to three hundred feet from the place the van came to a stop. He testified that he had a revolver with a two-inch barrel, and from that distance, he opened fire when the shooting started. I couldn't believe it! A handgun with a two-inch barrel could not be fired with a hope of accuracy at that distance. Anyone who had ever seen a *High Noon*-type movie would know that even with the long-barrelled guns of the Old West, the duelists stalked each other until only a few yards separated them before they tried to shoot it out.

Apparently the defense attorney had difficulty believing it also, since he asked what he was shooting at, the van? And the officer replied, "Yes, the front window of the van."

With that kind of shooting going on, no wonder the third-floor window of the Civic Center was shot out.

An occasional witness was the exception to what had become the typical officer. Timothy Miller was a handsome young California Highway Patrol officer. He told of standing next to the building at the North Arch and watching the van go past. When the shooting started, he stepped out into the road and shouted, "Stop shooting!" When Mr. Branton asked him why he had shouted this, he replied, "I didn't want people killed."

In the whole series of witnesses, only this one expressed concern for the people involved. We were shown a picture of Miller kneeling beside Mrs. Graham applying first aid to her wounded arm. His concern did not interfere with his functioning as a policeman. When a co-officer stopped by his side and asked if he could do anything, Tim Miller told him to go over to where he had laid his shotgun down and check to confirm that it had not been fired.

It might have been just their personal mannerisms, but some of the lawmen appeared too slick, too much like the often maligned used car salesman. One of these was an investigator for the sheriff's department. He was so facile with his answers he seemed almost a professional witness. As he was being questioned by the defense, just before each answer, his eyes flicked over for a quick look at the prosecutor, Mr. Harris. I don't mean to imply that Harris was coaching him. Harris kept his face very impassive, but the officer checked each time. Where most of the officers seemed to be concerned with remembering all the things they were supposed to say, this man seemed to be answering the questions carefully so as *not* to say something.

His contribution to the case was that he had heard someone from the group say, "You have until twelve noon to release the Soledad Brothers." Under cross-examination he admitted that at the time he did not think that this was directed at anyone; he thought it sounded like the yell, *"Free the Soledad Brothers,"* that he had heard at the rallies in San Francisco.

Part of his assigned duties was to attend rallies and demonstrations in the Bay Area and identify the Marin County people who attended them. Amazing! If he were attending such meetings for Marin County, someone was probably attending them for my county (Santa Clara) and for each of the other counties around the bay. Perhaps representatives were sent from all the cities as well, and the states' Attorney Generals' offices and the FBI. I wondered if the officers knew each other and, like the demonstrators, would say to their colleagues as the rally broke up, "So long. See you next week at the Peace March!" I wondered if they ever listened to the ideas being expressed or if they only looked at faces.

In this first segment of the prosecution's case we heard the testimony of Gary Thomas, who had been the prosecuting attorney in the James McClain trial. He had been taken as a hostage and had been wounded in the shoot-out. A bullet had struck his spine; he will never walk again. Gary Thomas was allowed to testify from his wheel chair on the floor of the courtroom directly in front of the jury box. He told essentially the same details of the courtroom scene as had the other witnesses. He did not recall hearing any statement concerning the Soledad Brothers, either in the courtroom itself or at the elevator.

The dramatic portion of his testimony came when he was

telling about his recollection of what happened inside the van. When the van jerked to a stop, he saw Jonathan Jackson point his right hand, holding a gun, out the window. He heard one shot followed quickly by two other shots. He turned and looked at Judge Haley and saw the right side of the judge's face pull away from his skull, as though in slow motion. Seeing that, he reached forward and grabbed the gun from Jonathan Jackson's now bloody hand and started firing—first at Jackson, then McClain; then, turning to the back of the van, he fired at Christmas and Magee. The gun clicked as he tried to fire again, so he turned back to yell out the driver's window, "Stop firing!" At that moment he was hit in the back with a bullet.

The gun he used was a .357-magnum police revolver which had been taken from a deputy outside the courtroom just a few minutes before.

A very large question arose in my mind as to the accuracy of his memory. For example, his description of the judge's face falling apart as though in slow motion seemed highly improbable, especially to anyone familiar with the effect of a short-range shotgun blast. I had hunted wild game birds with my husband. One day when I was still learning the use of a shotgun, we were walking through a fallow pumpkin field. Art raised his gun and fired at a medium-sized pumpkin about six feet away. The pumpkin disappeared—instantly and totally! It happened so fast that I couldn't see it happen. The pumpkin was sitting there . . . and then it was gone. I observed no "slow motion" effect. That incident made me carefully consider the validity of Gary Thomas' perception.

The law-enforcement men who had handled the guns and other materials with reckless abandon after the shoot-out, taking no care to preserve fingerprints or even to make certain the guns and bullets were saved, were not alone in demonstrating a lack of professional efficiency. The doctor who had performed the autopsies for the coroner testified as to the wounds found in the bodies of the four victims. He carefully explained that the judge was shot two times, once with a shotgun blast to his head and once with a bullet in the chest, either of which could have been fatal. Christmas was shot in the back. Both Jackson and McClain were shot in a similar manner with the bullet entering the left side just in front of the shoulder blade, crossing through the chest and out the right side of the body at the upper right arm.

In cross-examination, Mr. Moore brought out that the original reports on Jackson and McClain described the course of the bullets as just the opposite, entering on the right side, crossing and exiting from the left. The doctor carefully explained that in no way could he make that determination with complete accuracy, and he had changed his report only after (a *year* after!) someone had told him that from the physical evidence of their clothing, the trajectory must have been as he now reported it.

Howard Moore reached out and picked up the extra court recorder's chair, set it in an open space in front of the witness stand and said, "You don't mind if I sit down?" Everyone murmured, "No," and Judge Arnason perked up and looked down at him.

Mr. Moore then said to the doctor, "Now, I'm a little confused as to just where these bullets are going in and out." He swung the chair around and sat. The doctor came down off the witness stand, walked over to him and pointed at Moore's body where the bullet that killed Jonathan Jackson would have entered. Mr. Moore then asked the jurors if we could see, and some of us shook our heads, "No." He picked up the chair, moved it over in front of the jury box with his back to us, and said, "Well, here—I'll sit just as though I were driving along the road in this yellow van . . . ." He raised his arms as though he were holding a steering wheel. The doctor leaned over and touched Moore's left side at the spot corresponding to Jackson's entry wound. He walked around and touched Moore's shoulder at the right side to show the point of exit.

Mr. Moore said, "Now if I were sitting up erect, then the bullet would have to have come from just opposite me, as though a man were crouching over at that side, and had shot up at the side of the van; this is where the path of the bullet would have been?" And of course it was; quite obviously it was. And McClain's wound was almost identical to Jackson's.

Howard Moore had again used his body to provide the jury with a more graphic presentation. He was laying the ground work for establishing that the first shot had been fired by the San Quentin officer crouched at the side of the road.

In this first segment of the prosecution's case, which was to give evidence of a kidnap and murder, the final witness was the Chief Criminalist from the California Department of Justice. A criminalist is a specialist who has been trained in the laboratory techniques of criminal investigation. The training is in ballistics, chemical determinations, blood typing and the like. This man had studied at the University of California and had received most of his training on the job as he worked in the Department of Justice for a number of years as an assistant. Sometime between the August 7, 1970, escape attempt and the trial, he had tried going into business for himself. He was rehired by the state as Chief Criminalist just two weeks before the trial started.

He identified all the bullets that had been found and linked them to the guns. He demonstrated the techniques used and he had his full report in front of him. He did not have any corroborative evidence of the results of his tests. He had not taken any pictures of matching bullets, nor had he checked the hands of any of the participants for nitrogen deposits which would show if they had recently fired a gun. His testimony was based on his report of what he had found, and since no evidence to the contrary existed, it must be accepted. I got the impression that his very convenient appointment as Chief Criminalist just two weeks before he was to testify made the defense team a little uneasy.

I tried to keep a careful record of all the bullets and guns by writing everything down on my note pad. But when the cross-examination started I became irreversibly confused. I decided that I couldn't rely on my notes. More guns than I could remember were mentioned as I tried to listen to the testimony. The questions and answers jumped from one to another and by the time I figured out which gun they were talking about they had moved on to the next. I quit trying to keep up.

As I remember the guns, they included:

1. A Browning automatic, short-barreled handgun, purchased by Angela Y. Davis in 1968. This gun was carried into court by Jonathan Jackson, given to McClain, then to Magee, and was found in the belt of Magee's pants after the shoot-out. It had not been fired.

2. A carbine with an extendible stock, which was bought by Angela Y. Davis in 1969. It was called the "beast" carbine by the prosecutor. It was carried into the courtroom by Jonathan Jackson, and kept by him during the escape attempt. It had been fired in the parking lot.

3. Another carbine which was bought by Angela Y. Davis in July, 1970, in Los Angeles. It was in the van but not fired.

4. The .12-gauge single-shot shotgun, sawed-off, which was purchased by Angela Y. Davis in San Francisco two days before the escape attempt.

5. Officer Morris' .357-magnum revolver, taken from him in the hall by Jonathan Jackson, and recovered from the van. All six bullets had been fired.

6. T. V. Hughes' .357-magnum revolver, loaded with military .38-caliber bullets. This gun was taken from him by Jonathan Jackson, and was recovered in the van. All six bullets had been fired.

7 and 8. Two shotguns taken from officers by Jonathan Jackson and one of the convicts as they came out of the building. One of these guns had been fired twice. They were both recovered from the van.

9. A pump-action .30-.30 rifle, which was the gun Officer Mathews used as he fired into the window of the van. He fired four times.

Other guns were mentioned, such as the revolver with the

two-inch barrel which had been fired from the South Arch, Timothy Miller's gun which he didn't fire, and the guns of the other San Quentin officers, some fired and some not.

Most of these guns were introduced as evidence during this part of the trial. Each one was brought in, shown to the witness for identification, given a number (such as Prosecution's Number 56), then laid on a wide table. The jumbled stack of weapons grew as the trial progressed, since each morning all the guns were brought back. Walking into the courtroom, I would pass by the table on my way to the far end of the jury box. I would glance down, check to see if they were still there, and try to ignore the cluttered arsenal for the rest of the day.

The guns had "trigger guards," which were circular pieces of wood bolted through the gun at the trigger site which would prevent their being fired. Even so, I felt uneasy when the guns were handled carelessly. I had been taught too well as a child never to point a gun, loaded or not, at anyone. One of the witnesses, as he looked for a serial number, inadvertantly pointed a revolver directly at Judge Arnason who instinctively flinched and ducked away.

When Mr. Harris needed to ask a witness about one or the other of the guns, he would rummage through the pile until he was able to pick out the right one.

Toward the end of the prosecution's case we came in one morning and the guns were gone! I felt a great lightening of spirit that morning when I walked past and saw the table empty.

The Dawn of a Juror

As the days dragged on, testimony about this part of the indictment in which Angela Davis played no active role was repeated constantly. We jurors had been duly impressed with the seriousness of the charges and the heavy responsibility we carried. We watched each witness in the parade very carefully, expecting each one to make some profound or significant statement. We listened to every detail of his testimony. We leaned forward in our seats as he strained to put his initials on the chart at the very spot where he was standing on that fateful day.

But as we listened to all the statements as to where "X" officer was standing in the corridor, what gun he was wearing and how long he had been on the police force, and watched all of the detailed initialing of the charts and pictures, and heard all the questioning relative to the shoot-out itself and the guns involved, it became obvious that all this testimony was repetitious, confusing and totally unnecessary.

For this trial, we on the jury needed to know simply: did a kidnap occur, and did a death result? The first five witnesses plus a coroner's report were surely sufficient to show these events had occurred. The hostages had been there throughout the whole affair; the photographer had documented it.

Once those basics were established, the important thing was to tie Angela Davis into the conspiracy. Other than the testimony as to her ownership of the guns, the only aspect of this segment of the trial that really pertained to her was the reports of the demand for freeing the Soledad Brothers.

Since so much of the testimony was not relevant, what was the purpose of presenting it? As I sat there becoming more and more bored, I came to suspect that the prosecutor was using the Angela Davis trial to present evidence that would be used in a second trial, the trial of Ruchell Magee. Magee's trial was scheduled to start shortly after the completion of this one. All of these witnesses would be repeating their testimony there. In a sense two trials were going on in our courtroom, but no one was defending Ruchell Magee.

Another possibility occurred to me. Perhaps it was thought necessary that every bit of testimony be presented to the jury to satisfy some legal requirement.

While we were sitting in our jury box the whole ritual of a trial took shape. The court was run by men, and men had long,

long ago worked out trial procedures to make it possible for them to function with a minimum of conflict. Court processes have become so formalized and established that sometimes the purpose of it all becomes lost in the routine. Like the game of baseball, the ground rules were set and past performances were recorded in minute detail. It was as though, once started, the orderly progression could not be stopped.

I occasionally fantasized about what would happen if I were just to stand up and start walking out of the courtroom, right in the middle of some irrelevant bit of testimony—and when I was stopped (and I surely would be stopped!), I would turn and explain calmly and rationally that I was bored with the games these men were playing, and would be happy to return when they were ready to get down to the business at hand . . . which was, I thought, to prove that Ms. Davis was involved in kidnap, murder and/or conspiracy.

Another of my favorite fantasies was to wonder what the trial would be like if women were running the courts. This scene was so totally male dominated: the judge, robed and sitting on his raised dais and served by his uniformed bailiff who announced like an English lackey the judge's entrance into court; the prosecution attorneys representing "The People of the State of California;" the two principal defense attorneys, adversaries of the accusors; the clerk of the court, keeper of the records; the dozens of deputies; and, after the first day, the stream of witnesses —all men!

The roles of women were few and strictly secondary. The two court reporters were women. A very quiet young sheriff's matron sat every day behind the prosecutors. The other two defense attorneys were women, neither of whom uttered a single word during this part of the trial (at least not in the presence of the jury) and whose occasional absences from the courtroom were explained by, "They are running some errands," or "There is paper work to be done back at the office."

Of course Ms. Davis was present. But after her opening statement, she became less and less an obvious participant and seemed to fade into the background. In the opening days of the trial, during the questioning of the prospective jurors, she had joined in discussions at the table with the other attorneys, but when the body of the prosecution's case got under way, she assumed a less active role. She even moved back from the attorney's table and sat in the row of chairs in front of the railing that separated the spectators from the court.

The prosecution seemed consciously trying to ignore Angela Davis' existence as a human being. To them she was an object called "the defendant." The only times either of the prosecuting attorneys looked at her was when it became necessary for a witness to identify her in court. When that happened, the prosecutor would turn his head and follow the glance of the witness to Ms. Davis, look quickly away and say, "For the record, the witness has identified Angela Davis." He would then turn his back toward her and continue with his questioning.

At the very infrequent times when it was necessary to include her in the proceedings, Judge Arnason treated her with old-worldly courtly consideration and politeness, as did the other members of the court. Her own attorneys often became so engrossed in the work they were doing, they seemed to forget she was there. She sat quietly with her notebook in her lap, listening intently, taking notes—writing, always writing. She looked like a student attending a required class that she abhorred—but one she desperately needed to pass.

The atmosphere of male dominance did not carry over to the jury assembly room. Once we left the restrictions of the courtroom and the security area and arrived up in our own territory, we were autonomous. We had our own unspoken rules of behavior for our little society of twelve-plus-four. Racial and ethnic jokes had no place in our group, and any careless male chauvinist or sexist statements or acts were immediately pointed out to the offender with good-natured objections.

One day while we were waiting for court to reconvene, Michelle said thoughtfully, "Isn't the foreman of a jury always a man?"

"Not on *this* jury!" I called out.

Ruth explained that a man wasn't required, but choosing a man had become the custom in states which allowed the jurors to select their own foreman. In some states, Juror Number 1 is automatically the foreman.

Bob joined the conversation and informed us he had once served on a jury in a small civil case. He was the only man on the jury—eleven women and himself—but they had selected him to be the foreman. We talked about the implications of that decision, and how society forced us into roles. And how we were now forced into the role of jurors.

With all its formal language and ritualistic procedures, the court pushed and fitted us into the mold of THE JURY so that the mechanics of the trial could proceed.

Once we were chosen and the trial started, we lost our individuality and became THE JURY. The press ignored us. The judge, the attorneys and all the court personnel always spoke to and about us as a group: "The jury is excused . . . will you please bring the jury down? . . . the jury is reminded that . . . ."

We were never consulted about the hours we were to report, or whether dismissal at a certain time was convenient for us. We were never given any reasons for delays or early dismissals, other than the vague statements that court business needed to be taken care of.

We were told just where to sit and when to come and what we must not read and who we must not talk to. We agreed to accept the judge's ruling as to the interpretation of the law. We were told our duties.

We were not told our rights. We were not informed if we could take notes; one of us tried it and nothing happened, so we decided that was acceptable. We were not told whether or not we could ask questions during the proceedings; one of us tried that, and the judge looked at him and said rather stiffly, "I will not communicate directly with a member of the jury. If you have a question, write it down, give it to the bailiff, and I will read it." So we decided asking questions wasn't looked on with favor.

More importantly, we were not informed as to what actions
on our part would lead to our dismissal from the jury, or cause
a mistrial. Not knowing the limits put a lot of pressure on us.
Everyone else in the courtroom knew his or her job. They knew
what they were doing—everyone except us. We were overwhelmed.
We tried to conform and adjust and be perfect jurors, perfect
people.

But up in the jury assembly room we were able to relax together—which was fortunate, since throughout the trial there
were long, long periods of waiting. Occasionally we would arrive
in time for court to convene at the regular 9:00 time and then
would wait in the jury assembly room for an hour, or two, or
all morning. Other times our lunch hour would start at 11:00
and extend until 1:30 or 2:00. Sometimes we would be sent
home in the middle of the morning or the middle of the afternoon.

We jurors could in no way anticipate what the schedule would
be. For many of us this situation was very inconvenient. For all
of us it was frustrating. We were people who were used to working, used to being busy and functional. Wasting hour after hour
was difficult for people who felt they had better things to do
with their time.

One of the women had been informed by her employer that
any day she was dismissed before 3:00 p.m., she was expected
to report to work to finish out the afternoon. That meant she
had to rush home, change into her secretary's dress, and head
for the office. Another woman (one of the alternate jurors)
worked nights as a cocktail waitress in Santa Cruz, a beach town
twenty miles away. She worked until 2:00 a.m.; then, after a
few hours sleep, rose early to drive to San Jose. She would come
bursting through the door just before the scheduled starting time,
greet everyone, and then join us in what was often a long and
tedious wait.

We were occasionally given a day or two off. Since these breaks
were not anticipated, we had no way to plan for them. We were
able to make some arrangements for the regular Friday off, but

even those had to be tentative since we were given to understand that whenever the Court (meaning Judge Arnason) thought it necessary or desirable, sessions might be held on Friday. (Not having court on Fridays cut our weekly pay from $25 to $20, and every day that we weren't called to court, another $5 was lopped off. Some weeks we were paid nothing.)

I had arranged to use my accrued vacation time for the days that we were not in court. For me to continue with my research project on a schedule of one day a week would have been impossible. So my reaction whenever we had an extra day or a couple of half-days off was, "Damn, there goes another day's vacation time!"

Being kept in the jury assembly room for long periods meant we had the additional problem of adjusting to each other as we waited together. Fortunately we had lots of space and excellent facilities. The chairs were comfortable and couches and tables were available. I first tried reading to pass the time, and found that I couldn't concentrate on anything but very light, very short magazine pieces. I tried hobbies. I brought clay and worked on designing a chess set, but that was messy and I had to keep everyone waiting for me while I washed up whenever we were called down. Playing chess wasn't satisfactory either, except during the lunch breaks when we knew we would have time to finish a game. I hadn't done any knitting or embroidery for years, and didn't want to start on something I might not want to finish after the trial. Others in the group did knit and sew.

Some wrote letters or took care of their first-of-the-month bills. Bob paced the floor and smoked. Winona read quietly by herself in the large room. Nick spread the sports pages out over the desk in the large room and spent hours poring over the sports news. Roz, Jim and Luis talked or read. One of the alternates sat looking out the window and reporting to the rest of us any activity she noted. The rest of us tried playing games, and finally settled on penny-ante poker as the one game that fit our needs. Sometimes two or three were playing; other times as many as nine were crowded around the small table. The games went fast, with much good-natured joking and laughter. They relieved the tension and also kept the more sociable people from inadvertently starting to talk about something that had happened in court. When we were called down to court we left our cards and pennies on the table. For a while we left our little bags and jars of coins in the room overnight. One morning we came in and found our caches had disappeared! The only people allowed in the room at night were the cleaning crew and the sheriff's deputies.

On days when the lunch break was extended, I occasionally took long walks around the north side of San Jose. I enjoyed being outside and liked being by myself for a short while. The area around the Civic Center was part of the old section of town, and the houses and yards were very similar to the houses and yards of the town where I had grown up. I saw flower gardens with the old-fashioned plants in them: hollyhocks, nasturtiums, honey-suckle, pansies and sweet peas. The women working in their gardens were friendly and smiling and ready to stop for a moment and chat about the weather and their plants.

One lunch hour, I went to see an exhibit being presented at the Santa Clara County Library. In 1942, Executive Order 9066 sent all the people of Japanese ancestry on the west coast to internment camps for the duration of World War II. They were not allowed to have cameras in their possession, or to take pictures, but fortunately some official pictorial documentation and news photographs had been made of this tragic event, and an exhibit of these photos was now on tour. I had been living in California when this internment took place and I remember the emptiness of whole sections of valley towns. I wish I could claim that I understood the implications of the order at the time it happened. I didn't. I accepted the idea that such an act was necessary. Looking at the faces in the photographs, I wished I could in some way tell the people how sorry I was that I hadn't understood.

One April noon we were dismissed for a two-hour lunch break. The trial was reaching the end of the first section of the prosecution's case. A group of us decided to drive over and do some shopping and have lunch in the area's newest large shopping center. While we were on our way, Mary B. mentioned that she hoped we would be released early that afternoon, since she wanted to visit her doctor. She told us that she had developed a lower back condition that was being aggravated by the hours of sitting in the chair in the jury box. She apparently was not too uncomfortable at other times, but during court sessions the pain became almost unbearable and was no longer relieved by aspirin. It bothered her so much she felt she couldn't concentrate on the evidence. It was caused, she said, by the design and shape of the jury box chair.

We all started suggesting ways she could ease the pain, and I suggested she use pillows to make the chair more comfortable. She didn't want to.

We offered to carry them in for her or bring in a pillow for everybody, but she refused our offers, saying that the local and international press were watching our every move, so she just couldn't do it.

She said that it would be just too embarrassing, and that Angela Davis wasn't worth it.

I was shocked and disturbed. What chance would anyone have for a fair trial if all jurors held this attitude, if human life and freedom were not worth enduring the possible embarrassment of carrying a pillow into court to make a seat more comfortable?

I lay awake that night and wished there were something I could do. If I were on trial, I certainly wouldn't want a person with that attitude judging me. The next day I hurried over to ask her what her doctor had said. She was disappointed. He had told her the same thing we had suggested, to take pillows into court to make her chair more comfortable. When she refused to consider that solution, he had scolded her, saying she was part of a very important trial and she should be willing to make great sacrifices to do her part as a good citizen.

Mary was a middle-aged woman, born in San Francisco. She had worked for years as a bookkeeper for small businesses, but for the past year had not been employed outside the home. She had quit work to take care of her mother who had just recently died. She was married, and had three grown children. Her home and family seemed very important to her; she was certainly not a bad citizen. She had just reached her limits.

She continued for another week. She did not use a cushion. She spoke to the judge about her difficulty and he told her that at any time the pain became severe, she could signal him and he would call a recess for a few moments. He also suggested that she stand if sitting was uncomfortable.

When she told us what the judge had said, Ralph offered to stand with her so she wouldn't be alone. Others of the jurors joined in, saying that if they all stood, no one in the press would know the reason for the act. Mary refused that offer too.

I didn't know what to do. By her statements and by her actions she was indicating that she had reached the point where she could no longer cope with the situation. I didn't see how she could be an effective juror. The pain she was suffering distracted her from the trial. She couldn't pay attention. The fact that she seemed to feel the trial wasn't worth a minor embarrassment indicated that she could not be really impartial or unbiased.

I considered all the possible actions I could take. If I were to contact any of the attorneys, there would be immediate cause for mistrial. So that course was out. I debated with myself about the advisability of contacting Judge Arnason to let him know what was going on. I had by then full confidence in his judgment and integrity, but what position would that put me in? I didn't know. Would I be suspect of "jury tampering" or some other heinous crime? God! What could I do? What *should* I do? Was this my responsibility? I could just shrug my shoulders and forget it. I didn't have to be involved . . . .

I certainly didn't want to encourage her to stay, so I didn't try to help her solve her immediate problem. I felt that justice would be better served if she were dismissed, but I couldn't suggest that to anyone.

So I showed great sympathy. I asked her how she felt after each session of court. I asked her what the judge had said, and said, "Tsk . . . tsk," when she told me. I frowned. I worried about her. I waited for her while she phoned her doctor again, and commiserated with her when he wasn't sympathetic.

Finally, after a week in which her distress built up, she insisted that she couldn't continue. Her doctor wrote her a letter providing her with an official medical excuse, and Judge Arnason acted to allow her to be released from jury duty.

The announcement was made at the morning session, and Mary rose from her seat and left the courtroom. I have never seen or heard from or about her since.

Bob moved over to her seat from his first alternate chair, becoming Juror Number 4. At the next recess we clustered around him to tell him how happy we were that he was officially one of us, and asked him how he felt. He replied, "Pretty good, but a little scared, you know. Now I, too, will have to be in on the last day, the day of decision."

On April 17, 1972, I picked up the morning *Chronicle*. The trial stories had been cut out as usual. The remaining headlines were about the resumption of full-scale bombing of North Vietnam!

All the protests, all the letters, all the petitions had been for nothing. We were right back where we had been a year ago.

As a juror, I felt that I didn't dare go to a peace rally or to any type of protest meeting. If an "incident" were to happen, I might be arrested and thrown off the jury—and this might be grounds for a mistrial. It seemed I could do nothing. I wasn't free to be myself. I was a juror.

Wait a minute! True, I had a responsibility to do nothing that would in any way interfere with the trial. But did that really mean I couldn't be myself while I was functioning as a juror? Did I have to mimic all the other jurors and play the role as it was interpreted by the average person? I had been picked for this jury because I was myself, not because I would conform to someone's stereotype of a juror. I decided to be myself.

I went to my dressing table and picked up my "peace pin." It was a unique and beautiful pin. It had been designed by a medical student at Stanford during the Cambodia crisis in 1971. It incorporated the symbol of medicine (the winged staff) with the peace sign, blue on white. I wore it to court that morning.

It was a big decision for me: to quit pretending. Now I could laugh openly at the humorous episodes; I could show my irritation at the overt expressions of male chauvinism; I could even weep if I became overwhelmed with sorrow, despair. It was a big relief.

Judge Arnason, whenever he opened court, swept the jury box with a glance and then announced the jury was all present and in their assigned seats. On the day I started wearing the peace pin, I smiled a big "good morning" at him as he scanned the row of jurors. He was almost startled; he did a quick double take, swung back to look directly at me, and smiled.

After that, judge and jury smiled at each other in greeting every morning.

The escalation of the war was the principal topic of conversation in the jury assembly room for the next few days. Most of us were very disturbed by President Nixon's decision to bomb North Vietnam.

A mass rally was held at the Stanford campus, and the main thoroughfare through Palo Alto was blocked by demonstrators. The sheriff's department was called to control them; the men involved in the security of the trial were sent down. Anger and violence erupted, and the officers came into work the next morning full of excited stories about their brave adventures. Our own Captain Johnson was the hero of the day. His picture was in all the papers, showing him stretched out on the sidewalk. He said he had been struck on the right temple by a rock. I looked carefully at his face that morning as he was telling us about it, and

and I could see no sign of a bruise or a scrape. I guess he must have been hit by something, but it didn't leave a mark.

The enjoyment the officers showed as they described chasing the students across the campus appalled me. A great gap separated their thinking and mine. They seemed to have no concept at all of what was going on; the protest was just another local disturbance that they had to contain. The law officers demonstrated by their reactions to the anti-war activists the same exaggerated responses that existed in their security measures for the Davis trial. I was no longer impressed.

The events of that week enabled me to rid myself of the uncertainties and sense of inadequacy I had felt for the past month and a half. The Angela Davis trial was important, but so was I.

The pressures I felt at the start of the trial were no longer overwhelming. If no job was waiting when I came back, I could find something else. If my family and friends felt betrayed, my husband and children would still trust me.

For the first time in six weeks, I was at ease.

The Conspiracy Unfolds

Conspiracy to commit a crime makes each person equally guilty with all others in all aspects of a crime. So the prosecutor need not show that Angela Davis was any more involved in the escape attempt than that she knew of the plot and that she intended to help in its execution by some overt act. The overt act could be as simple as giving money to one of the active participants for the purpose of assisting in the commission of the crime.

My understanding was that the components of an act of conspiracy were motive, means, opportunity, knowledge and intent.

Mr. Harris, the prosecutor, added "awareness of guilt," which
he said was shown by flight.

But first he must show motive.

On August 15, 1970, eight days after the events of Marin County,
an announcement was made that a warrant for the arrest of Angela
Davis was issued. That same afternoon the FBI had searched her
apartment. She was not there. They had returned the following
day with a search warrant which gave them the right to look through
her possessions for any information that might lead to her whereabouts (names of friends, addresses, letters and such).

In the search they had found a cardboard box in the hallway
containing, among other things, photocopies of two handwritten
letters to George Jackson. They were dated June 1 and June 10,
1970. They were photocopies—flat, unwrinkled, no creases. I wondered at their being copies. If they were love letters, as Harris
had indicated in his opening statement, why had Ms. Davis xeroxed
them? I thought about love letters that I'd written—I certainly
wouldn't have kept copies for my files!

The cross-examination of the FBI agent was conducted by Doris
Walker. She questioned him about the manner in which the
search had been conducted, and the use of warrants. The FBI
had searched the empty apartment without a warrant the first
time, then returned the next day with a warrant and removed
the letters. She asked what else he had seen in the apartment—a
typewriter? books? many, many books? books of academic interest?

Jonathan Jackson had used books belonging to Angela Davis
as a cover for the guns in his briefcase. The defense attorney was
establishing that Jackson's use of those books was not significant.
Angela Davis had many, many books of a similar type.

When Ms. Walker finished with her cross-examination, the
prosecutor rose and asked, on redirect examination, "Well, did
you see any printed matter of *non*academic interest?"

The agent thought for a moment, then answered very carefully, "Yes, I saw a newspaper."

The reporters present picked up on that answer and a murmur

moved through the court. In the interval between this witness and the next, Leo Branton stood up and addressed the judge with exaggerated formality, "While we are waiting, Your Honor, I am just wondering if this historical record should leave the inference that a newspaper is not of academic interest?"

Judge Arnason smiled and said that he would leave that decision to a higher court. Leo Branton and Judge Arnason seemed to have a mutual admiration and to delight in the same style of humorous verbal repartee.

The third letter, which had been written on June 22, 1970, to George Jackson, had been found by a prison guard who was in charge of checking the mail of all prisoners. All mail was checked to determine if contraband was being sent to a prisoner. "Contraband" included letters from persons not on a particular prisoner's list of approved correspondents. Angela Davis had not been on the guard's list for George Jackson. When the mail clerk found a letter from her included in an envelope from Jackson's attorney, he turned the whole package over to his superior. The defense questioned the propriety of his opening and checking correspondence between a prisoner and his attorney. I could understand that mail from an attorney might well be opened to see if it contained a weapon or drugs. But to read written or printed material sent by an attorney to a client appeared to me to be an infringement of that client's right to legal counsel.

The jury had been sent home for a day and half before the witnesses who identified these letters testified. When we came into the courtroom that morning, I looked at the faces of the defense group. Usually they gave the appearance of a fairly close, happy team. They talked to each other, they were alert, they looked up at the jurors and smiled when we came in. The prosecutors, on the other hand, were more phlegmatic. When it was obvious that "points of law" were being argued outside the presence of the jury, I checked the faces and demeanor of the defense as we reconvened. If they were smiling and happy, it meant that all had gone well for them. This day, they were grim.

From the tenor of the questioning that followed, I suspected that they must have been objecting to the introduction of these letters because of the ways they were obtained.

"Examiner of Questioned Documents" is a very impressive title, and Sherwood Morrell was a very impressive witness. As an employee of the State Department of Justice, he was the expert on determining the authenticity of all kinds of documents. He has to identify handwriting, typewriting, signatures and the like. For the Davis case, he reported that the three letters were indeed written by Angela Y. Davis; that the signatures on all the gun registrations were hers; that the signatures on a series of personal checks were hers. None of this testimony was disputed by the defense.

He also stated that all of the pages of an eighteen-page letter which had been found in George Jackson's cell after his death had been typed on the typewriter that Angela Davis had been using in her cell.

My mind flashed back to Mr. Harris' opening statement. This letter must be the one he said Ms. Davis wrote after her meeting with George Jackson in the Marin jail—the meeting with the "close, passionate, physical involvement"—after which she called herself Jackson's wife. This letter was supposed to show "in her own words" that the escape attempt wasn't a political act, but the result of uncontrollable passion. Wow! Apparently finding this eighteen-page letter in Jackson's cell a year after the Marin County escape attempt convinced the prosecution that the motive was passion.

While I had been musing about the implications of the letter, Sherwood Morrell had continued with his testimony. He was reporting on other items, some of which had not been introduced: signatures on the San Quentin gate visitor's register on August 4, 1970, and August 5, 1970, of Jonathan Jackson and Diane Robinson, both of whom were written by Jonathan Jackson; a gate registration of July 26, 1970, of Jonathan Jackson and Penelope McKenzie, neither written by Jonathan Jackson nor by Angela Davis; a signature "Jon" on a postscript of a letter by Ms. Davis, which was not conclusive one way or the other.

It was very reassuring to watch and listen to a state employee who was so obviously competent and apparently unbiased in his report. But his reporting on materials that had not been introduced in the case was confusing. Apparently once a witness was called he testified as to everything he knew about the case at that time. This procedure really messes up the sequence of the presentation of the case, and makes it difficult for the jurors to tie it all together. So you try to remember everything!

Another State Department of Justice expert who testified was Spiro T. Vasos, the latent-fingerprint expert. He was a jolly little man, very precise, very eager, round-faced with quick little movements; I wouldn't have been surprised to see him break into a skip as he came down the aisle. He was the only person involved in identifying fingerprints on the van, the guns and all the other physical evidence from the Marin County escape attempt. He had also been called in to go over George Jackson's cell and possessions after his death.

Mr. Vasos reported (and pointed out that a report was *always* made, whether fingerprints were found or not!) that the only fingerprint of Angela Davis found on all the pieces of evidence was a left thumb print on page two of the eighteen-page letter. He found fifty or more prints of George Jackson on this document, and one other print of a former cell mate of Jackson's. This odd print was never explained.

Mr. Vasos found a print of Jonathan Jackson's on the right front mirror of the van, and a couple on the Hertz rental slip.

Other than a single print of hers on a letter that had been written almost a year after the crime, no fingerprints of Angela Davis were found on any of the evidence!

The eighteen-page letter was then identified by the Attorney General's Investigator who found it in Jackson's cell; Mr. Harris moved for admission of all the letters into evidence. The defense immediately objected to having any or all of them admitted. In order that this point could be argued in depth, the jury was dismissed for the day.

The letters had been identified by the men who found them. They had been talked about and waved in front of the jury but they had not been "admitted into evidence." I really didn't understand this technicality. Apparently after an item has been identified thoroughly, the attorney requests that it be admitted into evidence and, if the opposing attorney objects, then arguments pro and con are presented. The judge then rules whether to admit it or not. So we, the jury, were not to be allowed to hear what was in these letters until those steps were taken. We had to sit and pretend that we didn't have any idea what was going on . . . though Mr. Harris had carefully told us in his opening statement (which, of course, was not to be considered testimony) that these letters would prove the motive.

When we entered court the following day, I looked quickly at the faces of the defense team. They seemed to feel pretty good. The prosecutors were quiet and stony-faced. When the formalities of opening court were over, Albert Harris moved that the three handwritten letters be admitted for evidence. He did not mention the eighteen-page document. If my interpretation of the facial clues of the attorneys was correct, then that document was the most important one.

Mr. Harris started to read each of the three letters.

I think we were all prepared for letters of tremendous passion and violence and sex, probably full of four-letter words. After all, these letters were from an angry black militant woman to a San Quentin convict.

They were beautiful, fantastically beautiful, compositions—very natural and direct. While they did contain passages of love and glimpses of her feelings toward George Jackson, the greater part of the letters was concerned with philosophical discussions of the Black Liberation Movement, and the role of the black woman. She presented the concept that black women should not allow themselves to be caught in the trap of the home in order to build up the ego of the black male. This would delay the freedom of all peoples. Rather, they should continue to be strong and work side by side with their black brothers. They should go out and accomplish as much as possible and not be afraid.

That concept was new to me and I found it very interesting. I had assumed that the theory which advocated that black women mimic the role of the white middle-class housewife for the purpose of establishing the black man as head of the household was acceptable. Now I was not so sure.

A number of contradictions appeared in the letters. Angela Davis spoke of violence, made allusions to "killing pigs" and to her willingness to do anything to help George Jackson gain his freedom. As Mr. Harris read these lines in which she described her total commitment, it sounded as though she might be leading up to something like an escape attempt. However, she then talked about the futility of one slave escaping from the slave master, that what was needed was for all subjugated peoples to band together and work to throw off their bonds. She also emphasized the importance of staying alive, and pointed out that the passive nonviolence in South Africa which led to the machine-gun slaughter of hundreds of blacks was suicidal.

So while some phrases seemed to support the theory of passion and violence being the guiding force in Angela Davis' life, other phrases equally as strongly supported a very different view of her motivation. She referred to legal documents to be filed, speeches to be given, papers to be written. In the last of the letters read to us, she stated that she would get to work on an essay that she felt was the most important thing she could be doing right then. She would have time to work on it, she said, since she had finished with her job and had her grades in and all the school paper work completed. She said it gave her a "great sense of freedom" to have it done.

She told of attending a meeting for the Defense Committee with her roommate. While they were there the news came that

a comrade of hers, a student at UCLA who had been active in
the Black Liberation Movement, had been found that day dumped
off the side of the road with a couple of bullèt holes in his head
—" . . . an execution . . . who knows who did it? . . . the police?
. . . militia men? . . . there's no way of knowing . . . ." But she
would go to the funeral on Monday and continue her work.

Jonathan Jackson was mentioned in one of the letters. She
said that they had made a pact. He would try to stop acting like
a male chauvinist if she would agree to stop mentioning his youth-
fulness. Jonathan was very sensitive about his age and, in a postscript to one of the letters, he asked his brother to stop telling
everyone that he was only seventeen, that no one would look to
him as a leader if they knew how young he was. Angela explained
to George that she hadn't been putting him down because he was
so young, but had merely mentioned that she was amazed that he
had avoided being caught in typical adolescence.

When Mr. Harris read this paragraph he emphasized the phrase,
"I never said that he was too young for anything," and with his
reading he added a verbal exclamation point, hoping that we
jurors would take that phrase and give it a more sinister application—that is, that Angela Davis didn't think that Jonathan was
too young to join in the conspiracy to kidnap and kill.

Albert Harris did not read easily or well. The reading of these
three letters took him almost forty-five minutes, and it was a
real chore for him. He stumbled and sweated and had difficulty
pronouncing words (he mispronounced "omnipotent" to the
amazement of Juror Number 8; she obviously thought everyone knew that word). Time and time again he reached into his
back pocket for his folded white handkerchief. He brought it
out and swabbed his forehead, his cheeks, and the back of his
neck. He put it back in his pocket and a few seconds later was
reaching for it again. Sometimes his right hand was in continuous
movement from the rostrum, to the pocket, to his face, back
to the pocket, up to the rostrum, down again to the pocket . . . .

The content of the letters was not what disturbed him, it was
the act of reading aloud. I wondered why it was necessary that

these letters be read to us, since it would have been so much easier to xerox them and give copies to everyone: the jurors, the judge, and most particularly to the poor court reporters whose little fingers just flew to keep up with his steady reading. It was another rule of the game, I guess.

The eighteen-page letter/diary was not read. I wished I knew why. Did that mean that the judge had ruled it inadmissable? Or perhaps Mr. Harris was keeping it for a later date, when it would have a more spectacular effect; or perhaps he needed to rest up for that. Harris reading eighteen pages of anything would be a difficult experience for everyone, reader and listeners alike.

The letters from Angela Davis to George Jackson did show that she felt a love and physical desire for him, which was apparently the purpose for presenting them to us. They also showed that she used revolutionary slogans in her writing. More importantly they showed that she was a deeply thoughtful woman struggling to resolve conflicts in her own life and philosophy.

If they had been presented to convince the jurors that her emotions before the abortive escape were of sufficient intensity to compel her to involve herself in such violence, they fell far short of such a goal. If that was "mad passion," I had been going to the wrong movies. If they were to be the only evidence on which Harris planned to stake the motive of the case, his approach was a miserable failure, as far as I was concerned.

Four of us jurors went to lunch together that day. We were out in the car, waiting the few seconds for Bob's Mercedes to warm up when he turned and said, "I know we aren't supposed to talk about the case, but those were beautiful letters!"

"Fantastic!"

"Beautiful!"

"Great!"

The prosecution moved on to "means and opportunity." Did Angela Davis have the means to conspire with Jonathan Jackson? Did she aid and abet the kidnap? Did she have available the guns

to give to him? Was their relationship such that she could have
helped him? Did Angela Davis have the opportunity to conspire
with Jonathan Jackson?

In the prosecution's entire case, only five black witnesses testified. One was a teller in a bank in Los Angeles; he had cashed
a check for Angela Davis in July.

A black guard from San Quentin, on his fourth day on the
job, had found himself crouched across the street from the Civic
Center, firing his rifle at a yellow Hertz van. On the witness stand
he qualified every answer with "It seemed to be . . . " and "It
looks like that . . . ." He wouldn't even admit positively that the
gun he "seemed to be" firing was an M-1 rifle. He was trying to
walk the tightrope, trying not to antagonize his superiors, but
also not to admit to anything that would incriminate anyone.

A young black man working at the Civic Center witnessed the
shoot-out. His early statement indicated that the first shot he
had heard was muffled shotgun blast. He had retracted that statement in a television interview. When he had reported for work
at a new assignment on the Monday following the escape attempt,
he had been met by police officers who questioned him in front
of his new boss, and who also brought up incidents in his past
which he had no chance to explain or discuss. As a result of
this confrontation, he had not been given the promised job, and
had not been able to get another job in Marin County. He had
moved to San Francisco and was employed by the San Francisco
School District as a teaching aide.

I couldn't understand why the prosecution called him as a
witness. The testimony he could give was not vital to this case,
as far as I could tell. What was important to me was the story
he told of the pressures exerted on him when he didn't conform
to the authorities' version of what happened. Whether or not
what he was saying had any validity, he strongly felt that he
had lost his job and had been prevented from getting another
because he refused to swear that he had heard a shotgun blast
first.

A black police officer from Los Angeles had seen a Rambler station wagon stalled in the left lane of a boulevard of that city. He had pulled over to check it out and Jonathan Jackson raised his head up from below the dashboard where he had been "hot-wiring" the car. The car was registered to Angela Davis. Jonathan's parents, Georgia and Lester Jackson, and Angela Davis had come to the police station and identified Jonathan and said that he had permission to use the car. This occurred on August 1st, just after midnight.

Another black prosecution witness was Ms. Otelia Young. Mr. Harris had said that he would present evidence to show that Angela Davis moved into a new apartment in July and that Jonathan Jackson lived with her in this apartment. The implication was that she moved into the apartment so that they could live together . . . and conspire together. Ms. Otelia Young was brought from Los Angeles to San Jose to testify that she lived downstairs in a four-unit apartment building, and Angela Davis moved into the upstairs apartment in July. Ms. Young was a small woman, perhaps sixty to sixty-five years old. She said she knew Ms. Davis and had spoken to her a number of times. She marked a picture of the building after Mr. Harris, in the manner of a person talking to a child, very carefully explained just what he wanted. She wrote her initials quickly, looked up at him, and said disdainfully, "Is *that* what you want?"

Mr. Harris then asked if she recalled a young man living with Ms. Davis, and Ms. Young replied, "Yes, he was in and out, but not too much." She wouldn't say that he seemed to be living there. Mr. Harris asked about the day Ms. Davis moved into the apartment; did she remember the white station wagon and had she seen anything carried in or out? Before the defense attorney could get his objection out, she answered, "No." The objection was withdrawn.

She did mention that she had seen Ms. Davis carrying in books. The prosecutor asked if Jonathan Jackson had carried in her books. "No, Miss Davis had a lot of books, and what books she had, she carried them in herself!" Ms. Young answered positively.

The last time she had seen Angela Davis was on Monday, the Monday before the escape attempt. Mr. Harris asked her how she could be sure that it was Monday; did she work on the other days?

"Yes, I work. I work from seven in the morning until eight o'clock at night, five days a week." She said it defiantly, looking him straight in the face. And she was poor. Her clothes were old and ill-fitting, her shoes worn—and those apartments rented for $75 a month.

On her way out of court, Otelia Young, the prosecution witness, turned and waved her hand and smiled at the defendant, Angela Davis. It was a gesture of support from one oppressed black woman to another. What courage it took to defy the Court, the police—even the power of the State of California!

No other "evidence" was produced that Jonathan Jackson had lived with Angela Davis. Much evidence was presented that they were closely associated in the month preceding the escape attempt. They had been stopped at the Mexican border as they returned home from Mexico about midnight on July 30, 1970. They had attended court hearings for the Soledad Brothers together. She had gone to the police station with his parents when he had been picked up for hot-wiring her car.

Those of us on the jury whose seats were near the front of the courtroom usually walked past the jury box, up the two steps and, instead of turning to the right into the witness stand, would turn left into the jury box. This saved stumbling over people's feet as we found our seats. One day after the midmorning break the jury was returning to the box. As I approached the steps, Ms. Davis came out from the chambers behind the courtroom.

I've mentioned that I wondered why Angela Davis was so frequently referred to as beautiful. I thought she had an interesting face, but not a beautiful one. She reached the top of the steps just as I reached the bottom of them. We were both preoccupied with our own thoughts and looked up at each other simultaneously.

It was such an awkward situation—who should step aside for whom? What would Emily Post or Amy Vanderbilt say? Angela Davis and I looked at each other and smiled, amused. For a part of a second, we weren't the accused and the juror. We were two women wordlessly sharing a response to this slightly ridiculous situation. For the first time the warmth and joyousness of her personality came through to me, and I knew why she was called beautiful.

The next section of the prosecution's case dealt with the activities of Angela Davis and Jonathan Jackson during the week of August 3, 1970—the "crucial week," as Mr. Harris called it.

Angela Y. Davis had bought a ticket on a United Airlines flight from Los Angeles to San Francisco which left L.A. at 8:30 p.m. on the evening of August 3rd. She had paid for the ticket with a personal check. The clerk who OK'd the check remembered the transaction and remembered noticing the gap between her front teeth. Mr. Harris emphasized the point that the clerk remembered the gap in the teeth. He kept coming back to it, making certain that we understood that this witness had never seen Angela Davis in person before but, when he identified her as she cashed her check, he noticed she had a gap between her front teeth.

I frequently found it hard to figure just what Mr. Harris was driving at. Why was it even mentioned? Surely the fact that she had cashed a check was not incriminating. Was the defense going to question that it really was Angela Davis taking that flight? Was that what Harris was preparing for? Hmm . . . maybe Angela Davis *wasn't* the person cashing the check.

After listening to the first weeks of testimony concerning who had what gun and where and when, I had come to the conclusion that Mr. Harris asked a lot of questions just to make the witnesses feel important.

Visitors to San Quentin prison park in an open parking lot, walk up an incline to the outer gate, sign in, then continue along a walk for about a quarter of a mile to the next gate. They enter the building and go into a waiting room where they stop and identify themselves at a desk by the door and give the name of the prisoner they wish to visit. They remain in the waiting room, which is filled with benches, while the prisoner is being brought from his cell. Then they are summoned into an adjoining room, the visiting room proper, which has long tables connected in a kind of squared "S" design with chairs on either side of the tables. The arrangement is such that the prisoners are always on the inside, or prison side, of the tables.

People who accompany visitors, but who themselves are not allowed to communicate with the prisoners, remain in the waiting room and do not have to identify themselves at the desk.

After establishing that Angela Davis had come to the Bay Area, Mr. Harris brought on a series of witnesses who said they had seen her with Jonathan Jackson at San Quentin on the 4th, 5th and 6th of August.

The prosecution's first witness in this group was Officer Robert West, who had been in charge of supervising the waiting room and visiting room. He had walked through and checked the action in the two rooms every hour or so. He testified that he had seen Jonathan Jackson on Tuesday, August 4th, on a bench in the waiting room sitting next to a young woman with an Afro. Their backs were toward him—he did not see the young woman's face. The following day, Wednesday, the 5th, he saw Jonathan Jackson in the visiting room talking to his brother. As the officer came through the door between the rooms, he saw a young woman with an Afro, waiting in the doorway, wave to someone in the visiting room. He felt that she was waving to George Jackson.

Later, a week after the escape attempt, West was home watching the news on TV when he saw a picture of Angela Davis on the screen. He recognized her as being the young woman he had seen in the doorway, and so he immediately telephoned his superior officer to report. This call was made on the 14th of August.

Mr. Moore conducted the cross-examination. He was very intense, acting as though this man were a personal enemy whom he had been waiting for the chance to confront. Mr. Moore brought out that Officer West was a supporter of George Wallace in 1968, which implied the possibility that this man could have racist and strong anti-Communist feelings. But Moore could not shake his testimony. He finished the interrogation with the question, "In fact, isn't it true that what you said when you saw Angela Davis' picture on television was 'This is my chance to get that Commie'?"

Of course, Harris objected immediately, and Judge Arnason sustained the objection.

The next witness was the young guard who had been behind the table at the entrance to the visiting room. He too testified that Jonathan Jackson and a young "colored" woman were in the visiting room on both the 4th and the 5th. This officer left for military reserve camp on the 7th, so he missed the events of the escape attempt. While he was at camp on August 13th, a friend showed him the newspaper with a picture of Angela Davis. He testified he recognized her as being the woman with Jonathan, and phoned his superior officer, Officer West, immediately.

The friend who showed him the paper was a news reporter for the *San Francisco Examiner.* When this bit of information was brought out during cross-examination, a sudden silence fell, and then all of the people at the tables of the defense team turned and looked into the spectator section at one young man. They apparently knew him. The reaction was so spontaneous, I wondered if they were each saying to themselves, "I might have known it! It figures he would be the one to do that!"

One other guard said that he had seen Jonathan Jackson talking to his brother and a "colored" woman standing in the doorway waving to George Jackson on the 5th. He could not identify her as being Angela Davis.

Another very pleasant, young, round-faced guard testified that he saw George Jackson visiting with a Mrs. Hammer on Thursday, the 6th, the day before the escape attempt. After a while Jonathan came in and joined them. Mrs. Hammer remained while George and Jonathan conversed, and was still there after Jonathan left.

Mr. Harris asked him to mark on the chart where the three people were sitting. The officer very carefully marked the initials of the prisoner George Jackson on the visitor's side. When it was pointed out to him, he saw his mistake and changed it around. But as he was being questioned, he kept looking back at the chart, and finally said, "I know this is going to mess everyone up, but the way I remember it—the people were sitting as I originally placed them."

He was great. He knew it couldn't possibly be accurate, but he wasn't going to swear to something he couldn't remember. His complete honesty on a minor point made all the rest of his testimony very believable.

A middle-aged woman who was called as a witness resented very much having to appear. She and her mother and her husband had come to San Quentin to visit her stepson who was a prisoner. Their visit was on the 4th of August, Tuesday. On the way out of the prison she and her mother were walking ahead together and they passed a "young Negro couple." She said that she recognized Angela Davis and told her mother, "That's Angela Davis."

She thought the young man might be Angela's brother. She claimed to have been familiar with the appearance of Ms. Davis from the newscasts in San Diego where she lived. (Angela Davis had been a student at San Diego before she was hired at UCLA.) She was a very believable witness.

Louis "Bob" May had been a convict at San Quentin prison in August of 1970. He had a long history of criminal activity. At the time of the escape attempt, Bob May's prison job was to drive a "donkey train" from the entrance gate by the parking lot up to the actual prison for the convenience of the visitors.

He said he came to know who Jonathan Jackson was because he had seen him coming to visit his brother frequently. And he also knew who Angela Davis was because he had lived in San Diego when she was getting all the publicity there. This man testified that he saw the yellow Hertz van in the parking lot on Thursday the 6th and saw both Jonathan Jackson and Angela Davis come up the ramp from the parking lot and go on up to the prison. He later saw the yellow van leaving the parking lot with Jonathan Jackson driving and Angela Davis seated beside him facing the prison. They were arguing loudly as they passed by.

He testified that he had seen Jonathan every day that week and had noticed him in a black Jaguar sports car one of those days. He also testified he had seen Angela Davis every day but one that week. He said he had seen her on Monday (when according to previous testimony she was still in Los Angeles). And he saw a yellow van on Wednesday (when the van had not yet been rented).

Cross-examination by Mr. Moore revealed that this convict had been paroled very shortly after he made this statement to the Attorney General's Office. At the time of the trial, he was a free man.

Bob May had complete control of every muscle in his body. Where other witnesses fidgeted or twitched, he sat perfectly still. It was something learned in prison, I guess. However, he could not control the flushing of his face and neck when he was angry or cornered—and Mr. Moore angered him.

He questioned May in great detail about his past and about the convenient parole he got. Mr. Moore asked about an interview with a defense investigator to whom May made the statement, "I would turn in my own mother to get out of here [San Quentin]!" May denied making that statement.

Mr. Moore kept after him very doggedly, very quietly. He stood directly in front of the witness, leaning on the lectern. They stared at each other as though no one else was in the room. Moore asked a series of questions, trying to break down the story of his seeing Angela Davis. He spoke more and more softly. The courtroom quieted down—no one moved, everyone strained to hear.

Bob May finally admitted almost with relief that he was not sure that it had been Ms. Davis who walked up the ramp with Jonathan Jackson. That was what Mr. Moore wanted to hear. He turned away. He had destroyed the credibility of the witness —he had also destroyed the man's carefully contrived facade of respectability.

Jonathan Jackson had borrowed a Volkswagen from a friend on the morning of August 5th. This car was found later in the parking garage at the San Francisco airport. Prosecutor Harris' theory was that Angela Davis had driven the car to the airport and abandoned it on August 7th. One of the more dramatic episodes of the trial was the appearance of the owner of this car. A woman in her early thirties, attractive, apparently well-educated and intelligent, arrived in the courtroom accompanied by her attorney.

Mabel Magers had come from Kansas City. During the summer of 1970 she lived in the home of Mrs. Joan Hammer in San Jose. (The name "Hammer" and the "Hammer house" kept popping up throughout the trial. Mrs. Hammer had visited George Jackson the afternoon before the escape attempt and was there while Jonathan talked to him—but she was never called as a witness.)

When Ms. Magers started to testify, Defense Attorney Branton rose to his feet, interrupting and saying that he had read the pretrial statement of this woman and had serious questions concerning her testimony, and that she should be advised of her constitutional right not to testify—and that she might be in serious jeopardy if she were allowed to testify without that warning. He was reassured that she had been properly warned and had her personal attorney present. (What was Mr. Branton doing? Telling us on the jury to watch out, we might have reason to suspect the involvement of this witness?)

Mabel Magers testified she had moved into the Hammer house and lived there during the summer, along with other unrelated individuals. While she was living there she met Angela Davis and

Jonathan Jackson. She only saw Ms. Davis once, when she came there with Jonathan and his mother, Georgia Jackson, to pick up some art objects for an auction for the benefit of the Soledad Brothers Defense Fund. This meeting was in the middle of July.

Ms. Magers saw Jonathan at the house a number of times. On July 28th she took Mrs. Hammer to San Quentin and picked her up later in the day. Mrs. Hammer was accompanied by Jonathan Jackson when she came out. They all drove back to San Jose together, stopping for dinner in San Francisco. She then took Jonathan to the San Jose airport. She saw him again on Sunday, August 2nd, at the opening of the Soledad house, and once more in the Hammer house on the 4th. On August 5th, Jonathan asked to borrow her VW. She gave him the key, did not go out to the car with him—and so did not know if he was accompanied by anyone.

She did not see Jonathan again. About three weeks after the escape attempt, Mrs. Jackson came to the Hammer house and told her that the VW had been located in the garage of the San Francisco airport. They went down to the garage, picked the car up and paid the $43 parking bill.

In cross-examination, Mr. Moore brought out that she had used the name "Mickey Jackson" as an "affectionate gesture toward someone." That fact was a surprise—could that have been what Mr. Branton was hinting at when he warned Ms. Magers about testifying?

Mr. Moore then asked her if she had been the person who spent the night with Jonathan at the Holland Motel the night before the escape attempt.

"Objection!"

Her attorney jumped up, protesting the line of questioning.

Everyone turned and looked at Judge Arnason. He hesitated a moment, then called a short recess so this could be argued in chambers. We were dismissed—just when it was getting good.

When court reconvened, I took a good look at Ms. Magers. She was fairly tall, attractive—her skin was tanned—I wondered how she would look in an Afro wig . . . . Then I stopped

myself—I was beginning to think like a script writer. It wasn't
my responsibility to find someone else to suspect.

She denied she had ever spent a night in a motel with Jonathan
Jackson.

Her appearance on the stand disturbed me. Something about
her testimony was false or incomplete. It was as though another
whole big story was going on that everybody knew about, but
no one would tell the jury. I wished I knew just how deeply
she had been involved in the events of that week.

The prosecutor was leading up to the final days and the incriminating evidence. Frank Blumenthal and David Lipson were salesmen in the Eagle Loan Company in San Francisco. On Wednesday,
August 5th, they sold a .12-gauge shotgun to Angela Davis. She
was accompanied by a young "light-complected" black man. Frank
Blumenthal waited on her. He testified, under direct examination
by Albert Harris, that she had asked for "an inexpensive shotgun,"
and he had showed her a couple of guns. She decided to take the
single-shot, .12-gauge "Spanish-make" gun.

He knew the name of Angela Davis, but he didn't recognize
her until she showed him her driver's license. He then asked her
if she were still teaching at UCLA, and they chatted a little.

In cross-examination Leo Branton had him reinforce his testimony that Angela Davis had not asked for a specific gun, just
an "inexpensive one"—and also that the only identification needed
was a Social Security card, or something similar.

The other salesman, David Lipson, was a middle-aged man, a
San Francisco character—a movie version of a typical pawnbroker
who spoke with a New York accent. He thoroughly enjoyed being the center of attention on the witness stand. His responses
to the questioning of Mr. Harris were so spontaneous and humorous, the whole courtroom burst into laughter several times. When
he was explaining that he could not be absolutely sure the young
man was really accompanying her, he said:

"You see, in our place of business we have a lot of kibitzers
come in too. Now, you can be waiting on a customer and,

especially when it comes to guns, you will be displaying a gun, and there will be two—three walk in off the street, and they will stand there. Now, I can't say, 'Are you with the customer?' or—sometimes I will—'are you?'—I don't want to queer my sale, so consequently, in this case, I don't know a hundred percent. Now I want to be a hundred percent here. I don't know whether for sure he was with her or he wasn't with her, but I would say he was with her. I would be 99 and 9/10 sure he was because they—they discussed things together, and he was very much interested in the gun, and that is all I remember."

He was obviously an admirer of Angela Davis and, in fact, asked her for her autograph when she was in the store. She had, he said, signed his business card, "'Angela Davis' in flowing letters." He had put the card in his wallet, but now said sadly, "I must have lost it. It isn't there now."

When it was time for cross-examination, Mr. Branton asked the salesman, very seriously, if he had indeed gotten Ms. Davis' autograph. And he no longer had it? He had lost it? Mr. Lipson answered yes to each question.

"Would you like to have another one?" Mr. Branton asked.

"Huh?"

"Would you like to have another one?" Branton was grinning broadly now.

"Sure! I'd like to have another one!"

"You'll get it."

Leo Branton's ability to control the tone or the mood of the trial was fantastic. He was aware of everything that went on in the courtroom and was able to interpret and react almost instantaneously. With his chair turned sideways, his back was to the rest of the defense group, his right arm rested on the table, his left elbow was hooked carelessly over the back of the chair—almost a slouch, but with the controlled elegance of a natural athlete.

He had the voice and the movements of an experienced actor and he utilized the stage of the court effectively. He knew where his props were and how to work with them; he never fumbled for papers or exhibits and he used his microphone efficiently, although he had no real need for one.

Mr. Branton was a master showman who played to his audience, the jury. Always polite, he would break into the testimony of a prosecution witness apologetically to ask a quick clarifying question—or with an offer to "speed things up a little" by stipulating to the truth of the evidence. He never interrupted enough to cause the judge to censure him—but just enough to keep Mr. Harris from establishing momentum and continuity in the story he was trying to unfold.

Prosecutor Harris was getting us closer to the fatal Friday. Jonathan Jackson had rented a yellow Ford Econoline van at about 8:30 in the morning of Thursday, August 6th, from the Hertz Rental Agency in San Francisco. He had come into the agency alone and had paid for the rental with two $20 bills.

About 10:00 a.m. Thursday he had made a phone call from Fleming's Mobil Service Station across the street from the Marin Civic Center to the Hertz agency, requesting authorization for mechanical repairs to the van.

That night he had rented a room for two in the Holland Motel in San Francisco. This fact was not disputed by the defense. They did take issue with the implication that the second person at the motel was Ms. Davis. No evidence was presented that she or anyone else was ever in the motel with Jonathan.

These events were documented with physical evidence as well as witness testimony.

The other happenings of that Thursday were brought out through the testimony of four men who were in and around the filling station.

Alden Fleming, the proprietor of the Mobil station, testified that he noticed a young black couple enter the station, walking in from the sidewalk. The young man came into the office to get help in starting a Hertz van which was stalled in the Civic Center parking lot. The young woman, who had been waiting outside, joined them and Mr. Fleming arranged for his son, Peter, to take the couple back to the lot in the station's pickup. Mr. Fleming identified the young woman as Angela Davis from a picture he saw in the newspaper on August 15th, eight days after the escape attempt.

During cross-examination, Mr. Branton asked him about his experience with black people. Had he known many? Fleming replied that he had a lot of black customers, probably twenty percent of all his customers were black.

I wondered about that. I had been in Marin a number of times and had always been vaguely aware that I passed very few non-white faces in the streets. Twenty percent seemed way out of line.

In trying to show that Mr. Fleming was not too familiar with black people, Mr. Branton queried him about some of the defense people sitting in the court, "Have you ever seen Ms. Kendra Alexander before?"

"I think I may have seen her picture."

"You don't recall ever seeing her in person?"

"No."

"How about Howard Moore?"

"Yes, he has been in the station a lot since August 1970."

"Was he in the station a couple of weeks ago, on a Friday?"

"Yes."

" . . . accompanied by a young woman?"

"Yes."

"And wasn't that young woman Kendra Alexander?"

"I don't know."

It was brought out that Howard Moore and a young woman drove into the station in a Volkswagen. Mr. Moore got out of the car and left the area. Mr. Fleming asked the young woman about checking the oil and she handed him the keys. She then got out of the car and walked around the station for a few minutes.

Now, in court—just two weeks later—Fleming, looking at her across the courtroom, could not say whether or not the young woman was Kendra Alexander.

And yet he positively, absolutely identified Angela Davis as the woman who had accompanied Jonathan Jackson—from a newspaper picture.

Kendra Alexander had been sitting beside Angela Davis throughout the trial. All of us on the jury had been a little confused when we first saw the two of them. We weren't sure which one was Ms. Davis.

But as the days and weeks of the trial passed, Ms. Davis grew thinner and thinner—and Ms. Alexander grew heavier and heavier. By the time the trial reached the point where prosecution witnesses were identifying Angela Davis as the woman they had seen —the two young black women with Afros were no longer almost identical.

Much discussion centered about a series of nine pictures that the Attorney General's staff had shown witnesses for the purpose of identifying the young woman. The jury was shown this set of pictures. I noticed that the series included three pictures of Angela Davis, one of her sister, Fania Jordan, and five of other women (who were not all black, nor all young, none of whom had Afros and most of whom had names or numbers under the faces—these were police mug shots). The only pictures that fit the physical description of being a young, light-complexioned black woman with an Afro were those of Angela Davis and her sister. Alden Fleming, on the witness stand, with Angela Davis sitting just a few feet away, picked out the photo of Fania Jordan, and said that it was the picture of the woman he saw!

However, he did manage to point to Angela Davis in the courtroom as the woman he had seen.

Peter Fleming, son of the proprietor—who drove Jonathan Jackson and the young woman over to the parking lot, helped them get the van started, and talked to them after they returned to the station—had not been able to identify Angela Davis as the young woman from this same set of pictures—but two years later, he did identify her in court.

A friend of Alden Fleming's had been in the station that morning. He stood around outside the office for a few minutes and had said "Hello" to the woman whom he described as young, black, tall, with an Afro. She was wearing a fatigue jacket, a mini-skirt and was smoking a medium-sized cigar. He also noticed that she had a gap in her front teeth. (Aha! That remark was the reason for the emphasis on the gap in the teeth by the man who had cashed her check!)

He identified her from a television picture he saw of Angela Davis. He was very positive. He said that he didn't bother to inform the law-enforcement authorities, but had just casually mentioned it to Alden Fleming later in the day. Fleming told him that he had already called the sheriff about it.

Branton asked if he knew that no record had been made in the sheriff's office of such a call; if such an important call for such an important case had come in, wouldn't such a record be most likely to exist?

A fourth man, the station mechanic, could and did identify Jonathan Jackson from photos but could not identify Ms. Davis as the woman he saw in the station that day.

When the effects of Jonathan Jackson were collected after his death, he had fifty-seven cents in one pocket, fifty cents in his wallet and a dollar bill tucked into his jockey shorts. The wallet contained no bills but did have a driver's license, a high school student-body card, a couple of passes to a theater, a library card and some pictures—the same things one would find in the wallets of high school kids all over the country. I came close to weeping as Prosecutor Harris itemized the effects.

All together he was carrying two dollars and seven cents . . . .

A scrap of paper with what appeared to be a phone number written on it was also found in the wallet. A representative from the telephone company testified that the number was that of a pay phone at the American Airlines terminal at the San Francisco airport.

We were shown a photograph of the actual phone booth—one

of the modern plastic-hooded open phones. It was the first in a wall of pay phones. The surrounding area wasn't shown in the picture.

When Mr. Moore cross-examined this witness he showed the jury a different picture of the row of pay phones—they were out in the open, just a few feet from a row of chairs in front of windows—and right behind them was the desk of the terminal entrance. People were working within eighteen inches of the back of the open phone booth.

The prosecution's picture was not "doctored"—it was not dishonest. They thought of the phone as a part of a sinister plot, and so they represented it as hidden.

In contrast, the defense saw it as a perfectly ordinary phone booth—out in the open, not at all sinister—and that was how they presented it to us.

The pay phone booth at the American Airlines terminal introduced us to the San Francisco airport. From that airport Mr. Harris said Angela Davis had started her flight—the flight which was a manifestation of guilt.

Marcia Brewer was the ticket agent at the gate desk of the PSA terminal. She was very attractive, very helpful—a "fly-me" stewardess type. She testified that Angela Davis bought a ticket from her, paying with a personal check, and left in a hurry to board the two o'clock flight to Los Angeles. She had no baggage.

As Ms. Brewer was testifying, she smiled sweetly and apologetically at Ms. Davis. She was a very helpful and cooperative witness for the prosecution.

During cross-examination she testified that she had no recollection of the incident when she had first been questioned; she had recalled the events only after checking her records. She vaguely remembered Ms. Davis saying that someone had told her she could catch the two o'clock plane if she hurried. She said that customarily passengers boarding the planes left their baggage out at the main ticket counter, and that on her original statement she had said that she didn't recall if Ms. Davis had any baggage—rather than stating flatly that she had no luggage.

She was asked whether passengers taking the hourly commuter flights were not frequently in a hurry. Marcia Brewer agreed. She was a very helpful and cooperative witness for the defense.

Prosecutor Harris announced that he had reached the end of this section of his presentation, and since the next section would entail bringing witnesses from out of state, he felt that if he and Mr. Branton could get together, perhaps a great deal of time and effort would be saved by stipulating to certain facts. Mr. Branton agreed—Judge Arnason said they were both to be commended and this stipulation should be a much more rapid way of handling it—time could be saved.

Mr. Branton said rather sardonically, "Yes, Your Honor, we might be able to save quite a bit of time—perhaps even days of testimony." He apparently got pretty frustrated and irritated with Mr. Harris' deliberate method of questioning and his inability to formulate the questions that would elicit the desired response. The witness often didn't know what Mr. Harris was getting at, which led to much unnecessary repetition.

The following morning it was rapidly stipulated (agreed to by both sides) that if the witnesses were called, they would testify that a man named Poindexter had said that Angela Davis was coming to his apartment in Chicago, that she did indeed arrive, that they left together and rented a room in a Howard Johnson's Motel in Detroit on the 17th of August. She got a new pair of glasses on the 19th. Next, they were apparently in Florida for a while, then registered in another motel as George Gilbert and wife in New York City.

When we were brought down into court the following morning, an additional attorney sat in the court. Charles Garry, a well-known civil rights attorney from San Francisco, was there to act as counsel for the next witness, John Thorne—another attorney. I counted quickly: five for the defense, two for the prosecution, the witness and his counsel and Judge Arnason—ten lawyers in court that morning.

Mr. Thorne had a client-attorney relationship with both George Jackson and Angela Davis. The testimony he gave related to a phone call he had previously admitted to having received from Angela Davis. In this call, she was supposed to have made a comment that she was driving Jonathan over to Santa Cruz to pick up his things. On the stand, Mr. Thorne testified that while it was true that he had said previously the call could have been on August 5th, he now wished to modify that statement and say that it was highly unlikely it was made that day.

He based the change on what he said was the purpose of the call. Angela Davis was calling in regard to the status of the motion that she be allowed to become an investigator in the George Jackson case. She had phoned Mr. Thorne to ask about the results of an appeal which had been filed. After checking the dates of the filing of the appeal, he realized that the phone call must have been made in late July, not on August 5th.

I couldn't understand the importance of the testimony. The point seemed to me to be a very trivial one. The prosecution had already placed Ms. Davis and Jonathan together earlier on the 5th. They bought the shotgun that day. Perhaps the prosecutor would have liked to ask John Thorne other questions, but was prevented by legal rulings.

Mr. Harris then announced he had only three more witnesses to call. They were out of town and could not be called until Monday. So we were dismissed early Thursday for a long weekend.

Only three more witnesses? The prosecution's case was almost over.

A single morning session could take care of three witnesses. So Monday might be the last day of the prosecution—then what?

I began to speculate on the possibilities. I knew enough about legal procedures to realize that at the end of the prosecution's case, the defense normally asks the judge to dismiss all charges on the basis that these charges have not been proved. We, the jury, would probably be sent out of the courtroom during this argument. Could Judge Arnason rule on this issue immediately after it was presented? I thought not—he would probably take it "under advisement" and go back into his chambers—returning later with his decision. I wondered how long that would take.

Suppose he were to rule that the prosecution had not proven its case and then dismissed all charges. Then the whole thing would be over! Wouldn't that be fantastic? The decision would be made and we jurors wouldn't have that burden. Fantastic, but not likely. Could any judge take that responsibility himself in a trial with so many political overtones? I doubted it.

If Judge Arnason decided the case must continue, then the defense would start their presentation of witnesses—but wait a minute! They didn't have to present any defense at all. They didn't have to put Angela Davis on the stand. They didn't have to provide her with alibi witnesses, character witnesses or anything else, if they thought the prosecution had not proved the case—at least not enough to convince the jury.

Then what would happen? Would it go right to the final closing arguments? I wondered how long that would take—probably a day or two. After that, the judge would give instructions to the jury and drop the case in our laps.

That possibility was pretty frightening! We might have to begin deliberating next week. I wasn't ready for that.

I began to wonder about my fellow jurors. Were they too beginning to worry about possibly having to make the final decision in just a few days?

This jury was not the same as the one that Ms. Davis and Mr. Harris had accepted two months ago. The make-up of the jury was different. The two other Marys had left and Bob and Michelle had taken their places. But the biggest change was within the group. We had been strangers when the trial started, but now we were friends. I no longer thought about the others in terms of their ages, jobs, family backgrounds and personal appearances.

I wondered how each of my friends would vote if she or he had to make the decision right now, this very day. I thought about each of them and what I had learned about them these last few weeks—their mannerisms, their attitudes, their reactions to events—then tried to guess whether each person would vote for acquittal or conviction. I felt they would all vote on the evidence that had been presented, but how had they heard that evidence? Had they heard it the same as I?

I listed the names of the jurors on a sheet of paper and, after thinking about each one, I made a note beside the name as to how I thought that juror would vote.

I came to the conclusion that two of them would definitely vote for acquittal and three others might also vote for acquittal. Three would probably vote for conviction. And the other three? I couldn't even hazard a guess as to their leanings.

If I were correct in my analysis—and nothing else happened in the rest of the trial to change things—conflicts would arise in the jury deliberations. Perhaps we might even be a hung jury.

Well, these thoughts were just speculation on my part. I had no way of knowing what would happen. But if we were going to be facing arguments when deliberations started, I wanted to be sure of the testimony and the evidence.

I began reviewing my notes. I had kept a daily record in a little nickel notebook which was fairly dog-eared after a month and a half. I decided to type the notes on three-inch by five-inch cards—a card for each witness with the date of appearance and a few relevant facts, including my personal impressions of the testimony. This chore gave me a chance to review and remember each witness. I felt more confident having that bunch of cards. I now had a quick reminder for each witness if I ever needed it.

I wondered about the three last witnesses Mr. Harris had mentioned. Some things were missing from what he had initially told us we could expect to hear. First of all, a woman, Joyce Redoni, had been on the list of prospective witnesses which he had read to us the first day of the trial. What had happened to her? She had been one of the three women who had been taken hostage during the Marin escape attempt. She had been in pictures we were shown and many of the early witnesses had said that they knew her personally. Why hadn't he brought her in to testify? He had brought in everyone else from that day. Maybe he was saving her for the final witness—to make a dramatic impact at the end of his case. That possibility meant she could be one of the remaining three.

We hadn't heard any testimony about the actual arrest of Angela Davis in New York. I was sure that technical point had to be covered. Maybe another witness would do that.

We had been told that evidence would show that Angela Davis and George Jackson, in the meeting in the Marin jail a year after the escape attempt, had "close physical contact." Without actually saying it, Mr. Harris had implied a lot more than huggin' and kissin'—since she referred to herself as George's wife after that meeting. No evidence concerning the meeting had been presented. Maybe that would be done by another of the remaining three witnesses.

Without testimony about this meeting and without additional documentation of her deep personal involvement with George Jackson, the efforts of Prosecutor Harris to establish passion as the motive will have been pretty ineffectual. This motive was to have been substantiated by the eighteen-page letter written after this meeting. Harris had never implied that this document (called a "letter" by the prosecutor and a "diary" by the defense) did more than establish the motive for the conspiracy. It was not supposed to be a confession of guilt.

How we, the jury, were to determine the emotions of Ms. Davis at the time of the crime, from either the way she acted or what she wrote a year later, I couldn't imagine.

Angela Davis had been through terrific pressures during the year. A youngster she had been very fond of had been killed along with a number of others under shocking circumstances. Her friends and family were subjected to much grief and harassment. She fled across the country, was caught and brought back and locked up in a jail for a year, having a very limited number of visitors. Then she was allowed a meeting with the man to whom she had professed love and affection—himself a prisoner for years, also accused of murder—both of them under heavy guard and in the presence of their attorneys. I wondered why anyone was surprised that such a meeting would be an emotional one . . . .

I decided to stop right there. The prosecution had not finished its case. I had not heard the letter read. I must not start making judgments on something that had not been admitted for evidence.

The first witness on Monday morning (the first of the final three witnesses for the prosecution) was an FBI agent from the New York office. He told us about the arrest of Angela Davis.

This agent had been in charge of the investigation for that area. They had received a report that she and David Poindexter were in New York and were driving a Toyota station wagon. The agent was checking all of the downtown hotel and motel parking lots for this particular car and, on October 13, 1970, it was found at a Howard Johnson's Motel. The FBI agents, after determining the room in which Ms. Davis was registered, stationed themselves in adjoining rooms and waited until she returned.

Ms. Davis was wearing a "pixie wig" but the FBI was able to identify her absolutely by matching fingerprints.

Mr. Harris pulled from a plastic bag the wig that she had been wearing, and it was identified by the agent. Mr. Harris then asked Judge Arnason for permission to show the wig to the jury.

So we were "allowed" to examine the actual pixie wig that had been worn by Angela Davis during her flight from the law. It smacked of a circus sideshow. I saw no need to take it in my hand, examine it and say to myself, "Yes, sir, that is a real pixie wig. It sure is proof that she was fleeing from the law. So she must have known that she was guilty!" All that from looking at a black pixie wig? How ridiculous.

Mr. Branton conducted the cross-examination. For the first time he hesitated a few seconds. He seemed a little at a loss as to what issue to raise in his questioning. A sudden movement behind him caught my eye. Margaret Burnham, the tiny, round-faced, quiet attorney who hadn't said a word out loud in this entire trial, leaned over to Howard Moore and buzz-buzz-buzzed. Mr. Branton turned to them and the three of them put their heads together for a few seconds.

Mr. Branton came back to the rostrum and queried the FBI agent as though he doubted the accuracy of the identification of Angela Davis. The agent admitted that while he was in charge of the investigation, and during the month in which he was actually looking for Ms. Davis, a number of people had called or sent notice that they had seen her in various places. Eight or ten reports were made and each of them had to be checked out.

Eyewitness identification of Angela Davis was crucial to the prosecution's case, and the defense had maneuvered an FBI agent into testifying under oath that on numerous occasions, Angela Davis had been falsely identified by eyewitnesses.

It was beautifully done. I'm sure the agent didn't know what Mr. Branton was getting at, because he was very open and answered, "Yes, there were false reports all over the United States."

And when Branton asked, "In fact, you would get two different reports from two different places right at the same time, that people had seen Angela Davis at widely separated sections of the country?" the agent replied, "Yes."

Of course, no one questioned that Angela Davis was the one he had arrested. She sat there in the courtroom as a result of that arrest.

The remaining two witnesses testified that an automobile had been parked in the San Francisco airport garage. The car had come in about 8:30 in the morning of August 7th and had left about 9:30 in the evening of August 22nd. The bill for this car was $43.25. This car was supposed to be the Volkswagen of Mabel Magers which she had loaned to Jonathan Jackson on the 5th. Harris' theory was that Angela Davis had driven that car to the airport and waited around (for a phone call at the American Airlines terminal?) until she left hurriedly on the two o'clock flight from the PSA terminal. No link was made between Angela Davis and the VW. The prosecution had only established that some unidentified car had been parked in the airport garage at

8:30 on the morning of August 7th and was left there for three weeks. Even the amount due was different from the amount Mabel Magers had said she paid.

The defense brought out that the prosecution stopped looking once they found the data that roughly matched the evidence they were looking for. Out of seven or eight thousand parking tickets per day that were processed, they were willing to settle for the one that fit their preconceived ideas as to what had happened—even though Ms. Magers had testified that the bill was $43.00, not $43.25.

They had looked for cars that had entered on the 3rd, 4th, 5th, 6th and 7th—and which had left on the 18th through the 22nd. They did not look for cars that might have entered after the 7th, or left after the 22nd.

Mr. Branton asked about cars that left on later dates—the 24th and the 25th and the 27th—all with charges of approximately $43.00 and some with the exact amount. The airport official and the investigator for the Attorney General both admitted that they had not even considered looking beyond the date of the escape attempt.

The jury was then allowed to examine all the pieces of evidence that Mr. Harris thought were relevant. We were handed all the guns, all the boxes and plastic baggies of bullets, the briefcase and the attaché case, the books and the letters. Mr. Harris gave each of the exhibits to the alternate juror who sat on my left. As soon as she looked at one, she passed it to me, then I started it on down the front row of the jury box.

There seemed to be no way I could say, "No thanks, I don't care to handle all that junk." I had seen the exhibits in court as they were brought in and identified. I didn't have to hold the guns and bullets in my hand to understand what they were and what they stood for.

But just because I had no need to touch and examine the exhibits didn't mean that all the jurors felt the same way. It seemed important to some that they examine each gun and each box of shells.

Ralph, sitting directly behind me, made little jokes about slipping an occasional bullet into his pocket in order to have souvenirs of the trial to exhibit . . . "And on this table, ladies and gentlemen, you can see the bullet from the very gun that was carried by Angela Davis . . . and on this wall is the gun removed from the actual yellow Hertz Econoline rent-a-van." He said it all under his breath as we passed the exhibits back and forth around the jury box.

We had a two-hour lunch break that day. Ruth and I went to a downtown restaurant and after lunch we wandered around the streets of that part of San Jose. We went into a pawnshop. Neither of us had ever been in one before. We looked around at the watches and musical instruments—and the guns. I bought a watchband and we strolled across the street to a Goodwill Store to look at the used odds and ends.

Ruth found a children's book to take home to her daughter. While she was waiting to pay for it, I stood in front of an old black-and-white television set watching a game show. A news flash interrupted the show: Governor Wallace had been the object of an assassination attempt. He had been terribly wounded and it was not known whether he would live. We watched and listened for a few minutes and then hurried back to the security of our juror's assembly room.

One of the jurors brought in a small radio and the jurors and deputies gathered around it trying to get the latest word on the shooting. No one knew yet who had done it. Someone finally voiced what was in all our minds, "I hope it wasn't a black man."

Just as we were called back to court, the radio announcer mentioned that the assailant had been a blond young man.

We were still upset as we filed into court for the afternoon session. In this atmosphere, Albert Harris completed the prosecution's case by reading what appeared to be an edited version of the eighteen-page letter.

I had felt certain that Mr. Harris would end his presentation of the case with something dramatic. I suspected that it might be the eighteen-page letter, so I planned how I would comport myself during the reading of it.

Most of the time, I had just sat in the juror's seat as though I were in a movie theater, watching what was going on and responding openly to the testimony. But with the world press watching the jury's response to this document, I planned to remain as impassive as possible. The end of the prosecution's case was at hand. I was not going to give anyone a clue as to what I was thinking at that time.

The edited version was about two or three pages long. Even read in Mr. Harris' monotone, the words of love were beautiful. Nothing in them would make me believe that the woman who wrote them was consumed with a passion that knew no bounds —and would become violent and destructive if her love was frustrated.

If everyone who said to another, "I love you, you are wonderful," was suspected of being a potential murderer, not many of us would be left.

The presentation was over. Albert Harris said quietly, "Your Honor, the People rest their case."

Judge Arnason turned to the jury and announced that certain points of law would now be handled by the Court. These discussions had to be held outside the presence of the jury, so we would be dismissed for two days. We were to return on Thursday morning when the next phase of the trial would commence with the witnesses for the defense.

Again, we, the jury, were sent off to wait.

I knew from casual conversations between jurors during the periods of waiting up in the assembly room that no one had any idea how deliberations should proceed. No one seemed to be concerned about it, either. But it bothered me. I felt that many things could probably be done to facilitate the deliberations. It was just a matter of knowing about them. None of us had ever served on a jury before (except Bob, who had served on a short civil case) so we had no way to draw on past experience. But this problem was surely not a new one. Books must have been written on the subject.

So, I headed for the library to find some reference material. Palo Alto has an excellent city library, but not much material was available on the subject of juries. I checked out those volumes I felt might be of some value. At that particular moment, I was not interested in the history of the jury system or the need for reform of the jury system. What I wanted were guidelines for deliberations.

The first book I picked out sounded great: *What Every Person Should Know about Jury Trials.* It was written by a Washington, D.C., judge. He knew all about jury trials—from the standpoint of an attorney and a judge. He knew nothing about what it was like to be a juror, what the problems were and how best to solve them. He said, "The first duty is to select a foreman." Great. Now how does one do that? Which one of the twelve equal jurors stands up and says, "Our first duty is to select a foreman, so I will now pass out the papers and we will have a secret ballot," or " . . . let's match pennies to decide who shall be the foreman"?

I wasn't going to find the answers I needed from treatises written by members of the legal society. None of them had ever been a juror.

What You Need to Know for Jury Duty (Chicago: Cowles Book Corporation, Inc., 1968), by Godfrey Lehman, was the very book I was looking for. I glanced through the first chapters. It was well written, the manner was easy and very readable. My eye was caught by a phrase here and there that showed that Mr. Lehman had the experience. He knew what it meant to serve on a jury.

I looked at the back cover and read the publisher's blurb about him. He was a San Franciscan and had served on a number of juries. The book was published in 1968, so it was recent enough to be relevant.

I turned to the section on deliberations. And there I found exactly what I needed. Mr. Lehman had worked out an outline guide for deliberations and discussed the reasons for each step. I read it carefully and thought about it in relation to our trial. It fit almost perfectly. I would wish to make very few changes.

I took his outline and made additions from some other books I had read and from some of the thinking I had done. I typed a copy for myself and then decided it might be a good idea to have copies for some of the other jurors. So I took it down to the corner drugstore and photocopied a half-dozen sets.

Then I settled back and read the entire book. I wished I had found it before the trial started. It would have helped solve many little problems and explained things that I found out by trial and error. It was a delightful and informative book.

When I arrived at the jury assembly room on Thursday, I had the copies of the outline and gave them to some of the others. I was a little hesitant; I didn't want them to think I was trying to tell them how to handle themselves. As they read the outline, I gave a short description of the book and author. They were all interested and asked what other suggestions he had made.

The one I felt was most important for us to use was *never start the proceedings by taking a vote* or in any other way force the jurors to commit themselves before ample opportunity has been given for discussion. The rationale for this was that once people commit themselves they feel compelled to defend their positions. And as they do this, they further cement their opinions. Besides, no one should make a firm decision on the verdict without listening to a thorough discussion of all the evidence. One of the other jurors might remember something that could change one's thinking completely.

We all agreed to the validity of that argument and planned to follow the suggestion. About that time we were summoned down to court, and that effectively stopped our discussion of the book.

After the usual opening formalities, Mr. Moore rose from his seat and addressed the judge. I held my breath. Suppose he

announced that the defense would present no witnesses? The
trial would then be over.

He didn't. He asked Judge Arnason if the defense could be
given a few more days in which to review the prosecution's case.
He stated that instead of presenting the lengthy defense which
had been planned, it was possible they would be able to answer
the prosecution's case with a very abbreviated defense. In the
interest of saving time, if they were allowed a few more days
for review, the trial might be shortened.

As he spoke and the meaning became clear to us all, the jury
give a unanimous sigh of relief.

De-fense! De-fense! Defense!

I was really looking forward to testimony from the defense,
hoping to be given some answers to my uncertainties and maybe
further interpretations of what had happened.

The big question in everyone's mind was whether or not Angela
Davis would testify and perhaps respond to some of the allegations
of the prosecutor. Then, too, Mr. Harris could cross-examine her
and question her directly about all the times and places and incidents he had been hinting about. So, when Judge Arnason directed the defense attorney to call his first witness, I turned and
looked at Angela Davis. She made no move.

Instead, the first witness was the executive director of the
San Francisco Model Cities Day Care Center, Susan Castro. She
was very nervous, massaging her hands as she sat in the witness
chair.

She said she had become interested in the plight of the Soledad Brothers and had gone to a court hearing in Salinas with
some friends. She was shocked by the fact the prisoners were

brought into court shackled—chains around their waists, around their ankles, around their wrists. They couldn't move, even to reach out for something. She stated that she was horrified by this display and became active in the Soledad Brothers' Defense Committee. In this capacity, she went to Los Angeles to talk to members of their families, and there she met Angela Davis.

Ms. Castro testified that on Wednesday, August 5, 1970, Angela Davis had phoned her at work in San Francisco, suggesting that they have lunch together. She left around noon and went to a Ms. Wheeler's house where Ms. Davis was staying. They had lunch and talked until about 2:30 in the afternoon. When questioned about the subject they were discussing, Ms. Castro stated that Ms. Davis was concerned that few black people were involved in the defense committee work and they talked about methods of bringing more of them into the effort.

They left the Wheeler house and Ms. Castro drove Angela Davis over to the Soledad House which she had not visited since its opening the previous Sunday. Other people were around and they discussed, among other things, how best to provide protection—locks, guns, and the like. While they were there, Jonathan Jackson came in and offered to take Angela Davis back to Ms. Wheeler's, so Ms. Castro left and went back to work.

That meeting was on August 5th, from noon until after three o'clock. The prosecution had placed Angela Davis at San Quentin at that time, on that day.

The second witness was Juanita Wheeler, a middle-aged woman who had worked at *People's World* in San Francisco for twenty-one years. She testified that about a week before the escape, her boss, the editor of the newspaper, Carl Bloice, asked her if Angela Davis could stay at her house for a few days when she came north from Los Angeles. Ms. Wheeler said that would be fine, Ms. Davis had stayed with her before.

Angela Davis arrived about 10:30 Monday evening. She stayed there four days, sleeping there every night and having breakfast with Ms. Wheeler every morning. Some mornings she accompanied Ms. Wheeler to the office of *People's World* and met with Carl Bloice.

On Friday morning the two women had breakfast, put Angela Davis' weekender bag into the car, and drove to the offices of the paper. About noon Mr. Bloice asked if he could borrow the car to take Ms. Davis to the airport. Ms. Wheeler didn't know what time the keys were returned.

Marvin Stender, a San Francisco attorney, was the next witness. He had a thin face, fairly short hair, conservative dress and precise speech. He was the unofficial attorney for the Soledad Committee, and his wife had been an attorney for George Jackson. They lived in Berkeley.

He testified that on Thursday morning, August 6th, he received a phone call from Angela Davis at his office. She asked if he could give her a ride over to the East Bay. Since he had planned to go back to Berkeley to do some research at the law library there, he was willing to give her a ride. They met at a parking lot about 10:30 and he drove her to an Oregon Street address in Berkeley.

He testified he also knew Jonathan Jackson and had seen him the last weekend in July when young Jackson had stayed at the Stender house. They had discussed how best to protect the records and materials that were being stored at the new Soledad House. In this regard they had discussed the use of guns.

He was giving support to an alternate theory for the buying of the shotgun.

In cross-examination of these witnesses, Mr. Harris kept bringing out that none of them had ever told any law-enforcement agency the details of what they knew about Angela Davis' whereabouts during that critical week. Mr. Stender admitted that he hadn't, saying flatly that he felt the Attorney General's Office was not interested in the truth.

Most people in the area know that *People's World* is a newspaper of the Communist Party. I had heard of it but, like most people, had never read a copy. In fact, to the best of my knowledge, I had never seen a real live Communist before I became a juror on this trial. Carl Bloice, the editor of the paper and most surely a Communist, was the next witness. He was not a very good witness. He was so careful with his answers he gave the impression he was not answering openly and honestly. It was probably fear or nervousness that manifested itself through his impassive, deadpan look and slow, careful speech, but the effect was that I mistrusted his answers.

He testified he had been with Angela Davis on Tuesday morning, they had dinner together on Wednesday evening, she had been in the offices of the paper on Thursday morning, and he had taken her to the airport on Friday.

The airport incident was a very important part of his testimony. He stated that they went in Ms. Wheeler's car. They didn't have the radio on. He parked in a parking lot and they went into the terminal to the PSA desk. He had carried her bag in and he set it down on the weighing platform. She had a reservation for the 3:00 commuter flight to Los Angeles.

While she was preparing to purchase her ticket, she was told that if she hurried she might be able to catch the two o'clock flight, since it hadn't left yet. Ms. Davis then hurried off down to the boarding terminal for PSA and Mr. Bloice left the airport.

When he arrived back at the newspaper office later that day, someone told him that an escape attempt had been made. He stated that he had been very busy and had not paid too much attention to it until later that evening.

The cross-examination of Carl Bloice was really interesting. Albert Harris brought out that Mr. Bloice, too, had not informed the Attorney General's Office of any of these matters about which he had just testified. And then Mr. Harris asked if Bloice had heard from Angela Davis after she left. Mr. Bloice answered that he had not, until after she was in jail in Marin County.

Mr. Harris asked, " . . . didn't you receive a telephone call from her?"

"No, I don't recall receiving a telephone call from her," Bloice was answering very carefully now.

"Didn't you receive a phone call from her from the Los Angeles airport on August 15th?"

"No."

"You don't remember receiving a phone call, *any* phone call?"

"No . . . well, yes, I remember a phone call after August 7th."

I looked at the defense people. They were all leaning forward with their jaws slack, staring at Mr. Bloice in amazement. Something was going on. It looked as though Mr. Harris knew something they were not expecting to hear about.

Carl Bloice continued, "Yes, I remember the phone call from the Marin County jail." The defense group leaned back in their chairs, turning and smiling and shaking their heads at each other in relief.

That call wasn't what Harris was talking about. He asked Bloice if he'd received another phone call, this one from the Los Angeles airport to his home phone. A call had been charged to the phone of Kendra and Franklin Alexander, close friends of Angela Davis. The name of the person making the call was "Jamala."

Mr. Harris asked if "Jamala" was not in fact really Angela Davis. Bloice denied that it was Angela Davis. Harris asked if Bloice knew who it was and Bloice answered, "Yes, it is Jamala."

"Was that her first name or her last name?"

"Neither, just Jamala." Bloice was getting pretty nervous. Harris seemed to be closing in for the kill.

"Do you deny getting a phone call from the Los Angeles airport on August 15, 1970?"

"I don't remember . . . ."

Carl Bloice was so nervous while he was answering that I thought he must be lying. Leo Branton and Ms. Davis were whispering together. I couldn't see their faces.

When Mr. Harris finished his cross-examination, Mr. Branton rose for a redirect examination. He asked if the woman to whom Mr. Harris had referred, Ms. Jamala, was in the courtroom at that time? Everyone looked at Angela Davis. Branton laughed and said, "No, I don't mean Ms. Davis—elsewhere in the courtroom?"

When Carl Bloice answered that she was, Branton turned to the spectator's section and asked a young woman to stand, please. A happy-looking black woman stood up and smiled, and her friends around her tittered and laughed.

Mr. Branton asked if that was Jamala. Bloice answered that it was. Jamala smiled and sat down.

This episode was the only one in the entire trial that was anything like *Perry Mason* on TV.

It was fun, but it was also very important. I was watching Prosecutor Harris very closely throughout the whole episode. He had been so sure of himself. He could not believe he was wrong. In fact he rose and cross-examined Mr. Bloice again—insisting by his questioning that Angela Davis must really have made the call.

The incident was a perfect example of the thinking of all the law-enforcement people in this case, from the Attorney General on down. Here was an incident that they could put into their master plot, and as soon as they found it and made it fit, they looked no further. They not only stopped looking, they could not accept that another explanation for the incident might be possible.

Albert Harris' expression during this whole episode revealed clearly the thrust of his thinking and the inflexibility of his approach to the case. And it shed light on a number of areas which had been bothering me—for example, the treatment of the records at the airport garage, when no effort had been made to find out if the Volkswagen could have been brought into the lot at a later date. No, once they found a time span and receipt that fit their master plot, they stopped looking. They didn't think to look any farther and possibly find something that might cast doubt on the guilt of Angela Davis.

This attitude could explain, too, the set of pictures they showed eyewitnesses for identification of the "young, tall black woman with the Afro" they had seen. The investigators were sure that the woman in question must have been Angela Davis, so they felt no need to offer pictures of other women with similar physical characteristics.

Later that afternoon, Mr. Branton asked the court's permission to put the young woman known as Jamala on the stand even though he had not planned to do so.

She explained that her legal name was Carol Broadnax, but when she became interested in the Black Liberation Movement, she decided to adopt a Swahili name to help identify more strongly with her African origins.

She then admitted making the phone call to Carl Bloice on August 15th. The reason for the call was that a group of people were flying up to San Francisco to attend the funeral of Jonathan Jackson and they called to make sure someone would meet them at the airport when they arrived.

Another young woman who used a name of Swahili origin was the next witness. "Tamu" had been Angela Davis' roommate in an apartment in Los Angeles for more than a year—until Angela Davis moved out three weeks before the escape attempt. Leo Branton first questioned her about her name and she explained that Tamu means "sweetness," and that was why she chose it for her name. It suited her.

Having been such a close friend she was able to give details of Ms. Davis' life. She said that their apartment had become head-quarters for the Che-Lumumba Club (an all-black Communist collective) as well as the headquarters for the Soledad Defense Committee. The apartment was noisy and crowded, with no place for Ms. Davis to have the privacy and quiet to do her writing. For this reason she moved from the apartment in mid-July.

Tamu told of the purchase of the guns and ammunition and how all the club members used the guns for target practice out in the desert area near Los Angeles.

Mr. Branton brought into court a homemade gun rack which Tamu identified as having been in the closet of her apartment. The carbine and rifle had been kept in this rack, as well as the handgun and some shells.

Tamu testified that on the Saturday before the escape attempt, Jonathan Jackson had come to her apartment to do some work (they had typewriters, mimeograph machines, and the like). She had left him there alone. When she returned later in the day, he was gone. She had had no occasion to look in the closet; and the next day she drove up to San Francisco to attend the opening of the Soledad House. Jonathan Jackson was there. Angela Davis was not.

Tamu returned to Los Angeles on the following day. During that week, she had no reason to look in the closet and so did not know if the guns were there or not.

The following Saturday, the day after the escape attempt, Tamu testified that Angela Davis and Franklin Alexander came to the apartment about noon and asked her if the guns were still there. She answered that she didn't know, so they went to the closet and looked. The guns were gone.

Mr. Branton asked her to repeat exactly what was said by Franklin Alexander. Tamu didn't want to say the word in court, but at Branton's insistence, she answered, "Franklin said, 'Oh, shit!' . . . and Angela said, 'Oh, no!'"

Tamu was the last witness to testify on Monday, the first day of the defense. We had heard testimony that Angela Davis could not have been at the places where the prosecution's witnesses had said they had seen her. She could not have been at San Quentin all the times she was supposed to have accompanied Jonathan to see his brother. And she was in the car with attorney Marvin Stender when the men at the Mobil station supposedly had seen her in the yellow Hertz van with Jonathan Jackson.

We had also been given testimony that she had not driven a Volkswagen to the airport at 8:30 in the morning and waited around near a pay phone until 2:00. Instead, she had been taken to the airport, arriving just in time to catch the 2:00 p.m. plane.

We had heard that Jonathan Jackson had an opportunity to take the guns and ammunition without her knowledge, and that she had been surprised when she found they had in fact been taken.

When we were called down to the courtroom the next morning, the first witness was a woman named Ellen Broms, a social worker in L.A. She testified that she had known Franklin and Kendra Alexander for years and had met Angela Davis a number of times.

Ellen Broms testified that Angela Davis and Franklin Alexander were guests at her house for dinner on Friday, August 7th. They had arrived about 5:30 or 6:00. She and her husband had planned an early dinner so they could all go to a movie. They couldn't find one they all agreed on, so they just sat around and talked and listened to records and played scrabble until about 10:30 when the phone rang.

It was Kendra Alexander—calling to break the news of the escape attempt. Franklin came back into the room and told them what had happened, and Angela Davis said, "Oh, no! I can't believe it—he's so young."

They turned on the radio and television to get the news reports. Ms. Broms said that Ms. Davis was extremely distraught, very upset about the event, saying over and over that she couldn't believe it, "He was so young."

A shotgun was mentioned in the broadcast and Angela Davis said that she had bought a shotgun two days before; she wondered if it could be the same one.

Ms. Broms insisted that they both spend the night with her. She gave Ms. Davis a tranquilizer.

The next morning they read in the paper about the escape attempt and saw the picture of Jonathan Jackson with a carbine. It looked like the one that had been kept at the Che-Lumumba Club, so Franklin Alexander and Angela Davis left the Broms house and went to find out if in fact it was that gun. That was the last she saw Ms. Davis.

In cross-examination of these witnesses, Mr. Harris stressed two points: first, that none of them had come forward to tell these stories to any law-enforcement agencies and, second, that they were all friends or close acquaintances of Angela Davis.

He very carefully phrased a series of questions to each of

them asking if they belonged to any clubs or organizations to which Angela Davis also belonged. All of them except Tamu denied this. What he was really asking seemed to me to be, "Aren't you too a Communist?"

The defense presented two more witnesses that afternoon. One was the investigator for the Attorney General who had testified earlier for the prosecution about the telephone number found in Jonathan Jackson's wallet—the one that was for the pay phone at the American Airlines terminal. He was asked if there had been an area code included on the number. There hadn't been.

Mr. Branton then asked if any other area code had been investigated? After all, Jonathan had lived in southern California—had they made any attempt to see if such a number was in service down there? They had not.

The next witness was the representative from the phone company who had testified for the prosecution that the number belonged to the pay phone. This time he testified that the same number was operative in southern California as well—a number which would not have been listed in the phone book, since the phone was installed in June and removed in August of that same year.

The number was listed for a house in the Huntington Park area. (I was familiar enough with the Los Angeles area to know that the Huntington Park area was near Watts and was heavily populated with minorities—a ghetto.)

The prosecution had done it again. Just as with the airport parking lot incident, the phone call from Jamala and the set of pictures, they had not looked beyond what they thought fit their master plan. It apparently never occurred to them that the phone number could have been from a different area code.

We spent most of the next day listening to a lecture by Dr. Robert Buckout, an associate professor at one of the nearby state colleges. His special area of interest was social and experimental psychology, specifically the social and perceptual factors in eyewitness identification.

Dr. Buckout used visual aids such as graphs and slides to demonstrate points he was making. He had electronic devices to show how experiments were conducted and he presented data derived from these experiments.

Probably the best-known type of experiment he told us about was performed in his class at college. On the first day of each semester a short skit would be enacted before the students. They did not know this skit was prearranged so they believed it to be an actual confrontation. A "former student" entered the class room, loudly upbraided Dr. Buckout because his grade was so poor, then shoved or struck the professor and left the room. The entire event was videotaped.

Dr. Buckout then had the class describe the incident and the individual involved in it. He recorded their answers and was able to demonstrate the very great disparities in their eyewitness accounts of the incident. And the videotape showed them what really had happened.

He then presented us with a dozen or so different factors which might influence a person's ability to perceive and recall accurately what had been seen. The first was *insignificance of event,* in which experiments had demonstrated that details remembered correlated with the importance placed on the observance. If an event was not considered significant at the time it happened, it could not be recalled accurately, no matter how important the event later proved to be.

Dr. Buckout brought into the court an instrument called a tachistoscope, which flashed an image on a screen for a measured interval. He showed us how much more detail could be picked up and remembered the longer a subject was viewed—so *length of viewing time* was important.

Accurate observation was also affected by the *physical condition of the viewer*—color blindness, defects in vision, and the like. Whether the observer was distracted or otherwise occupied affected the accuracy of reporting.

Conditioning was important. Dr. Buckout gave an example:
If a reporter is sent out to "cover a riot," he or she sees a "riot"
in what might otherwise be reported as a meeting. Since we are
all conditioned to expect certain things, we are open to suggestions that support our own biases and stereotyping.

People also have a tendency to *follow the leader* and agree
with what a person in a position of leadership—such as a parent,
teacher or government official—states is true. Experimental data
showed that this tendency often caused subjects to deny something very obvious, about which an outside observer felt no possibility of error could exist.

One of the most amusing stories he told concerned the *desire
to be part of history*. Dr. Buckout recounted an experiment in
which a psychologist planted a story in the papers about a baby-
sitter in a small Midwestern town who had become stuck to a
freshly painted toilet in the bathroom of a house where she was
working. The local fire department had to be called to relieve
her from her predicament.

This whole tale was the figment of the psychologist's imagi-
nation, but it received wide publicity. The town was named,
but the girl was not identified. After a suitable interval, the
psychologist, pretending he was a reporter, went to the town
and interviewed some of the citizens. He found that many of
them "remembered" the incident, claiming to have known the
baby-sitter or the home where it had happened. A local fireman
even claimed to have been one of those sent out on the call who
had helped release the girl. Amazing!

The spectators, the court personnel including the attorneys
and the defendant, as well as the jury, were quiet and interested.
This lecture was not one that a student would sleep through.
The material was informative and the manner in which it was
presented was interesting.

We were shown slides depicting the result of experimental
data showing the effect of *conformity* and the *need for approval*
and how strong those influences are even on important issues.

In discussing *personal bias* he mentioned that some of the

professors at his college think that all short-haired students were athletes.

People see what they want to see. The example mentioned was of a picture flashed briefly before a class of a white man with a knife attacking a black man on a subway. If the picture were shown long enough, very little error resulted, but if the time of viewing was shortened the observers reversed the characters; the black man became the one with the knife. Theoretically, the observers found it easier to accept the idea that a black man would attack the white man with a knife.

Another variable which the professor called *passing on a theory* dealt both with experimental animals and with school children. When an experimenter was told that one group of rats was more intelligent than another, the group labeled "intelligent" did better on all learning tasks. When a teacher was told that one group of children was more intelligent, that group did much better in their school work. These experiments were carefully controlled, using different groups and different teachers.

I had heard of many of these experiments in psychology courses I had taken, or had read about them in journals. But it was important that I was reminded of them within the context of this trial. While I might have felt distrustful of some of the eyewitness testimony, I would not have been able to isolate and articulate the reasons for such mistrust.

One experiment I had never heard of before dealt with *filling in detail.* Observers were given drawings to examine. They came back at different intervals and tried to reproduce the drawings. When the observer returned in just a few hours the reproductions were very accurate, but as time passed changes appeared. The changes were gradual and always went from the unusual to the usual shapes.

In the cross-examination of Dr. Buckout, Mr. Harris attempted to show that the witness was not really qualified to discuss a subject such as color blindness since he wasn't an ophthalmologist or even an oculist. But anyone who has taken a college psych course knows that much of the knowledge of the eye specialists has come from the work of experimental psychologists or physiologists.

Prosecutor Harris suggested that the reason for Dr. Buckout's appearing as a defense witness might be a "desire to be a part of history"—one of the variables Dr. Buckout had listed. The professor did not directly deny this possibility, but suggested with a smile that he might very well turn the question around and direct it toward Mr. Harris.

The atmosphere had been tense all day in the courtroom. Ten or twelve armed sheriff's deputies were in the courtroom at all times—looking grim and determined. Right behind the witness stand chair was a locked door with a small window at eye level. We had asked about it early in the trial and been told it led into a holding cell in which prisoners who were to testify could be kept.

When we entered court that morning we caught glimpses of a black man inside the room. Names floated in the air—Ruchell Magee? Soledad Brothers? Fleeta Drumgo? John Cluchette?

The nervousness of the deputies was fairly contagious. I wasn't frightened but the situation was tense. Some of the other jurors showed that they, too, were more than normally edgy. They kept glancing up at the little window, straining to see who was in there.

We were released for a short recess in the middle of the afternoon. When we returned to the jury box, a black man sat in the witness chair, smiling at us as we filed in.

I could see that he was chained. His legs were shackled with about eighteen inches of chain between the ankles. Handcuffs were attached to another chain around his waist. His right hand was free, but the left was held in the cuff.

He gave his name as Fleeta Drumgo and he said he was one of the Soledad Brothers. He did not stand when taking the oath, but was able to raise his right hand. I couldn't see if his chains were attached to the bolts on the chair and the floor.

Why was he chained? A dozen armed deputies guarded a

courtroom designed for maximum security, and still they chained the man.

He was appearing as a witness for the defense—to help free his black sister, Angela Davis. Surely not even the Attorney General would suspect him, under these circumstances, of planning anything violent.

Fleeta Drumgo was the only witness who was not brought into court from the central doors of the courtroom. He was the only witness who was seated at the witness stand when the jury was brought in. Were they afraid the jury would become angered at seeing a man brought into court in shackles —a man who just two months before had been acquitted of murder?

Well, I could see the chains—and I was angered!

Mr. Drumgo testified he was now residing at San Quentin prison, in the adjustment center. The adjustment center is the name of the section of the prison where the most "difficult" prisoners are confined. It has the strictest security of any of the prison blocks. Mr. Drumgo's cell was right next to the cell of James McClain. He testified that he had heard nothing of any escape attempt until after the event. He heard about it on the news broadcast that evening. He, as one of the Soledad Brothers, knew of no conspiracy to stage the escape attempt in order to free the Soledad Brothers.

Attorney Branton then asked to submit into evidence a photostatic copy of the acquittal of the Soledad Brothers. Mr. Harris objected, saying that the document had nothing to do with the case.

Mr. Branton replied, "You read their indictment and implied that this whole escape was because time had run out for them, and I wish to say that rather than time running out, time was just beginning for them!"

The statement was beautifully phrased—and there was no answer to it.

I looked at Fleeta Drumgo—a small man, weighted with chains —he looked almost joyous at that moment.

Mrs. Elsie Gluck was the executive secretary for the Department of Philosophy, University of California at Los Angeles. She testified that during the months of publicity about the regents of the university having fired Ms. Davis, the department had received a tremendous increase in phone calls. The phone system had broken down and new lines had to be installed to allow the regular business of the department to carry on. These calls were largely calls of harassment.

The daily mail also increased tremendously—so much that additional help was required to handle it. Ms. Gluck brought into court a stack of manila folders containing the files of "hate mail." Angela Davis had read these letters.

When the witness left the stand, Attorney Branton said, "The defense rests."

He sat down, turned to the jury and smiled.

The time had come to pause and get an overview of the case. I wanted to do some independent thinking now that the testimony was completed. I didn't want my decisions to be influenced by any emotional rhetoric which might be a part of the attorneys' summations. These summations, like the opening statements, were not to be considered as evidence.

I didn't think about the details of the testimony, but rather how I felt about the people involved in the events that had occurred. No one of them could be considered as an isolated entity.

Jonathan Jackson was the central figure in all the interpersonal relationships. Jonathan communicated with James McClain through his brother, George, one of the Soledad Brothers. Jonathan was directly involved with the people and activities at the Soledad Brothers Defense Committee headquarters both in San Francisco and Los Angeles. He also had a close relationship with the young woman at the Hammer house and borrowed her car. Jonathan knew Angela Davis and used her books and guns.

Jonathan Jackson was seventeen years old. That fact is almost enough to explain the rashness of his actions. It was August—getting toward the end of summer vacation. In just a few weeks he would be back in school with all the restrictions of his movements that going to high school imposes.

Probably no other group in the world is as idealistic as high school seniors. They volunteer for all the wars and join all the marches. They carelessly sacrifice their lives for ideals which their elders treat with casual intellectual scepticism. Very little suggestion is required to cause them to become involved in a righteous cause. The greatest problem in dealing with seventeen-year-olds is containing their energy and directing it toward a goal which can be reached by less extreme measures than martyrdom.

Another thing—so many young people are so sure of themselves and the rightness of their ideas that the older people who have doubts credit the young with more knowledge and experience than they could possibly have. Jonathan spoke and acted with authority. But when I looked at the *Mini-Manual of Guerrilla Warfare* he had carried in his attaché case, I could tell by the fingerprinting stains that he had read only the first quarter of the book.

I thought about Angela Davis, whose family still lived in Birmingham where she was born in 1944. She grew up in a racist community, where frequent bombings occurred in her neighborhood—in the town where the four little girls were killed while they were attending church one Sunday morning.

She was the same age as my oldest child, so she too must have grown up with the civil rights movement, must have been in college when President Kennedy was assassinated. She must have been affected by the academic rebellions and must have protested against the war in Vietnam.

She was doing graduate work when Martin Luther King was assassinated. She stayed in school and finished all the course work for her PhD. She had only to write her dissertation when she was offered a position as Assistant Professor of Philosophy at the University of California at Los Angeles. No one reaches that point without a good deal of self-discipline. Being black and a woman, to have reached that point she must have overcome tremendous odds and exhibited tremendous dedication.

Would anyone as obviously sensitive as Angela Davis sacrifice a seventeen-year-old kid—one with great potential—by sending him into an adventure which could only destroy him? Mr. Harris seemed to think she would. I wondered.

Would anyone as intelligent as Angela Davis get involved in such a stupid plot: If the rescue of the Soledad Brothers was the object of the escape attempt, why use such an involved procedure? Why didn't they just wait a few days or weeks until the Soledad Brothers themselves were in court and pull the same caper? The plan wasn't well thought out—no real demands were made, confusion and disorder marked that day in Marin.

This exploit seemed to me to be the action of a very young person—not the action of a woman who had always succeeded by using her mind and her ability to speak and write to accomplish her ends. No evidence had been brought out that Angela Davis had ever used force to make her point—rhetoric, yes, but not violence.

Following this line of thought, I began to wonder whether Jonathan could have done the whole thing without Angela Davis' knowledge or approval.

He was the central figure. He rented the van, visited his brother at San Quentin, signed in at the prison gate register, handled the transaction at the Mobil station, made two or three "dry runs" at the courthouse the day before the attempt.

He borrowed the Volkswagen, he was present when the shotgun was purchased, his fingerprints were all over the *Mini-Manual of Guerrilla Warfare,* and he entered the courtroom on the 7th and initiated the escape attempt when he stood up and drew the gun. He had brought the guns, the ammunition, the tape and the wire. He had the van waiting outside in the parking lot.

So Jonathan Jackson was the central figure in the events of

the week. Someone was probably with him on Thursday, a young black woman with an Afro, but it could have been someone other than Ms. Davis. Jonathan could have planned and executed all of the necessary acts by himself. So, it wasn't important that an unknown woman was with him. What was important was whether or not that unknown woman was Angela Davis.

I thought not. . . . I suddenly realized that I didn't believe that Angela Davis was involved in the conspiracy. I felt this very strongly. I wasn't absolutely sure just why, but right then I knew that the escape was the action of a seventeen-year-old youth acting in concert with men who had been imprisoned since they were about that age—men who were desperate, who could no longer believe that they could ever achieve freedom within the mechanics of the system. I didn't believe that Angela Davis was guilty.

A great feeling of relief and joy came over me. I had reached my own personal decision. I still had to do a lot of thinking and organizing to be able to justify my beliefs to others. And I had to be careful not to block out other ideas that might be in conflict. I must be reasonable and logical, but I need no longer be in this limbo of indecision and uncertainty.

I had found her not guilty.

The courtroom was overcrowded. Extra chairs were placed in the court area and against the walls. Albert Harris was going to make his final summation.

I went into court that morning with a large notebook and two pens, not wanting to have to depend on the little notepads I had been using. I had carefully reviewed my notes and couldn't believe that I had accurately recorded the whole case. I must have missed something important if he had proved Angela Davis was involved.

The court session was opened the usual way. Judge Arnason commented that the summation was always one of the more interesting parts of any trial. He called on Mr. Harris and then leaned back in his swivel chair and prepared to enjoy the final summation by the prosecutor.

Mr. Harris brought the lectern over in front of the jury box and started. Just as in the first days of the trial, the jury suddenly became all-important. Mr. Harris ignored the rest of the court, the press and all the spectators. It was the jury to whom he spoke.

I sat with my pen at the ready. I was prepared to take notes if he reminded me of the evidence that I had missed. But I had missed none. He told the same story over again—only this time with omissions. Some of the "evidence" he had planned to present had not materialized; for example evidence that Jonathan Jackson lived with Angela Davis for the three weeks preceding the escape attempt, and evidence of "close physical contact" between George Jackson and Angela Davis. But essentially his story was the same one he had told in the introductory statement. But I wasn't the same.

This time I was prepared. I watched for the inconsistencies; I saw the false logic. When Mr. Harris said, "If it was Angela Davis in the van, then she had to have known of the plan," my trial experience forced me to hold back and to question the validity of the conclusions he was drawing from the evidence he had presented.

Mr. Harris did a fine job of summarizing all those weeks of testimony, fitting the pieces together, blending it all into what could almost be thought of as the working outline of a tragic Russian novel.

He dealt with it in an unemotional, factual manner. He told the story—it was up to us on the jury to accept or reject it. He did not try to disguise the possible weak points of his case by covering them with emotional tirades or bombastic rhetoric. I did not know whether this was Mr. Harris' usual style but it was the only way he could have dealt effectively with us. I, for one, was grateful for his factual, professional approach.

I waited for Mr. Harris to include the three crucial elements of the crime of conspiracy—agreement, knowledge and intent. When he did, he merely stated that if the evidence which had been presented were accepted, then no other logical interpretation could be made but that Angela Davis must have known about the escape attempt and agreed to it and, by the "overt acts," shown her intent.

He emphasized again that the motive for the attempted escape must have been to free the Soledad Brothers, since by his very acts Jonathan Jackson would cut himself off from ever being able to help his brother, George Jackson—and the driving force in the young man's life was to obtain the freedom of his brother.

I went home that afternoon satisfied that I had understood the prosecution's case throughout the trial, and had not ignored any salient points. I had needed no reminders from Mr. Harris' summation.

During the trial when one of our friends or relatives wanted to attend a court session, they had to arrive at the gates of the security fence hours before court began.

Ralph brought his "darlin' daughters" down to the security fence at 4:30 Thursday morning, the day the defense was to present their final summation. The girls were the 15th and 16th in line. They were the last ones to get in. As we waited for our day to begin, Ralph said he had told the others in line that he was going to look for his kids when he entered the courtroom and if they weren't in the spectators' section, the whole trial was going to come to a grinding halt!

Many of the extra seats were taken by visiting friends and relatives of the court personnel, of the attorneys and of the judge. We recognized the wives of Mr. Harris and Mr. Branton whom we had seen in court before. The court had been crowded the day before, but today the place seemed jammed. We all checked quickly to see if Ralph's children had gotten seats. They had— the trial could go on.

Strangely enough, the atmosphere in the courtroom was very similar to that of the first day of the trial. It was filled with the same sense of excitement and anticipation.

Today was to be the big show. No one knew if Angela Davis would speak in her own defense. I thought she would. This would give her an opportunity to refute any testimony she wished to, without worrying about cross-examination. Of course her speech could not be considered testimony, but it could be impressive.

I knew I wouldn't need to take any notes this day. This day was one for listening.

After the usual opening rituals, Judge Arnason turned to Howard Moore and said he understood Mr. Moore was to begin the defense summation.

Mr. Moore opened rather formally, thanking the jury for our attention and then giving a brief discussion of the importance of the jury in the evolution of our legal system.

He talked about reasonable doubt—two of the most important words in American jurisprudence, the two words that more than any others decide who shall go free.

The duty of the jury to presume that the defendant is innocent was discussed, and we were reminded that unless every vestige of that cloak of innocence was removed by evidence, the defendant remained innocent.

Mr. Moore discussed circumstantial evidence and how it must not be confused with mere coincidence. He gave as an example the arrival in San Francisco of Angela Davis on Monday, August 3, 1970, and her departure on Friday, August 7, 1970.

"People watchers" was the name that Howard Moore used to describe many of the law-enforcement personnel. He said that some of them called themselves "San Quentin Correctional Officers" but in fact they were prison guards, and he preferred to call them "people watchers" since that was their primary function. Mr. Moore said that he was concerned and disturbed that the descriptions given by these trained professional people watchers fit the racial stereotypes most commonly associated with black people. He asked us to think back about all the black people who had appeared in court and think of them in terms of skin color (were they light-complexioned?) or irregularities of teeth (did they have a gap between the front teeth?). I tried to remember the black witnesses, and what their facial characteristics were.

I wasn't sure I could have recognized any of them.

Eyewitness identification and all the various factors which interfere with accurate identification by an observer—the points brought out by Dr. Buckout—was the main thrust of his final statement. He reminded us that Alden Fleming was color-blind, which would have interfered with his ability to make identification. And Officer West at San Quentin could have been "filling in" when he identified Angela Davis after having heard Officer Ayers make the identification two or three days earlier.

Mr. Moore reminded us of the photographs used by investigators to show witnesses for identification of the woman they had seen. These photographs made the odds almost insurmountable that anyone other than Angela Davis would be picked from the stack.

He quoted a decision of the Supreme Court of the United States saying that, "A major factor contributing to the high incidence of miscarriage of justice from mistaken identification has been the degree of suggestion inherent in the manner in which the prosecution presents the suspect to witnesses for pretrial identification."

Mr. Moore added, "Perhaps it is responsible for more such errors than all other factors combined."

He stopped, looked down at his notes for a moment, then, abruptly turning away from the jury, he suggested to the judge that this would be a good time for a break. The judge agreed and we headed up to our jury assembly room. Our conversation dealt largely with the unfamiliar people in the courtroom—guessing at their identities.

When we settled down in our chairs for the continuation of the defense summation, Mr. Branton came to the lectern.

Throughout the trial, Judge Richard Arnason did not interject his opinions or impose his will unless he was forced to do so. Leo Branton, Jr., seemed in charge. He was the one who controlled the tempo, the mood. Handsome, urbane, charming, never at a loss for the proper word or phrase, giving almost too polished a performance, being almost too much the "Hollywood lawyer," Mr. Branton in cross-examination had been casual when luring the witness, sharply incisive when making an important point. Only on occasion did he display the depth of his personal involvement or his sensitive understanding of the people he dealt with. This morning was one of those occasions.

As he opened his summation, he seemed a different man. He even looked different. Serious, his face ashen, his hands shaking slightly as he set his notes down, he began speaking softly. "May it please the court, gentlemen of the prosecution, my colleagues and Angela Davis, ladies and gentlemen of the jury, I rise to speak to you today on one of the most important days of my life, one of the most important days of the life of my client.

"I rise to address you as an officer of this court, a member of a very noble profession. But, more importantly, I rise to address you as a black man, a black man to defend my black sister, Angela."

He reminded us that we weren't black, that no black face was present on the jury. In order for us to be able to understand what makes an Angela Davis, we had to know what it has meant to be black throughout the history of our country. He asked us to "think black—to *be* black for a few minutes . . . don't worry. When the case is over I am going to let you revert back to the safety of being what you are."

Mr. Branton asked us—me—to *be* black. What did he mean? After all these weeks, their blackness and our whiteness had become unimportant, forgotten. Now suddenly we were pushed back again—separated and forced to remember where we came from, and what we were when the trial started.

He asked me to be black. I couldn't. In no way in this world could I know what it is to be black. I could understand parts of it, I could sympathize, I could forget color—but I couldn't *be* black.

"If you are black, you know that 300 years ago your forbears were brought to this country in chains on slave ships, and you know that only the strongest of them survived. You know that

the weak died in the holds of those ships because of the fact
that they died of their own vomit and their own stink and their
own stench."

Branton's voice was intense. He held out his right hand, turned
it over and looked at his bare wrist—light against his suit. "Every
time you look at the color of the skin, you realize that it's the
result of some white man having raped your grandmother.

"You come to this country, and they pass a law. They call
it the Fugitive Slave Law. It means that they can chase a slave
across every border, bring him back in chains, no trial, no jury,
just sign an affidavit that this slave is mine.

"Then when this country declares its independence, it speaks
in a document, which has gone down in history as one of the
greatest documents of our time. It's a document which was
drafted and written by men who owned hundreds of slaves. It
says, 'We declare that all men are created equal'—all *white* men
are created equal, not black . . . .

"Then there was a man by the name of Frederick Douglass,
who was a great abolitionist, one of the greatest people that
this world has ever seen. When John Brown had his raid at
Harper's Ferry, the Governor of the State of Virginia started
looking for Frederick Douglass to charge him with a conspiracy
to free the slaves. Frederick Douglass fled this country and went
to Canada. He fled it because of the fact that he feared what
might happen to him if he were charged with a conspiracy to
free the slaves, having spoken out so eloquently on the right of
all men to be free."

Mr. Branton continued, "If you are an Angela Davis who
grew up in the South, you know also about the struggle that
went on in the South where any man who dared speak out for
liberation of black people was assassinated in cold blood. You
recall Medgar Evers who was assassinated. You recall Martin
Luther King. You recall Malcolm X. You remember four little
girls in Birmingham, Alabama—Angela Davis' home town—who
were at church, and the church was dynamited by people who
didn't like what the preacher was preaching in that church—

the equality of man—and four little girls lost their lives."

Mr. Branton walked over to the table in front of the clerk of the court and pointed to the stack of manila folders which had been introduced as evidence and which contained mail received at the Department of Philosophy at UCLA during the few months that the controversy of Angela Y. Davis' employment was in the news. Those folders must have held hundreds of letters; the stack was a foot and a half high.

Some of them were selected to be read to us. They were incredible—filled with hate and venom. I had never heard such language: " . . . Hey you, with the FIJI hairstyle," " . . . We haven't forgotten the old days, big-mouthed Angela Davis. The Ku Klux didn't fool around with courts and judges. They acted and then asked questions. Thank God there are still some left in America," " . . . If you black woolly-headed militant throwbacks to humanity knew how filthy, dirty, nasty and repulsive you appear," " . . . Listen you Commie bitch, get your burrhead out of UCLA. We don't need your Commie nigger shit talk . . . ."

The jury was being shown that all these factors created a climate that made her fear for her life. She might have reason for flight, reason other than guilt.

Mr. Branton then dealt with the case and the accusations of the prosecution. He said that we could all agree on one thing: Ms. Davis was no fool. We had heard her writings read to us by Mr. Harris; we had listened to her opening statement; we knew she was a college professor. But to be involved in the events as described by the prosecution, she would have to be a fool. She would have to be a fool to go into a pawnshop and buy a gun, give her own name, talk to the salesman about getting her job back at UCLA, give him her autograph—if she were planning to use that gun to blow off a judge's head two days later. She would have to be a fool if she went to visit San Quentin with Jonathan and signed the gate register "Diane Robinson" but made no other attempt to disguise herself by pulling back her hair, or wearing a wig, or changing her glasses.

With the resumption of Mr. Branton's summation after the lunch break the tension of the morning was broken. Mr. Branton was again his usual amiable self as he told us that he had neglected to release us from the responsibility of being black. "Well, now that you have had a nice lunch and you are back here this afternoon, I relieve you of that responsibility for the rest of the trial."

He turned to one of the two large stands that had been brought into court while we were out to lunch. It held a drawing of Ms. Davis, surrounded by a circle of chains. The links were labeled, MOTIVE, OBJECT, AGREEMENT, KNOWLEDGE, INTENT, and FLIGHT.

He went through the links, showing the weaknesses of the evidence supporting each element of the conspiracy. As he concluded, he turned to the second stand, ripped off the covering sheet of paper, and displayed another drawing of Ms. Davis— with the links of chain broken and lying at her feet, and Angela Davis symbolically free.

It was very dramatic.

But the most dramatic moment came when he read phrases from the eighteen-page diary that Mr. Harris had used as evidence of passion, which was the motive for the crimes. Mr. Branton had taken these same phrases and had them arranged in poetic form.

He read this poem to the jury:

> Do you know how elated I was
> When I first discovered you loved me?
> I did not know George Jackson;
> He was an abstract figure,
> A brother I had to fight for;
> I didn't know how to respond
> To something so remote
> Until I saw you
> And, stunned, I stared
> Like a love-struck girl.
>
> After the court appearance in Salinas
> I was struck with a sense of—of you
> That beautiful man with whom I had

Instantly and unexpectedly
Fallen in love.

During the trip back
(We took the seaside road
Through fog and curving mountains
And green woods—and water—)

I was beside myself with happiness,
Loving you and growing ever more impatient . . .

I love you
I love you totally
I love you to the end
I love you, George

I'm glad we saw each other when we did;
It makes me realize that I have not always
Been as alone as I feel at this moment . . .

I'm intoxicated,
Overflowing with you,
Wanting you more than ever.

Since that last embrace
You're still here
I see you
We are one
They'll never wrest away from us
Those feelings—
Feelings accumulating over centuries,
Today infinitely magnified,
Undiminished in their intensity.

That so much love could exist
Anywhere
In any two people
Even between us
I never realized.

It makes me feel weak,
Though not in the sense of
Succumbing to weakness,
For it makes me stronger,
Stronger with your strength without end—
So terrible is this love.

This morning—this morning—
As I walked the few yards
(Treading in the air, it seemed)
From this cell toward you—toward you—

The millions of pieces
I had tried to fit together
Into a picture which would reflect
The reality of the man I love
Would all be there—these and more—
In an arrangement more perfect
Than the perfection
I had already conceived.
Though time seemed short—
Eight hours but a moment—
It was a moment containing eternity.

Typing out these words,
My mind wanders into other worlds,
Worlds full of you;
Reality fantasies lure me away
From this machine,
And before I know it,
The minute-hand on this other
Machine they've installed
Has made half a revolution.

Goodbye—goodnight
I'm going early to
That other cell
To rejoin you.

I love you
I love you with love
Unbounded
Unconquerable.

Leo Branton said that we could not know the depth of Angela Davis' love for George Jackson, we could only know how deeply she was able to express that feeling.

That concept was important to me. I might well have attributed to Angela Davis the same emotions I would have been feeling if I had written those words.

He then spoke to each of us jurors, calling us by name, "Mr. DeLange, Mr. Gaetoni, Mrs. Timothy, Mrs. Ryon . . . ." And he transferred the burden of responsibility that he and his colleagues had been carrying on their shoulders.

That was it. We, the jury, were dismissed to go home and return in the morning prepared to spend a few days in deliberations. We would be living in a motel. No communication with our families would be allowed except in emergencies, and even then only through a deputy. We should make arrangements to be driven to court; since the parking lot across the street was not kept under police surveillance at night, it wouldn't be a safe place to leave our cars.

Roz had told me that she and some of the others had been talking about whom they wanted to have act as foreman of the jury, and they had decided that they wanted me. She explained that since Angela Davis was black, a woman and a Communist, and we had no black jurors, and also no Communists (as far as any of us knew), she felt that it was crucially important that a woman be selected. Electing a woman was the closest we could come to electing a peer of Ms. Davis.

Also, since the trial was being covered so thoroughly by the press, the selection of a woman for the role would be given wide publicity. And it would open the doors for women to be chosen more frequently in the future. She said if I agreed to accept the office, Bob was prepared to make the nomination.

With completely false modesty, I said that if they were sure that I would be the best possible choice, I would of course be willing to serve—but how about someone else? How about herself? Or Ruth? Or . . . ? Well, if she and Bob were sure . . . and would help me . . . and if the others agreed . . . of course I would be honored to be chosen.

We then discussed what we would do if the group were to decide that I was not the one they wanted. We agreed to push very hard for one of the other women, and decided that Ruth would be our second choice. She was well-liked by everyone, had a good logical mind, was not easily flustered and would represent the women's point of view with insight.

June 2, 1972—my birthday—fifty-two years old. I woke up early, excited and eager, almost in a holiday mood, starting off on a new adventure. I was all set to go. My bag was by the door. It had been packed for three days. I was prepared. And I had enough confidence in the other jurors that I was sure we could work out any conflicts that might come up.

Birthdays have always been big events in our home. The rest of the family tries to honor any desire or whim of the celebrant. They made a fuss over me at breakfast, but today wasn't going to be a typical birthday. Art asked me when I thought I would be home; how long would it take to reach a verdict? I answered that I didn't know; I was ready to vote right now, but I wanted to hear what all the others thought. I had packed clothes for a couple of days. If we had to stay longer he would probably hear from me through a deputy. The deliberation might take weeks. Then again, I might be home for dinner.

Then I asked, "What do you suppose would happen if I showed up at the courthouse with no bags?"

"What do you mean?"

"Well, if I showed up with no bags, that would tell everyone that I was ready to vote, that I didn't want to spend a lot of time debating."

Even though the temptation to ask me how I was going to

vote must have been great, Art restrained himself. (He probably guessed; he knew me so well he could tell by my moods what I was thinking. He must have known by my laughing and teasing this morning that I couldn't be planning to send anyone to prison for life.)

"Mary, don't take a chance on how the other jurors might react to that. Don't do anything to foul it up. Play it straight. You have come this far, don't do anything foolish." He sounded really concerned, but I had just been fantasizing again.

The trip to San Jose was very similar to the one we took on the first day of the trial, March 27th, except that my son, John, did the driving and Ruth, Roz and I all had bags to bring. Other jurors were arriving at the courthouse and unloading their luggage when we drove up.

The scene looked like the front of a Hilton. There were no bellhops, so we started lugging our things up the walk. We stashed our bags along the walls of the assembly room and stood around drinking coffee. Ralph was one of the last to arrive. He strolled in with his hands in his pockets. He had no bag, not even a flight bag. When asked where he had left his bag, he looked surprised. "What bag? I didn't bring one. We aren't going to be here that long."

Ralph had done the very thing I had thought about! But Ralph was such a joker, no one was upset about it. (He'd really brought a suitcase and left it outside the door.)

I remember very little of the details of that morning. The jury assembly room was noisy and confusing. I remember that someone had brought cupcakes in honor of my birthday, and everyone stood around singing "Happy Birthday to You."

The courtroom was very quiet. Everyone was waiting, even the newspeople. Judge Arnason entered and went through the usual formalities. He smiled at the jurors and explained that he would now give us certain rules of law that applied to this particular case. He had a stack of papers before him and he started to read. We jurors settled back and listened carefully. We had sworn to accept his interpretation of the law as the only valid interpretation, so it was important that we pay attention.

Judge Arnason had reached the final day of a potentially explosive trial. I had watched him in court every day for three months. In that time I had never seen him lose his composure. He would look quickly at everyone, checking to make sure each of the necessary people was in the proper place. He would start the proceedings and then lean back in his swivel chair, cross his legs, fold his arms and listen. He seemed to let the procedures of the trial take over, without interjecting his own personality into them. Of what went on behind the scenes or when the jury was dismissed, I had no idea. But when the jury was in its box, Judge Richard Arnason was the perfect judge. Never emotional, never authoritarian, he sat quietly watching and listening. When called upon to make a decision he remained calm and unhurried, frequently taking the problem back to his chambers for reflection before announcing his decision.

I had brought my pad and pen into court again. I wanted some precise definitions of "reasonable doubt" and "conspiracy."

Judge Arnason read well, clearly and with ease. He tried to make the formal wording of the legal writing interesting and understandable to a group of twelve average citizens. But speaking strictly for myself, he was fighting a losing battle. I was able to pick up certain phrases that I thought were particularly relevant, and I scribbled them down on my notepad. But mostly I listened and tried to understand.

My attention was distracted for a moment early in the reading. Judge Arnason stated something to the effect that, from here on in his instructions, whenever he used the word "he" it was to be understood to mean "she" as well, whenever appropriate.

The language of the law is very masculine. I involuntarily raised my eyebrows and made a wry face. I glanced around the court. Everyone was looking intently at Judge Arnason, except Defense Attorney Doris Walker, who was looking at me and grinning. Apparently she had had the same reaction to the phrase as I.

Judge Arnason completed his reading of the instructions. As everyone sat silently, we, the jury, stood up and filed out of the courtroom.

The Deliberation

Foreman / Forewoman

We filed out of the courtroom through the center aisle. We walked past the faces of the press people, each one of them trying to read from our eyes what we were going to do; past the faces of the spectators—the impassive ones of the friends of the Attorney General (members of his staff, families), and the hopeful, pleading, excited ones of the friends of the defendant; past the alert, watchful faces of the court personnel and the sheriff's deputies. These people had all done their jobs in this trial. Now our turn was beginning.

As we entered the small alcove of the jury assembly room, I felt terribly isolated again. It was the same feeling I had on the opening day of the trial after Mr. Harris' introduction to his case, the case against Angela Y. Davis. I looked at the other jurors, these eleven people I had been spending my days with for the past three months. They were moving around the room, lighting cigarettes, getting coffee, lining up at the drinking fountain . . . strangers again.

Even the room had changed while we were in court. The disorder that made it "our" room was gone. All papers and magazines had been removed. Two tables had been placed end-to-end, making a single long table. Twelve chairs had been set neatly around this table—five on each side and one at each end.

No one wanted to sit down. No one knew how to get started. With all the others milling around the room, I wondered where I should sit, and how I should respond if Bob did nominate me for foreman. I went over to get a drink of water and when I straightened up from the fountain, the rest of the group had moved *en masse* to the table and were pulling out chairs and taking seats. I joined them and found that the only empty chair was at the head of the table. Each of the jurors had instinctively avoided that seat. I hesitated. I didn't want it to appear that I was assuming that I would be selected, or that I wanted the job, or that this election was fixed.

As I stood looking around the table, trying to avoid sitting in the only empty chair, Bob called out, "Mary, come sit here!" and he stood at the head of the table pulling out that chair for me to use. I sat down and he remained standing and started to speak. "I would ask the group's indulgence because I am the senior member, and would you allow me the honor of speaking first as we start our deliberations?"

No one objected—in fact, everyone seemed pleased that he took the initiative and got things moving. He spoke briefly, saying that he knew that we were all aware of the importance of the role that we, as jurors, were playing in this historic trial and that he felt it was time to add another footnote to history and select a woman to be foreman of this jury—and he would suggest that Mary Timothy be the one.

Roz agreed immediately—I could hear her voice, along with other murmurs of assent—and Jim, who was sitting immediately to my right, smiled and nodded agreement. I was relieved that he seemed to concur; I had thought he would be one of the persons more likely to be selected.

Then suddenly from the far left end of the table, Nick spoke up. "I feel that this should be done in a more democratic manner, and we should consider other candidates, and I want to nominate Jim for foreman."

Jim—the Annapolis graduate, ex-Navy pilot and officer, former commercial pilot who worked now as an airport controller—was the juror who during *voir dire* questioning had stated that he wasn't sure he could accept the testimony of a Communist with the same trust he could give a non-Communist. Leo Branton had asked the judge to dismiss Jim when he made that statement. The judge had disallowed it and Jim had remained on the jury.

I looked at Nick. Why had he nominated Jim? Was Nick personally antagonistic toward me? I couldn't recall any instance of real conflict. We had disagreed about the rights of athletes to negotiate with owners (he felt it might endanger sports financially). But that hadn't seemed important. I felt he was probably the most chauvinistic of all the males on the jury, but would my being a woman be enough reason for his nominating Jim? Possibly. But at this time and under these circumstances his most overriding consideration must be concern about the direction he thought the deliberations should take!

So that was where the center of opposition was going to be: quiet Nick—the man who didn't play poker with us, the man who read his sports page and joined conversations only when the subjects were general and superficial, the last to arrive in the mornings and the one who usually went home to lunch, the accountant whose hair was cut short and who coached Little League teams, the quiet man.

Winona walked over to the shelves and picked up an empty two-pound coffee can (this can was to be our ballot box throughout the deliberations) and Roz tore pages from a small notepad and we voted for jury foreman. I voted for myself. I thought that Jim would be a good foreman, but I was suddenly afraid that Nick knew something about him that I didn't; also I had promised Roz that I would do what was possible to insure that a woman be selected. (Besides, by then I had convinced myself that I was the best person for the job! A jury foreman should have confidence!)

The count showed eight votes for me and four for Jim. No one seemed upset at the way it went. I leaned over to Jim and asked him to stay beside me, at my right hand both literally and figuratively, to help me through any spots I couldn't handle. He smiled in agreement. I thanked the group and stated that if at any time they weren't satisfied with the way I was working, another vote could be taken and I could be replaced.

Ruth then suggested that I read to the group the outline I had made based on the chapter in Godfrey Lehman's book, *What You Need to Know for Jury Duty*.

I explained that I had read Mr. Lehman's book through the chapters that related to deliberations. I had been impressed with the care and thought he had put into it and the logic of many of his ideas. The most important concept I remembered from the book was that it was desirable to delay taking a vote until the various aspects of the case had been fully discussed. Even though we might be eager to reach a verdict, if a vote were taken too early, a juror who was undecided might be forced into a position which she or he would then have to defend. This situation could limit the free discussion and open exchange of ideas. It would tend to cause people to argue rather than discuss; it could polarize people and possibly result in a hung jury. And a hung jury was the last thing we wanted.

I read through the outline of suggested procedures and then passed the sheet of paper around the table:

A. Get organized; elect
 1. a foreperson to run the meetings
 2. a secretary to keep notes
 3. a tally counter to count and record voting

B. Prepare a list of topics for discussion
 1. Each juror should suggest topics on which discussion/clarification is wanted
 2. Secretary should write down each topic on a separate sheet
 3. Foreperson and secretary should arrange topics in a logical order
 4. Any juror can add subjects at any time

C. Discuss each item
1. Single subject at a time
2. Follow *Robert's Rules of Order*
3. Vote each item and record vote
4. Hand ballot for small items, but secret vote on all major issues
D. Open for overlooked topics
E. Review all voting
F. Question if anyone wishes to reopen discussion of any topic
G. Debate on verdict, encompassing all issues, close debate by vote
H. Secret ballot on each count
I. Everyone satisfied? ? ? –if not, review again.

We had already elected the foreperson; the next step was to pick a secretary. I asked Stef to be the official secretary acting for the group, if no one objected. She was one of the best organized young women I had ever met; she was efficient and clear-thinking. Twenty-two years old, she worked in the credit collection department at Sears and was a very independent person with positive opinions. I liked her because she was aggressive and had a good sense of humor.

Since she was a strong personality, and since I had no idea what her responses to the issues might be, I didn't want to isolate her. I wanted to be sure that she felt she was part of the group and so would feel free to discuss anything that might be bothering her.

Winona, saying that cigarette smoke bothered her, asked if all the smokers could please sit at one end of the table and the nonsmokers at the other. She and Bob exchanged seats, placing her at my left hand, sitting next to Roz. I asked those two women if they would work together to handle the voting–be our tally counters? They agreed. We went on then to discuss some points that were not clear in the outline.

The longest discussion was about the section concerning a

"point of order." For example, if the jury was discussing an issue (such as *motive*) and one of the group started talking about a subject (such as *flight*) that was not relevant, then the speaker could be ruled out of order by the foreman; or, if that ruling was protested, a second must be called for and a vote taken without discussion. We decided that no discussion should be cut off if three or more people wished to continue it. Anything bothering that many people should be resolved, even if it were technically out of order.

This change seemed reasonable, so we decided that following this outline would be a good way to proceed, but that we would feel free to change or adapt it to our particular needs.

All this discussion about methods of deliberating took a long time, but it served to get us started. We had all joined in the talk, and now felt secure in the way we would deliberate.

The next step was to write out questions about the issues that we wished to have discussed. OK. Well, how specific should the issues be? Well . . . they could be very specific if that was what the juror wanted, or they could be broad and general.

So we sat with sheets of paper in front of us, like a school composition class. Some started to write; others just sat there looking down at their papers. Those writing finished quickly and dropped their pages into our coffee can and sat back waiting. The others started to feel pressured. They really should have some questions to ask. They didn't want the others to think that they weren't cooperating, or that they were too dumb to have a question.

Just as the atmosphere was starting to get a little heavy and uncomfortable, a knock sounded at the door followed by a call, "Stop deliberating!" I was startled. What was happening? A key rattled in the lock and Captain Johnson stepped in to inform us that we were going to be taken to the motel now and assigned our rooms and allowed to get settled before lunch. No one would be allowed in this room while we were gone, so we could leave our notes on the table for now.

The Court seemed to be assuming we were not going to come to a quick decision.

We had been deliberating for an hour and had selected a foreman, gotten ourselves organized and started our procedures—but we had not yet mentioned the trial.

So we stood up, bustled around, gathered up our coats and purses, found our bags and lined up at the stairwell door again. Down we went, lugging our paraphernalia out the door and into the hot sunlight. Waiting for us just outside the wire security fence was a bus. This bus was something else! Dark green with wire mesh over the windows and SHERIFF DEPARTMENT in bold letters on the side, it was to be our transportation to and from the motel morning, noon and evening. It was old and rickety-noisy. It looked like the obsolete school busses that are repainted and used by farm-labor contractors to carry the workers to the fields in the San Joaquin Valley. It was in fact normally used to transport groups of prisoners around. The prisoners could be shackled to bars which ran along the inner walls under the windows, and a screen had been installed behind the driver for his protection. He also had a two-way radio communication as a part of the bus facilities, as well as his own ever-present walkie-talkie.

Our bags were loaded on the bus and we took our seats, joking about giving secret signals to the press people as we went past them. The bus started up, swaying and jerking, rattling and clanking, the radio sputtering and twelve jurors holding on to the sides, straining to see what was going on, laughing and acting as though we were going on a picnic. We were accompanied by a sheriff's matron and two deputies, one of whom was driving. The bus swung around the back of the Superior Court Building, turned behind the Municipal Court Building, and was suddenly out on Heading Street going toward First Street. We passed the front courtyard and saw a group of Angela Davis supporters around the central benches. No one looked up to watch as the bus went past.

The motel was about a half mile away from the court and was one of the large, new, plastic motels with swimming pool, bars, dining halls, lunchrooms and magazine stands. We waited

inside the bus in the parking lot until Captain Johnson and the
alternate jurors arrived. They had separated from us when we
left the courtroom to start deliberations and were isolated in a
small room, waiting for us to come to a decision. We smiled and
waved at them but did not speak. They were taken up to the
second-floor balcony of the motel and assigned rooms. We watched
from below as they were locked into their rooms before we jurors
started up the stairs. A deputy had a large wooden board with
the room numbers blocked in and nails with the room keys
hooked to them. In his other hand he had a sheet of paper with
our names and room assignments. We stood waiting at the corner
of the balcony and he escorted us one by one to our rooms, explaining that the television sets had been disconnected, and that
no phone calls would be allowed. We were to remain in our rooms
at all times unless we were under direct supervision of a member
of the sheriff's department. We each had a room to ourselves—
large, with a queen-sized bed, and large bathroom and attached
dressing room and closet. It was very comfortable even though
the decor was designed to appeal to traveling salesmen.

The second (top) floor of the south wing was reserved for the
jurors. The rooms at each end were used by the sheriff's deputies;
a large meeting room at one end was where we gathered each
morning for coffee and in the evening for conversation and cards;
and separate rooms were reserved for each of the twelve jurors
and three alternates. Each room opened onto a balcony which
extended the length of the building. There were outside stairs
at each end.

As soon as everyone was settled a deputy came down the balcony walk, knocked at each door and announced that we would
meet for lunch in five minutes. We were instructed to step outside our room, lock the door and hand the key to the deputy
as he came by. We did.

We were then escorted in a group down the stairs, into the
center of the motel, past the swimming pool. The question immediately arose, would we be allowed to use the pool? San Jose
was hot in June. We were told to take it up with Captain

Johnson. This became the answer to all our questions: "Talk to Captain Johnson."

We never followed through on this question and never had our swim.

Winona, the retired librarian, was a good person to start the discussions. She had kept voluminous notes and took her responsibility as a juror very seriously. She played the role and seemed to think Ralph and I and the others down at our end of the jury box were almost a disgrace because of the occasional jokes and hearty laughter.

She asked if anyone knew the times on the San Quentin gate registrations sheets. No one was absolutely sure of the times she was asking for, so we decided to call for the registration sheets and look them over.

As Stef started to write the note, Ruth suggested that we wait until we had been around the table at least once and so could send down at the same time for everything we needed.

The rest of the jurors' questions dealt largely with details of the evidence—times and places and names.

When it was Jim's turn he indicated that he felt very strongly that we should consider the charge of Kidnapping first—then Murder and then the charge of Conspiracy. He felt that this approach would be the easiest to use. He seemed certain that by using that approach he would be able to explain his thinking and show the others the logic of it.

I was afraid of starting with the Kidnap-Murder charges. All the testimony about the guns and the bullets, and all the testimony of the police witnesses and the hostages would have to be considered—as well as the evidence of Angela Davis' involvement. I didn't want to get caught up in that because it really didn't have anything to do with whether or not she was implicated.

I tried to stall Jim, but he repeated that he thought it would be a good approach. As he and I discussed the best method for doing it, he suggested that perhaps we could get a copy of the indictment sent up and work through it in our deliberations. The rest of the jurors agreed that they would like to have the indictment to read. So I agreed too. I didn't want to be too argumentative as the foreman of the jury. I wanted to get myself accepted in the role before I got into any hassles.

We had already decided to ask for the San Quentin gate registration sheets for Winona. I asked if anyone wanted to take a look at anything else.

Stef said that she would like to see the love letters—she said that she had a hard time interpreting something that someone had read to her—she wanted to read them herself.

I suggested that we take a look at the "hate mail" that Ms. Davis had received at the university—the samples of the seven volumes of mail the secretary of the school had brought into court. I thought it might be important to all of us actually to see just how deeply some people hated Angela Davis and to see the crudeness with which this hate was expressed. It had been hard for me to grasp that those were actual letters that Mr. Branton had read to us. That people would send such vileness through the mails was incomprehensible to me. (I also thought the "hate mail" would contrast and counterbalance the love letters.)

Stef was in charge of composing the note to the Court, requesting these exhibits. She wrote it all out and reached the point of my signature. She looked up and called out, "Hey, Mary! You don't want to sign this as 'Fore*man*,' do you?"

We all broke into laughter and I said, "Good Lord, *no*! Make it fore . . . woman . . . no . . . make it *foreperson*!"

So the first message went down signed, "Mary M. Timothy, Foreperson."

While we were waiting for our request to be answered the conversation became more general. We all wanted to talk. We were the only people in the world who hadn't been able to discuss the case or even mention it casually. Now we finally were given a chance to start saying some of the things that we had kept bottled up for all these weeks. We were suddenly finding that the others on the jury had reacted to much of the testimony in the same way. We talked very little about the kidnapping and murder—about the events at Marin County Civic Center and the escape attempt and shoot-out—except to touch on some of the highlights, the characters that we would never forget: T. V. Hughes; Mathews, who did the rifle firing; the officer with the gun with a two-inch barrel; the first witness, Mrs. Graham.

No one defended the validity of Mrs. Graham's statements. Most seemed to feel that her testimony was completely invalid because she changed her story so much from the original version. Another point, which was something that I hadn't thought important enough to mention in my evening taping sessions, was that Mrs. Graham was suing the County of Marin and the State of California for many thousands of dollars as a result of her having been injured during the escape attempt. There was resentment among the jurors about this and a strong feeling that since she was suing, she was a very subjective witness and her own financial interests might influence her testimony.

I didn't agree. I felt that she was a very unreliable witness but that confusion rather than cupidity had caused her to change her story.

We talked about the love letters and whether they demonstrated a motive for the crimes. We discussed whether the original three letters—those written *before* August 7th—were strong enough to prove a motive of sexual passion, and whether the excerpts from the eighteen-page letter/diary (that Mr. Harris had struggled through as his closing bit of evidence—and that Leo Branton had read so beautifully as a love poem in his closing argument) could express emotions which applied to actions of a year earlier.

I stated my opinion that a motive of consuming physical passion which would lead to so irrational an act would be highly unlikely for a woman of intellect and restraint. However, some of the others (all women) felt that this motive was very reasonable—that any woman could be suspect of acting in such a manner, an intellectual no less than any other woman. The expressed reactions were, "Sure, she could have done such a thing for love! Almost anyone could. But did the letters show that much passion?"

I decided that I was not as romantic as they.

Flight as an indication of knowledge of guilt was touched upon. Not one of the jurors expressed a feeling that the flight of Angela Davis to New York was of importance. Actually, everyone agreed that it was a reasonable thing to do and, given the same set of circumstances, each would probably have done the same thing.

We spent a little time talking about the San Francisco airport and the possibility that the phone number in the wallet of Jonathan Jackson could have been for the pay phone in the American Airlines terminal—but we had all flown from that airport and were all aware of the fact that the airport buildings at San Francisco were spread out, and the two terminals were a block or so apart. It was unrealistic to assume that she would wait around for a phone call at one terminal, then rush to the other terminal to catch a flight to Los Angeles. Someone mentioned that commuter flights left hourly from both terminals. She was hurrying, but we agreed that rushing to catch a plane is a fairly normal thing to do, particularly when taking a commuter flight, since no reservation is necessary.

The phone number that was found in Jonathan Jackson's wallet, and the possibility that it could have been a Los Angeles number as well as that of the pay phone at the American Airlines terminal, was talked about. A little confusion arose as to what the telephone company representative meant when he was explaining just why the phone was not listed in the book. We finally agreed that a phone installed for a couple of months in the summer would not be listed in the books which come out in late fall.

We talked about eyewitness identification, and we discussed the points made by Dr. Buckout. We had each been aware of some of the difficulties involved in judging the accuracy of eyewitness identification. Dr. Buckout hadn't brought out so much that was new. But he did remind us of things we might have forgotten, and he put into words our vague feelings. We didn't have to discuss what he said, but we did need to apply it to the issues under consideration.

In reviewing the reliability of the eyewitnesses, we naturally came to the conflicting testimony of the defense witnesses and prosecution witnesses. There was great hesitancy to accept the testimony of the defense. They were all friends of Angela Davis. Wouldn't they lie for her? That possibility seemed reasonable to many of the jurors since no evidence, either physical or from other witnesses (strangers or acquaintances), corroborated the testimony of her friends. The stories sounded natural and direct . . . at least some of them did . . . but, yes, some of them were very difficult to accept. I wondered that no one who knew her —and thus could really identify her—had testified against her. Was it possible that *all* her friends and acquaintances would lie for her?

I felt that the most important defense witness was the attorney, Marvin Stender. He provided an alibi for the morning that Angela Davis was supposed to be riding around in the van with Jonathan Jackson. I had listened to his testimony very carefully. He had answered the questions put to him with such careful phrasing, he might have seemed evasive to someone unaware of this mannerism common to attorneys.

When we were discussing the reliability of his testimony, I brought out that I felt that attorneys' statements could probably be taken at face value, since lying on the witness stand meant that they could be charged with perjury, as would any other witness, but they could also be disbarred and would be subject to much more severe disciplinary action because they were "officers of the court."

I mentioned that I was familiar with the manner in which attorneys answered questions and the care they used to keep from committing themselves on anything that wasn't absolutely necessary, and that this careful answering might give the impression of deceit.

Before I finished my sentence, other jurors were interrupting and saying that they wouldn't believe the testimony of any of them, that lawyers would make any kind of statement if there was no way of checking on them. No one used the term "shyster," but that was what was in their minds!

Frankly, this response was quite a shock to me, and made me realize the intensity and strength of our preconceived ideas about professions, occupations or lifestyles.

During *voir dire* examination of prospective jurors the defense attorneys were able, by very carefully formulated series of questions, to elicit meaningful reactions from all of us, which showed a wide gamut of prejudices and attitudes. We were queried on the primary points of racial prejudice and attitudes towards Communists and militant black persons—the obvious areas to cover in a trial of a "black militant Communist," as Ms. Davis was usually described in the press.

The more subtle points of a prospective juror's fears were also probed, but the *voir dire* was still not complete. No screening had been made for our reactions to witnesses against whom we were not expected to have any deep-seated negative feelings—like lawyers.

Four attorneys had appeared as witnesses. Three of them were prosecution witnesses: The Assistant District Attorney of Marin County, who was one of the hostages and was wounded in the shoot-out; a former FBI investigator; and a San Jose civil rights attorney. The defense presented one attorney, Marvin Stender, who stated that Ms. Davis was with him during the period of time the prosecution had placed her in Marin County in the escape van, the day before the escape attempt.

During deliberations, the evidence presented by the Assistant D.A. and the former FBI investigator was not discussed in any depth. Neither had any real bearing on the primary issue of conspiracy.

When the testimony of the other two attorneys was discussed, I found that while I might accept their statements readily because of my associations with attorneys (especially my husband), the others were guilty of stereotyping lawyers as artful, mendacious, deceitful and untrustworthy.

This attitude was frightening. If the other jurors did not believe attorney Marvin Stender, a real conflict might arise when we got down to seriously discussing Angela Davis' alibi.

Again a knock came at the door and a call, "Stop deliberating!" and the rattle of the key in the lock.The items we had requested were handed to me. Wait a minute—not everything; the love letters were there, the "hate-mail" and the gate registration sheets—but not the indictment. Instead a note from Judge Arnason explained:

> June 2, 1972
> 2:00 p.m.

> Members of the Jury:
> In response to your inquiry, the indictment was not introduced in evidence and, therefore, I cannot sent it in to the jury room.
> However, if you wish to have it read to you, I can have you brought into the courtroom for that purpose.

> Richard E. Arnason
> Judge

We agreed that it wasn't important enough to go down to court to have it read to us. That decision was fine with me. Now I would have time to get some support for my plan to begin deliberations with the charge of "conspiracy" without having to challenge Jim directly.

We used the material we had received to get our notes straightened out as to times and dates. I looked at the San Quentin visitor's registration sheets and wondered about them. Was "Diane Robinson" really Angela Davis? Looking at the pages of names didn't help. No faces jumped out at me.

The discussion returned to the conflict between the prosecution's eyewitnesses and the defense's witnesses who were personal friends of the defendant. Which would be the most likely —that the men at the filling station (two of whom were positive,

one hesitant and the other made no identification) would be
mistaken, or that a personal acquaintance of Ms. Davis would
be lying?

The tempo of the talk picked up. People were starting to express themselves more freely. I tried to listen to *who* was saying
what—to determine the direction the discussion was taking.

Ralph, the maintenance electrician who worked at Memorex,
who looked like a "hard hat," like a telephone lineman, and
who wore a bright red metallic helmet and a yellow windbreaker
when riding his motorcycle; who was interested in health foods,
the environment, local and national politics; who had always
been exuberant, full of nervous energy, loud, cracking jokes,
very liberal, very humanistic, was now sitting quietly, speaking
carefully, rationally and very seriously. I was surprised at his
patience and control. More and more, the others were turning
to him and asking his opinion of the issues they were discussing.

Roz was very intense, phrasing her statements very carefully,
but making very definite ones. She recognized and acknowledged
inconsistencies and was not easily "conned." She had been the
head of the household with the responsibility of caring for three
children since her divorce. She was politically liberal and very
much into the women's liberation movement, and was a very
independent person and willing to fight for her ideas. She seemed
to have thought through most of the issues and to have reached
her decisions. I concluded that she was showing there was grave
doubt in her mind as to the guilt of Angela Davis.

Ruth seemed to be discussing something almost removed from
her life, as though none of this was touching her. It was like
an abstract problem or a book she had read. Ruth had read all
the recent political and social books as well as the best-sellers.
She was restless and liked to play games and keep things stirred
up. She seemed to be enjoying the give-and-take of ideas and
concepts and observations.

Nick—I listened very carefully every time he said anything. I
still had no idea what he was thinking. His statements were
fairly ambiguous. He said such things as, "Well, that's possible,

maybe she was at San Quentin . . . ." Then as he finished his statement, he would drop in, "But that doesn't prove anything." He did this on two or three occasions. Each time I tried to figure out just what he was saying. Was he really saying, "Yes, I believe that it was Angela Davis at San Quentin! . . . Yes, I believe it was Angela Davis at Fleming's Mobil Station! . . . Yes, I believe it was Angela Davis in the van with Jonathan Jackson!"? And then only to keep from antagonizing anyone, he would add, "Of course that doesn't mean anything." Maybe it did mean something!

Or was he really saying, "Sure, she might have been there, but that certainly doesn't prove that she is guilty—it could very well be a perfectly innocent act!"? Maybe that was what he was really saying! I was still uneasy about Nick.

Luis sat quietly at the opposite end of the table. He still read and wrote and thought in his native language. He left Mexico when he was eighteen years old. He very carefully wrote down every word he heard in court that he didn't understand, to look up later. He was kind and gentle and very soft-spoken, but with great inner strength. He and Bob had become good friends.

Luis had said very little. He listened and he watched. He seemed to be interested in what everyone was saying and to consider each statement thoughtfully. I tried to watch for any indication that he might wish to speak but was too polite to break into the rapid-fire conversations that were going on. He gave no sign that I could see.

Around the table on the right side were Stef, Anne and Michelle. Stef agreed readily with Roz when Roz made the statement that she thought the whole attempted escape which resulted in the kidnap was something a seventeen-year-old kid would do. Stef had a younger brother whom she loved very much. He had come to the trial one day and she had pointed "her kid brother" out to us with lots of pride.

We discussed the relationship of the escape attempt of James McClain, William Christmas and Ruchell Magee to the Soledad Brothers (George Jackson, Fleeta Drumgo and John Cluchette).

The involvement seemed to be more than superficial, since Jonathan Jackson was the young brother of George and had visited him at San Quentin frequently. Since he had no way of communicating with James McClain directly, he probably had used George to contact him.

We speculated about the testimony relating to the demand for the freedom of the Soledad Brothers as a part and purpose of the escape plan. No absolute statements were made, but many tentative "feeling out" comments were made, such as, "Well, T. V. Hughes said that it was 'Free our brothers in Folsom!'" and "One of the witnesses said, 'Free all the political prisoners at San Quentin,'" and "Gary Thomas didn't remember hearing any such demand and he was right there."

Both Anne and Michelle seemed to me to be able to accept the eyewitness testimony and to wonder why the others hesitated. They turned to Jim for answers—or to Ruth—and more and more to Ralph.

Anne was a small quiet woman. Her father had died suddenly early in the trial which might have contributed to her reserve. She didn't join in the games or group discussions, but was always pleasant and friendly. She related well to Jim. I didn't feel that I knew her very well.

Michelle sat beside me throughout the trial. She didn't take notes, but listened and remembered everything that went on in the court. She had been very interested in examining the exhibits —she had looked at every gun and opened every box of shells. She had only recently moved away from home, and still seemed very young to me.

Even Anne and Michelle disbelieved the testimony of the ex-convict who had gotten his parole shortly after he swore that he had seen Angela Davis in the van with Jonathan Jackson. His details were too confused, and it looked like his testimony had been "bought."

We talked about the men at the service station, the father Fleming and his friend and fellow fireman who were both positive in their identification; the son Fleming who took the young black man and woman in the station's pickup over to the Civic Center parking lot, talked to them, helped them get the van started, and then on his original report could not identify the woman—even after being shown the set of stacked pictures of Angela Davis for his identification.

I said that I felt if he had spent that much time with Angela Davis he would have recognized her face in the pictures; but Stef said that the woman was supposed to have been wearing a mini-skirt, and his eyes probably never got up to her face.

Bob, who had a slight hearing difficulty, moved back to the head of the table and sat between Winona and me, but back a little from the corner of the table so his smoking wouldn't bother her. He said he wanted to get close so that he wouldn't miss anything that was said, but I think he wanted to be close to give me support and advice. It was good having him there. He had a rather dignified manner of speaking, precise and with a slight Scandinavian accent which added weight to his statements. Bob had been the object of prejudice when during World War II he had befriended Japanese people and stated publicly that they were being treated unconstitutionally when they were being sent to concentration camps. This led co-workers to tell him to "go home where you come from, if you don't like it here!"

Stef and Ruth hadn't brought their notes to the deliberating room. They weren't sure that we would be allowed to have them with us. Ralph said that he had thrown his away. Winona and I had ours, and I think Jim and Roz had brought theirs also. I asked that everyone who had notes back in the motel please bring them in the morning. It took so long to get a response from the Court it seemed a waste of time. If we could settle things ourselves it would be a lot easier.

Jim was at my right elbow, leaning forward in his chair, watching the faces of everyone, always smiling and alert. He understood immediately what a person was groping for, as he or she tried to formulate ideas. Jim would let someone else answer if he or she wanted to, but if the answer wasn't complete, or covered too much territory, he would bring the talk back to the point and make a beautifully clear statement.

The afternoon was almost over. We were getting tired. We weren't deliberating, we were talking about the case. Twelve good friends had been through three months of identical experiences and hadn't been able to share these experiences with anyone. We'd had no communication, no give-and-take, no questions and answers, no shared laughter and tears. And now we were afraid to open up on any but the most superficial points. Afraid to take important stands and chance antagonizing someone. We were tentatively searching among the rest of the group for confirmation of our own ideas and for kindred responses . . . and we were finding them. Yet even as we made these overtures, we pulled quickly back.

We broke up that afternoon for the day, almost with a sense of relief. No conflicts had arisen. No voices had been raised. Each person had been listened to with courtesy and attention. I thought we had made a good beginning. We had worked together.

Art Vanick, the clerk of the court, took charge of the exhibits we had asked for. He would return them to us in the morning. Nothing was to be left in the room overnight. We must be careful about giving any clues as to the way the deliberations were going. I smiled to myself—I wished someone would give me some clues!

We piled into the bus again for the trip back to the motel. This time, as we swung past the front of the courthouse, we saw that the supporters of Angela Davis had gathered with signs in the courtyard. There seemed to be about thirty to fifty people —not a large crowd. One long banner read VIGIL. Ralph intentionally misread it and said, "Virgil? Who is Virgil?"

That became a standing gag each time we passed the courtyard. "Who is Virgil?" "Is he a political prisoner?" "Isn't he free yet?" "FREE VIRGIL!"

We had time in our rooms to rest a little and clean up before dinner. Lord, I wished I had a drink! But we had been informed that no alcohol would be served to us, not even wine with our meals.

I stretched out across the bed. I was tired.

Undecided

Dinner was pleasant. The conversation was desultory. Winona had a headache—from the cigarette smoke, she said. I wasn't hungry, though the food was excellent. We all felt better after dinner and were in reasonably good spirits as we were escorted back up to our second-story complex of rooms. Some congregated in the meeting room for coffee and conversation. It was still early in the evening and still hot. We knew it would be a long night if we went to our rooms right away, but we could do nothing in our lounge except talk and we were pretty well talked out. Before long, a deck of cards appeared and we started playing poker again.

Jim joined us for a little while. Strangely, this young man who had spent years in the Navy had never learned to play cards. Nick stood around and kibitzed for a while and then went off to his room. Bob and Luis talked for a while, then Bob went out on the balcony to stroll back and forth. Ralph, Ruth, Stef and I were the nucleus of the card game that night. Michelle played for a while and then wandered off to her room. Winona left early because of her headache.

We were all ready to quit when, a few minutes before ten o'clock, Captain Johnson came by—no longer in uniform and looking relaxed and more human in a tee shirt and deck shoes —to "tuck us in for the night."

I thought I would have trouble going to sleep, but I was able to read for only a few minutes before I started nodding off.

I slept well for about three hours, then I started hearing the footsteps of the deputies as they patrolled the balcony walk. I lay awake waiting for them to come past and trying to guess the time by their patrols. At about 3:30 I gave up trying to block the deliberations from my mind. I turned on the light, fluffed the pillows behind me, got my pad and pen and my stack of file cards and went to work.

First I wrote out the notes I had made from the instructions given by Judge Arnason—notes that I felt pertained to this case:

> Motive is not an element of the crime of conspiracy and
> need not be shown.
> Flight is not in itself a sign of guilt, but can be con-
> sidered in light of other evidence.
> Reasonable doubt is no abiding conviction of moral
> certainty.
> Conspiracy is a union of two or more, of thought and
> act . . . with certain specific intent to commit a
> crime.
> Indirect evidence proves a fact that leads to an inference
> consistent with the theory for which it is presented.
> It cannot be reconciled with any other theory—if
> so, it must be weighed toward the theory of innocence.
> It must be proved that there was an illegal plan or agree-
> ment—mere association is not enough.
> Any statement made by one of the conspirators (oral or
> written expression) is not relevant unless it is part of
> the knowledge of the other conspirators. So, unless
> it is an *agreed* part of the conspiracy, it is not part
> of the conspiracy.

I read these notes over and over as I thought about the evidence again. Other definitions of reasonable doubt had been given us—"doubt that a reasonable person might have,"

" . . . not merely a personal doubt, but one for which a reason can be given"—but this definition I could relate to and accept: *"No abiding conviction of moral certainty."*

I absolutely did not have an abiding conviction of moral certainty; I wasn't certain at all—no way!

I felt that the instructions that "any statement made by one of the conspirators is not relevant unless it is part of the knowledge of the other conspirators" meant that even if a demand had been made for the release of the Soledad Brothers, unless it had been shown beyond a reasonable doubt that this statement was agreed upon, then it was not to be considered part of the conspiracy.

Certainly the prosecution had shown a close association between Angela Davis and Jonathan Jackson, but the instructions stated that "mere association is not enough," and that the existence of an illegal plan or agreement must be proven beyond all reasonable doubt.

To make sure that I was not overlooking anything, I went through my card files and listed in chronological order the evidence against Angela Y. Davis.

If everything in the prosecution's testimony was true, then (AYD stands for Angela Y. Davis, and JJ stands for Jonathan Jackson):

1. AYD bought a handgun at the Brass Rail Gun Shop in January, 1968.
2. AYD bought the "beast" carbine at Western Surplus in April, 1969.
3. AYD was working for the release of the Soledad Brothers and had attended two hearings in Salinas in May-June, 1970.
4. AYD wrote three letters to George Jackson professing love in June (2nd, 10th and 22nd).
5. AYD was in close contact with Jonathan Jackson in late July and attended a hearing with him and his father in San Francisco on July 16th.

6. AYD exchanged a defective rifle for a carbine July 25th.

7. JJ was at San Quentin and returned to San Jose with Mabel Magers and Mrs. Hammer on July 17th.

8. JJ and AYD were at the Mexican border about midnight, July 30th.

9. JJ was in AYD's car which he had "hot-wired" at midnight on July 31st.

10. JJ was at the Soledad House on afternoon of August 2nd.

11. AYD flew from Los Angeles to San Francisco at 8:30 p.m., August 3rd.

12. JJ was at San Quentin 12:30 to 2:20 on August 3rd.

13. JJ was in Hammer kitchen in late morning August 4th.

14. JJ and Diane Robinson (AYD?) were at San Quentin 2:15-3:10 p.m., August 4th.

15. AYD cashed a check in Oakland on August 4th.

16. JJ and Diane Robinson (AYD?) were at San Quentin 11:50-2:15 p.m., August 5th.

17. JJ borrowed VW from Mabel Magers on morning of August 5th.

18. AYD and JJ bought shotgun at 5:00 p.m., August 5th.

19. JJ rented Hertz van in San Francisco at 8:30 a.m., August 6th.

20. JJ and AYD made phone call at Mobil station at 10:34 a.m., August 6th.

21. JJ was in courtroom in morning of August 6th.

22. JJ and AYD were in San Quentin parking lot in van August 6th.

23. JJ was in Marin court in afternoon of August 6th.

24. JJ rented a room at Holland Motel (for two) evening of August 6th.

25. JJ was involved in escape attempt at 10:45 a.m., August 7th.

26. AYD took plane to LA from SF at 2:20 p.m., August 7th.

27. The VW had been in the garage from 8:30 a.m., August 7th.

As I sat and looked at the list, I was suddenly struck by the fact that most of it was evidence of what Jonathan Jackson had been doing! The implication had been that Jonathan Jackson and Angela Davis were one and the same person.

Fantastic! I became really excited! I looked at my watch. It was after five o'clock and it was light outside. If I hurried, I could work this out before it was time to go to breakfast. I started on a new list; this time it contained only the testimony that related to Angela Davis herself:

1. January, 1968   Bought a handgun
2. April, 1969   Bought a "beast" carbine
3. May, 1970   Attended two hearings in Salinas
                    for Soledad Brothers
4. June 2, 10, 22   Wrote letters to George Jackson,
                    professing (among other things)
                    her love
5. July 15   Was in Berkeley motel with Jonathan
                    and his father and attended a hear-
                    ing regarding her request to act as
                    an investigator for George Jackson
6. July 25   Exchanged defective rifle for carbine
7. July 30   Was at Mexican border with Jonathan
                    at midnight
8. July 31   Went to LA police station to pick
                    up her car that Jonathan had
                    "hot-wired"
9. August 3   Flew to SF, leaving LA at 8:30 p.m.
10. August 4   Cashed check in Oakland
11. August 4   Was in waiting room at San Quentin
                    2:15-3:10 p.m.
12. August 5   Was in waiting room at San Quentin
                    1:30-2:15 p.m.
13. August 5   Bought shotgun in SF at 5:00 p.m.
14. August 6   Was at Mobil station in van at 10:34 p.m.
15. August 6   Was in San Quentin parking lot in van

16. August 7   Took plane to LA at 2:20 from SF
                      airport

This list, then, was the evidence against Angela Davis. When looked at separately from the activities of Jonathan Jackson, the list was not so overwhelming. I started to think about each item, viewing her as innocent and looking for proof of guilt.

Items 1 and 2 were the purchases of guns years before the escape attempt. True, the guns had been used in the attempt, but no evidence had been presented to show how they had arrived at that point—throw them out!

3. The fact that she had attended two hearings in Salinas for the Soledad Brothers was admitted by the defense. Surely this act was normal for a person involved in their legal defense. She had never before seen any of the Soledad Brothers; for the first time, she saw George Jackson. Surely her attendance could not be construed as evidence of part of the plot—throw it out!

4. The three letters written by Angela Davis to George Jackson in which she professed her love for him and for all her people, and in which she spoke of devoting her efforts to freeing him (but she spoke of papers to write and speeches to make), surely could not be construed as evidence of an all-consuming passion —throw it out!

5. She was in Berkeley with Jonathan and Lester Jackson, the father of the Jackson family, simply because they were going to attend a hearing the next day at which George Jackson's attorney was to make a request that she be allowed to act as an investigator for the case. This event certainly seemed to me to be within the normal activities of a person involved in the legal defense of the Soledad Brothers, and certainly not a part of a criminal conspiracy—throw it out!

6. This item was another in the series of gun and ammunition purchases. Since her purchases began in 1968 there could be no possible way of determining that this particular purchase was part of a conspiracy—out!

7. She and Jonathan were stopped at the border when they

were returning from Mexico. All that this evidence showed was that they were together on a trip. I have lived in southern California, and going over the border into Tijuana isn't all that big a trip. People go there for dinner, or to the bullfights, or to buy items not available in the States. It could have been a perfectly innocent trip—throw it out!

8. Jonathan Jackson had "hot-wired" her car; a person "hot-wires" a car either because he has lost the keys or because he is taking the car without the owner's permission. Since he might have taken the car without her permission, it was not evidence of her involvement—out!

9. On August 3rd, Angela Davis flew to San Francisco on the 8:30 p.m. flight from Los Angeles. Surely flying to San Francisco from Los Angeles does not show any criminal involvement—out.

10. On August 4, Angela Davis cashed a check in Oakland, just across the bay from San Francisco. This item of information had no bearing on any other bit of information presented. I could see no relevance to anything else. So she cashed a check. I have no idea why this event was mentioned at all. Out.

Items 11 and 12 are the reports that Angela Davis accompanied Jonathan Jackson to San Quentin on August 4th and 5th and stayed in the waiting room while Jonathan visited his brother. The name signed on the visitor's registration sheet was Diane Robinson, and it was written by Jonathan Jackson. The identification of the young woman was made by San Quentin officers only after Angela Davis had been implicated through ownership of the guns and her picture had been published on the front pages of the papers. Very big questions remained in my mind as to the authenticity of their identifications. But then I thought, so what if Angela Davis *were* in the waiting room at San Quentin on those two afternoons? Could it have been the act of a person who was working through legal channels for the release of the Soledad Brothers? Did it have to mean that she was a party to a criminal conspiracy?—leave these items in for more debate.

13. Angela Davis, probably accompanied by Jonathan Jackson,

purchased a .12-gauge single-shot shotgun at about five o'clock on August 5th. She paid for it and signed the gun registration sheet, and identified herself to the salesman. She talked to the salesman and gave him her autograph. She had asked for an inexpensive shotgun. She didn't ask for a single-shot, .12-gauge gun. This gun could have been bought by her for the protection of the newly opened Soledad House. Because it was used for another purpose does not prove that it was purchased for that purpose. The purchase could have been the act of an innocent person. Which version was more reasonable? Well, if I had wanted to buy a single-shot gun, I would have asked for that specific type of gun. No evidence had been presented that Angela Davis had any experience with shotguns, or knowledge of sizes or styles —leave this item in for further debate.

14. The Mobil station episode was probably the most involved part of all the evidence. Much testimony was given about what Jonathan Jackson did on August 6th. The men at the service station testified that Angela Davis was there with him in the van on August 6th. Their identification, like the San Quentin guards', was made after Ms. Davis had been implicated through ownership of the guns. This episode was an almost classic example of the possible contribution of factors which can influence eyewitness identification as enumerated by Dr. Buckout: *Insignificance of event*—surely the young woman who accompanied the young man who was driving a Hertz van was not significant in the day's work at the station. Why should they remember her? *Conditioning, desire to follow the leader, desire to be part of history, conformity, personal bias, need for approval, filling in details and passing on a theory*—all these factors could be applied to the testimony of these men. This item needed more discussion, so leave it in for now.

15. The convict who testified that he saw Angela Davis with Jonathan Jackson in the yellow van on August 6th was a highly unreliable witness. His testimony was confused and his motives were highly suspect—throw it out!

16. Angela Davis took a plane to Los Angeles, leaving the San

Francisco airport at 2:20 p.m. on August 7th. Even if she rushed and had had no baggage and seemed to be in a great hurry, it certainly would not indicate guilt or consciousness of guilt. Her behavior wouldn't be unusual for a passenger on a commuter flight—throw it out.

I reviewed my list. All I had left was the purchase of the shotgun and the testimony relating to her presence at San Quentin and at the Mobil station. All right! These were the issues to be considered.

The next step was to consider these three issues in relation to the elements of conspiracy. I looked at my watch again—not much time! I could hear the traffic noises on the nearby freeway increasing in volume, and the local truck and car noises—I wasn't going to have time to write it all down, so I reviewed it in my mind.

The defense had talked about "links in the chain" of the charge of conspiracy which included: *Motive, object, agreement, knowledge, intent, flight.*

Judge Arnason, in his final instructions to the jury, had said that it was not necessary to prove *motive,* but that it could be considered as part of the whole conspiracy. He also had told us that *flight* by itself was an acceptable way of showing knowledge of guilt, but was not necessarily proof of knowledge of guilt.

The prosecution defined the *object* of the escape attempt as an effort to obtain the release of the Soledad Brothers—ridiculous! Why in the world would such an involved plan be used when the Soledad Brothers themselves were appearing in court frequently? If their release was the object of the crime, then why didn't Jonathan wait until they were in court and organize the escape at that time? Besides, it was incredible to think he would expect San Quentin to release prisoners, no matter who was held as hostage.

That left *agreement, knowledge* and *intent.*

These three parts of the crime had to be proven by the evidence of the visit to San Quentin, the purchase of the shotgun, and the identification of Angela Davis by the men at the service station.

I had finished my lists and progressed this far in my review, when a knock sounded on the door and a voice called out, "Breakfast at 7:30. You have an hour."

After showering and dressing, I joined the others as we met again in the room at the end of the row. Hot water and instant coffee were available, and I fixed a cup to tide me over till breakfast. The group was pretty subdued. Slowly the stories started to come out. Bob hadn't slept well; he had gotten up every hour or so and gone out onto the balcony and paced back and forth during the night.

Luis said that he had awakened about three o'clock and hadn't been able to go back to sleep. When Nick came into the room, he asked if anyone had any Alka-Seltzer. He had been up all night with an upset stomach. Others talked of hearing the sheriff's patrol every hour. One deputy had worn hard-soled shoes so his every step rang loud as he paced up and down the walk. Another kept bumping the metal railing as he walked, which sent vibrations through the rooms.

Breakfast was a disappointment. We were given juice, coffee and a sweet roll. That was fine for me, but some of the other jurors were used to big breakfasts and did some grumbling about it. I had a long complicated attempt at communication with our waiter who didn't speak English. The fruit juices that were available were all citrus juices, and I was allergic to them. I wanted a glass of apple juice or pineapple or grape juice. He didn't understand. He brought me orange juice. I sent it back. He brought me grapefruit juice. He brought me half a grapefruit. Finally he came in with some apple juice. We all cheered and he seemed very pleased that he and I had finally broken the communication gap.

Our first order of business when we got to the jury room to start our Saturday deliberations was to make a request that the breakfast furnished us be a little more substantial.

While Stef was composing the note to the judge about our breakfast complaint, and Ruth was getting the coffeepot going, I went to the blackboard and listed the sixteen items of evidence that I had gleaned from my notes which related to Angela Davis. Then alongside that list I put down the elements of the crime of conspiracy.

When we were ready to begin, I stood at the head of the table and explained what I had done and what the list was. I asked if anyone else's notes showed that I had omitted anything of importance, or that my chronology was wrong. No one offered any corrections.

"Today I would like to start the deliberations a little differently. First, I think we should aim for a secret ballot on one of the charges before noon. Secondly, I think we should consider the charge of Conspiracy first, since the other charges hang on that. Thirdly, I think that since we have had a night to think about the events of yesterday, it would be a good idea if we go around the table again and each make any kind of statement he or she wishes, before we consider the specific charge . . . and I want to start off."

I asked the others to look at the list I had written on the blackboard, and then I held up the long list of items that included the activities of Jonathan Jackson. I explained how I had been struck by the mass of evidence that related only to him, and that I felt it was confusing—that we had been led to think that Jonathan Jackson and Angela Davis were one and the same.

I said that I had serious doubts about the validity of some of the items (those based on eyewitness testimony) but, if I looked at the list and assumed Ms. Davis was guilty, the list appeared damning. However, if I assumed she was not directly involved in a conspiracy to effect an escape, but was in fact merely working through legal channels—if I assumed she was innocent—the list might cause suspicion but was certainly not evidence beyond all reasonable doubt.

"Even if I accept as truth every item on the list, I feel that it is possible that these could be acts of an innocent person."

There was no response. The faces turned toward me were blank.

I then suggested that we consider the charge of Conspiracy strictly on the merits of the prosecution's case and, for the time being, ignore the defense testimony and consider alibi witnesses only if we needed to do so later.

I said that while it might be really interesting to talk about this trial with all of them for a week or two, people down in the court were waiting for our decision and I, for one, wanted to get it decided as soon as possible.

I sat down. Scared to death! Had I moved too fast? Were the others going to resent my taking over? But the talk went around the table. The tenor of the statements seemed supportive, but apparently some areas still needed clarification. Everyone seemed to agree that the Conspiracy charge should be decided first. Even Jim didn't object.

So we started with *motive*. I didn't join in the discussions myself to any extent. I didn't need to; the letters were there for us to read. One of the jurors reminded us that Judge Arnason had said that motive was not a necessary part of a conspiracy. After most of the jurors had had a chance to talk, a pause fell in the discussion. I suggested that we have a show of hands on this issue—not a formal vote, but just an indication as to whether we were going to need to discuss this issue any longer.

"Would everyone who feels that the prosecution did *not* prove beyond a reasonable doubt that the motive for the conspiracy was the love and passion of Angela Davis for George Jackson, please raise your hand?"

All twelve hands went up!

Without pausing for any further discussion on this point, I said, "Now let's consider *object*. Was the object of the escape attempt the release of the Soledad Brothers?"—and around the table we started again.

The chance seating that we had settled on at the first session of deliberation allowed Bob to speak first, followed by Winona, then three very strong jurors—Roz, Ruth and Ralph, then Nick

(Nick had raised his hand! He was with us on the first point.)—
and we ended with the final statement being made by Jim. This
order was very important since all wanted to know what Jim
felt about each issue—particularly after he had listened to all
the others. He was able to summarize and clarify what had been
said and add his own good comments.

We talked about the people who had heard the statement
"Free the Soledad Brothers by 12 o'clock," and about the people
who had not heard it. The evidence seemed to suggest that it
was said, but under what circumstances? Was it really part of
the conspiracy? Judge Arnason had said in his instructions to
the jury that "any statement made by one of the conspirators
is not relevant unless it is part of the knowledge of the other
conspirators." So if one or more of them decided during the
escape attempt to include a demand for the release of the Soledad
Brothers, this demand would not be a part of the conspiracy
unless the other members knew and approved of it.

The discussion seemed to have covered the issue pretty well
when someone spoke up and said, "If the object of the escape
attempt was to free the Soledad Brothers, why hadn't the escape
been set for a day when they were in court?"

Right then I called for another hand vote.

"Would everyone who feels that the prosecution has not
proved beyond all reasonable doubt that the object of the conspiracy was to obtain the freedom of the Soledad Brothers, please
raise your hand?"

Again! All hands went up.

Bob leaned over to me. "Great, Mary, you are doing fine, keep
it up!"

"Let's discuss whether there has been proof of *agreement*—
agreement between Angela Davis and Jonathan Jackson, or anyone else."

Someone said, "Well, there was no note, no reported conversation . . . ." The only evidence of agreement was the purchase of
the shotgun and the use of the guns and books. But an alternate theory for the purchase of the shotgun had been presented.

If two theories were presented and each of them was possible, then we must lean toward the defendant.

Let's have another show of hands. "Would all of those who feel that the prosecution has not proved beyond all reasonable doubt that there was agreement between Angela Davis and Jonathan Jackson or others, please raise your hand?"

Twelve hands again!

Great! Great! Great! If no one felt that it had been proved that an agreement existed, then there was no conspiracy.

Bob whispered again, "Keep going, Mary! You've got them going now!"

Knowledge was the next item on the list. The pattern of discussing in turn around the table was starting to fall apart. We were all getting excited. "Harris said that if Angela Davis had been in the van on August 6th, that meant that she must have had knowledge of what was going on . . . Well, we don't know that she was really in the van, do we? . . . Could she have just gone along for the ride? . . . There were no fingerprints on the van. . . . What about the testimony of the men at the service station; did you believe them?"

We had said all the things about eyewitness testimony yesterday. They were repeated again now. When I called for the vote on *knowledge* the hands went up more slowly. There were still twelve, but some had hesitated.

I moved quickly to *intent.* Too quickly. The others weren't ready to go that far yet. Winona said, "Wait a minute! What are we voting on—just the prosecution's case? Are we considering the defense? Are we accepting all the prosecution's testimony as true? What are we voting on?"

I answered that we were voting on just what I had said each time and quoted the last statement made—and, yes, we were essentially considering and discussing the prosecution's case since it was up to the prosecution to prove each point beyond all reasonable doubt.

Then I lost the group. Each one wanted to express his or her own ideas by talking back and forth to each other, not by going formally around the table. We had split again into individuals.

I sat back to listen. The discussions swirled around me. I was out of breath. I didn't think anything could possibly go wrong now. People had committed themselves; all that was necessary was to prevent a conflict from starting. I looked at my watch. It was almost 11:30. We had been working at high tension for two solid hours without a break.

Ruth was talking. I had no idea what she was saying. I leaned over to Jim and whispered, "Jim, as soon as she finishes, would you call for a formal vote?" He nodded, his eyes shining.

But before Ruth finished her final sentence, Nick had his hand up and as she stopped speaking, he said, "I want to call for a formal secret vote on the charge of conspiracy."

No one objected, so out came the coffee can and the slips of paper. Then suddenly we became cautious again. How should we vote— "Guilty"/"Not Guilty?" What if someone was still uncertain? Should that person just not vote?

No, we would make three choices: "Guilty," "Not Guilty," and "Undecided."

The slips were dropped into the coffee can.

Winona pulled them out and read them loud. Roz tallied: "Not Guilty," "Not Guilty," "Not Guilty," "Undecided," "Not Guilty," "Not . . . ."

GUILTY	NOT GUILTY	UNDECIDED
	⦊⦊⦊⦊⦊ ⦊⦊⦊⦊	⦊⦊⦊

"Guilty"=0, "Not Guilty"=9, "Undecided"=3. Not one juror had voted "Guilty"!

No juror thought that Angela Davis was guilty! As that realization sank in, I looked around the table. I found no expression of great emotion, but a kind of restrained joyous excitement was starting to grow. We were all just sitting there glancing back and forth at each other. We were afraid to look too closely at each other. We didn't know who the three were who were still undecided. We didn't want to isolate them now. We had come so far, and we were still friends. I didn't want to know who they were.

It was almost noon. We had done enough for this morning. Jurors started getting up from their chairs and moving around the room. Nick sat there quietly. He had called for the vote, so he was not one of the undecided. He must have voted "Not Guilty." I turned to Jim. He too had been willing to call for a vote, so he was not one of the undecided. He was smiling. We reached to each other simultaneously and clasped hands. Bob was standing behind me patting my shoulder and murmuring, "Good. Good, Mary."

We started chatting about lunch. Since breakfast had been so scant, we were hungry. We stretched and went over and looked out the windows at the area between the buildings. No one was there; but the bus—the rickety, rattling sheriff's bus—was waiting for us.

Back at the motel, I walked up the stairs with Luis. "It looks good, Luis," I said. I didn't know if he was one of the undecided voters, but we had been friends since we met on the first day.

Luis answered, "Mary, I want to say something to you. I want to say . . . as long as we have women like you, our country is going to be OK." We walked a few steps farther. I didn't know how to answer, except to say, "Thank you."

He went on, "Sometimes, I want to say something to someone—a beautiful woman—I want to tell her that she is beautiful—but I don't say anything, and I am always sorry. So I decided I would say this to you."

"Thank you, Luis. I am so happy we were both picked to be on the jury." We laughed.

Conversation at lunch was general and totally unrelated to the deliberations. We talked about food, restaurants we had eaten at, and vacations we were planning. The date was June 3rd; summer was here and it looked like it was going to be a nice one.

The young deputy at the head of the table called down to the matron at the other end, "Come on up here, Ginny, and serve the coffee." It wasn't a command; he was just being sociable.

We had had long conversations with Ginny about the working conditions for women in the law-enforcement field. She was a very independent young woman who was working toward the goal of getting equal training and advancement for the matrons.

So when the deputy implied that pouring coffee was a woman's job, we call called out, "Don't you do it, Ginny!," then turned on him, asking for an explanation. The poor young man hadn't realized what a hornet's nest he was opening and he started to blush and stammer his apologies. We were sorry we had said anything and Ginny said, "Let's not quarrel—you pour coffee at that end of the table and I will take care of this end," and she reached for a pitcher.

It was announced during lunch that arrangements would be made for attendance at any church any of us might desire to attend on Sunday. No deliberations were scheduled on Sunday, and some suitable entertainment would be provided for us— possibly a picnic at one of the lovely parks in the county.

We looked at each other. Roz spoke up, "Why Sunday? Sunday isn't my day of worship. Are they discriminating against the Jews on this jury?"

We started to laugh, then realized she was serious and was making a very good point. Why had it been assumed that Sunday would be the day we would want off? They should have consulted us.

I asked if anyone wanted to attend church the following day. No one did. Then someone suggested that we continue deliberations rather than take the day off. The idea of having a picnic while the responsibility for a decision hung over us seemed ridiculous. We decided to ask Judge Arnason if we could continue deliberations on Sunday—if we weren't through by then.

We were beginning to realize that we, the jury, were in a pretty powerful position. Everyone was waiting for our decision. All these weeks we had been doing the waiting while the court waded through the ponderous legal maneuverings—now it was our turn to make demands.

Nick was standing on the balcony when I came out of my room after lunch. I walked up to him and touched his arm, "That was perfect timing, Nick. You called for a vote right at the ideal moment. It was great!"

Nick reached out and hugged me. "Oh thanks, Mary . . . you know, I'm really a warm friendly guy . . . but I've been so scared . . . ." We stood there hugging each other for a few moments.

No wonder he had been vomiting all last night. He must have thought he was all alone in believing that Angela Davis was not guilty.

Ruth came up to us and joined in all the smiling. She reminded me that it wasn't over, that we must be careful not to upset the three who had voted "undecided." She suggested that perhaps we should use the original technique of writing out questions, so those three would not have to identify themselves. Nick agreed and as they moved away Ruth said, "Don't push too hard, Mary. We don't have to rush through this."

She was right. I had to slow down. We didn't want to lose the ground we had gained.

Saturday afternoon's deliberations started with my making the suggestion that since we didn't want to try to find out how people had voted, perhaps we should try again to write out some questions and put them into the coffee can, if everyone agreed?

Michelle spoke up, "Wait a minute. I don't mind you all knowing that I was one of those who voted 'Undecided' and I really don't have any question that I want to discuss. What I want to do—and I don't know if it is possible—is to go off by myself for a few minutes and do some thinking, quietly. Would that be OK?"

Ralph and Jim both turned to her and said, "Sure, that's OK."

Of course that would be all right. So Michelle picked up her notes and went off into the large room and sat in one of the easy chairs, quietly, by herself.

Then Stef said, "I'm another one and I'd like to take the love letters off and read them quietly by myself. I understand things better if I read them myself, rather than having them read to me." We gathered up the letters and she too went off into the adjoining room.

Winona stood up and said that she too would like to be by herself for a while in order to resolve her thinking—so off she went.

Those three were the undecided jurors. The rest of us started talking softly to each other. We were together. Now we were willing to open up and really express our feelings. Our conversation got a little louder and louder. I could see from where I sat that we were disturbing the three in the other room. So we sat quietly for a few more minutes and then started talking and laughing again.

This method wasn't going to work. Ralph said, "Let's play cards!" This game had worked for the past two months whenever we were tempted to talk too much. So out came the cards and the coins.

We had been playing about fifteen or twenty minutes when Michelle came up to the table and said quietly, "I'm ready to vote again, now."

We kept on playing and she watched. Another five minutes and Stef returned; then shortly after, Winona. We moved back to the table in our usual places. I asked if they wanted any further discussion. All three said, "No," so we took our second secret ballot: "Not Guilty," "Not Guilty," "Not Guilty," "*Guilty*," "Not . . . ."

GUILTY	NOT GUILTY	UNDECIDED
/	𝐼𝐻𝑇	
	𝐼𝐻𝑇	
	/.	

What had happened? What had I done wrong? Whose vote was it? Was this going to be a hung jury?

Before the enormity of it had sunk in, Winona spoke up. "I am the one who voted guilty. I want you all to stop and listen to me. I came in here thinking one thing and there has been so much said, now I don't know what to think. There are things that I want to say and I feel that I have been pressured terribly. I voted 'Guilty' to make you stop and listen to me!"

We stopped! Boy, did we stop! No one said a word.

Then Ruth took over. She agreed with Winona and said that we had been rushing but that we had plenty of time—"What was it you wanted to say, Winona?"

For a moment or two I sat there stunned as Winona started to speak. Then I decided that the best thing I could do was to keep my ideas to myself and not interrupt her, no matter what! I sat back quietly and Ruth took charge. We all deferred to her; she handled the situation.

The points that Winona brought up were the same ones we had been discussing since Friday morning. Winona, the retired librarian, was used to listening to others and responding to their ideas and requests. She was used to working in a calm, quiet environment. She seemed to want to work through the evidence in an orderly manner, reaching a firm conclusion on one item before moving on to the next. The introduction of a new idea, even if it were supportive, distracted her and disturbed the orderly progression of her thinking as she attempted to resolve her doubts.

She went on and on, reviewing her notes. The afternoon was wearing on. I looked at my watch. It was after 3:00. I would have liked to get the deliberations over with this afternoon.

During a short break from the discussion, I asked some of the others if they didn't think we would be able to finish the whole thing this afternoon? They agreed that once Winona got all her notes straight, it was likely that we could finish very rapidly. The murder and kidnap charges hung on the conspiracy charge. So once we were through that charge, we should be able to wrap it up quickly.

I wanted to send a message to Judge Arnason, letting him know how the deliberations were progressing and asking him if he would refrain from dismissing us this afternoon until we let him know we were ready to stop for the day. I hoped that we could finish the whole thing. Unfortunately, we had two problems. We didn't want the world press or the attorneys or spectators to know how the deliberations were progressing. We didn't know if there was any way we could communicate privately with the judge.

Also we didn't want Winona to feel that anyone was pressuring her to come to a decision before she was ready—and, if we made any kind of an estimate as to when we might finish, she could take that as a form of pressure.

So I sent down a very ambiguous note to Judge Arnason asking just what we were allowed to communicate to him. I planned to follow this note with a request that he not inform the press, but we thought we might be able to finish today if we were allowed to continue working.

His answer finally came back saying that we could direct any kind of message to him. By the time we received it, the rest of the jurors decided they didn't want anyone else, including Judge Arnason, in on what we were doing. So his answer was ignored. (I learned later that he had waited anxiously in his chambers for the next communication—which didn't come.)

Winona was reaching the end of her list. She asked, "If Diane Robinson—whose name was on the registration sheets at San Quentin on August 4th and 5th—if Diane Robinson were really Angela Davis, would that mean she was guilty?"

I said, "Let's go around the table, again. Roz?"

By the time Roz, Ruth, Ralph and Nick each said that they did not feel that that one thing would be enough to change their verdict—there were too many other areas of doubt—Winona was ready to vote again.

This time the vote was:

GUILTY   NOT GUILTY   UNDECIDED

             ~~LHT~~
             ~~LHT~~
             / /

I said, "Great! Now let's move right along to the charges of kidnapping and murder!"

I had moved too fast again. Winona grabbed her notes and said, "Oh, my. Do we have to?"

She wasn't ready to take the next step. She hadn't thought it through yet—that if Angela Davis was not guilty of conspiring, then she was not guilty of the other two counts.

Again Ruth came to the rescue. "Of course we don't. We have worked hard today. Why don't we break for the day and start in again in the morning?"

It was agreed. We got up from the table and stretched. Damn! I had wanted to finish and go home. Another night in the motel; another dinner, another breakfast . . . I didn't look forward to that.

I was even more concerned about Judge Arnason, all the attorneys, Angela Davis, all her supporters—but most of all, her family. They were all going to have to spend another twenty hours not knowing that we were going to find her innocent of all charges. God, I hated to do that.

Until that Saturday afternoon, I had not allowed myself to think about Angela Davis as a member of a family. In the early days of the trial I was aware that her family was not in the spectator section. But perhaps they were going to be witnesses for the defense and therefore were kept out of the courtroom during the testimony of other witnesses. Or perhaps they did not support her! I didn't know. In the last few days of the trial, however, there were people in the spectator section that we jurors guessed were members of her family.

I had been afraid it might be impossible for me to remain objective if I allowed myself to think about all the effects on other people the verdict might have. So I blocked it out of my mind.

That night after dinner, when we congregated in the meeting room at the end of the balcony, the realization hit us that it was all over but the formalities. We were sharing this fantastic secret! We were the only people in the world that knew that we had acquitted Angela Davis on the charge of conspiracy to commit the crimes of kidnapping and murder!

We would look at each other and break out into uproarious laughter—for no reason. We never mentioned any of the unpleasant things that had been brought out in the trial. We only remembered the funny happenings . . . how T. V. Hughes yelled out, "Free all political prisoners! Free our brothers in Folsom!" . . . the look on Harris' face when Jamala stood up in the courtroom *a la Perry Mason*! . . . the time that Leo Branton, when explaining to Judge Arnason that he wouldn't need much time to present his witnesses one afternoon, said that he had " . . . three short witnesses—well, I don't mean that the witnesses are physically short people, just that they won't be on the stand for long questioning!" and started laughing at his own horrible pun . . . how serious the officer was when he testified that he had aimed his revolver with a two-inch barrel at the window of the van which was two or three hundred feet away!

We had a grand party that night. We played silly card games and laughed and screamed and stamped our feet and pounded on the table when we won or lost. Nick joined the card players for the first time and tonight helped teach us some of the intricacies of the games.

We all tried to teach Jim how to shuffle the cards without fumbling and dropping the deck on the table. Each time it was his turn to deal, we cheered and applauded as he finally managed to get the cards properly shuffled.

When Captain Johnson came to send us to bed at ten o'clock, we persuaded him to let us stay up until eleven—after all, it was Saturday night.

Sunday! Sunday!

What a lovely day it was! Warm, sunny, a soft little morning breeze—the whole day glowed.

I went down to the motel meeting room early and watched the faces of each of the jurors as they came in for coffee. They all looked refreshed and rested. They were all still smiling. Nick said he felt fine—he didn't need any Alka-Seltzer this morning. Winona had set her hair and had on a bright summer print dress and white shoes. Her headache was gone.

When we got back to our rooms after breakfast, I packed my bag and set it by the door. I was going to be ready to leave the minute we were dismissed. Then I stepped out onto the balcony into the warm sun. I leaned on the rail and looked around. Cars and visitors filled the parking lot below. I looked out across the weedy field beyond the parking lot. I suddenly felt I had been there before—as though this whole scene was very familiar. Then I remembered. It was from the pictures that I had seen in the papers and magazines after April 4, 1968—the assassination of Martin Luther King, Jr. He had stood on just such a motel balcony talking to friends.

All the joy that I had been feeling disappeared and I was overcome by a sense of desolation. It was an extension of the sorrow I had felt in response to Leo Branton's closing statement when he asked us jurors to " . . . become black for a little while."

It seemed there would be no end to fear and hate.

The only change in our procedure for deliberating this morning was that I announced that we would have no smoking in the small anteroom and if anyone wanted to smoke, he or she would have to let me know and I would call a ten-minute break. (I wasn't going to take a chance on Winona getting a headache again.)

I opened it up for discussion on the charge of kidnapping. There was no response.

"Is everyone ready to vote?"

We voted—12-0, "Not Guilty."

I asked if anyone wanted to talk about the charge of murder. Did everyone understand the felony murder doctrine? They all understood, no one wanted to bother talking about it. They just wanted to vote!

The vote was 12-0, "Not Guilty."

It was over.

"Is everyone satisfied? This is our last chance to change our minds. Do any of you want to say anything before I sign the verdict?"

"No! Go ahead and sign it, Mary!"

I asked Jim to look over my shoulder and make sure I signed the correct sheets. We had been given a sheaf of forms for each of the three counts. For murder there was: "Not Guilty," "Guilty of Murder in the Second Degree," "Voluntary Manslaughter," and "Involuntary Manslaughter." The degrees of kidnapping were each on a separate page, and conspiracy, too: "Not Guilty" and "Guilty."

The foreman was to sign the appropriate sheet for each charge. The sheets for each charge were stapled together. The top sheet was always "Not Guilty." That was good; no attempt was made to subtly influence the jury's thinking by putting the "Guilty" sheet on the top.

At the bottom of each sheet was a line:

_____ _____
Foreman   Date

Stef asked me if I was going to change the word "Foreman" to "Fore-Ms."

"No way! This is too important to fool around with. I want this to be absolutely, perfectly legal." I wasn't about to take a chance.

I signed the appropriate sheets. Jim checked them. We sent our last note to Judge Arnason:

> **The jury has reached a verdict on all counts and is ready to report to the Court.**
>
> **Mary M. Timothy**
> **Fore-Ms.**

Jim said that he wanted to say something before we broke. "I want to make just one point. We are going to be asked a lot of questions by a lot of people, the press included, and I think we should be pretty careful just what we say. At least one more trial is coming up, Ruchell Magee's, and we don't want to do or say anything which would jeopardize his chances of getting a fair trial."

We all agreed—but we didn't know what would be OK to say, or what would be bad. What should we do? We decided that when in doubt, say nothing—at least until we had a chance to sort out our thoughts and decide what we could safely say.

The message had gone down. Nothing remained to be done. We waited.

I went over and looked out the window down at the security area between our building and the entrance to the court. No one was in sight. The concrete shimmered in the glaring sun. Captain Johnson, whom we had seen earlier in casual civies, reappeared in full dress uniform.

Then the deputies began entering the area from here and there, hurrying to their assigned duties. It began to look as though every deputy in the county would be on hand. The "security" was going to be complete.

The wife of Leo Branton was the first to arrive in the security area. She stood in the hot sun waiting quietly, patiently, for the officers to get their metal detectors and cameras and fingerprinting materials ready. Finally a deputy brought a chair to her, and she sat waiting—still in the sun. She was there a long time.

I left the window and went on back through the large room to the restroom. I wanted to make sure my hair was combed before we were called down to court.

Michelle was in the restroom crying softly. I asked her what was the matter. She said, between sobs, "I feel so sorry for Mr. Harris. He tried so hard, and now he has lost."

Most of the jurors felt somewhat as she did about the prosecutor. Mr. Harris had done a very professional job and there was no personal antagonism toward him at all. We talked about writing him a letter expressing our thanks for the manner in which he had conducted the trial, but we were afraid it might be misinterpreted. We were afraid he might resent it or suspect the sincerity of our thanks. So we decided against writing the letter.

By the time I looked out the window again, the deputies were letting the spectators enter the security area in groups of two or three. Most of them were dressed very casually in jeans, coveralls, overalls, tee shirts—no ties and suits or dresses. They were acting excited, eager—not fearful.

It took two hours for the court personnel to assemble, for the security clearance mechanism to be set up, and for everyone who was allowed into the area to be screened. For two hours we jurors waited.

At 12:30 we lined up—for the last time—and with Winona in the lead we filed down the stairs, across the open concrete area, through the temporary security building, into the corridor of the court, through the double doors, down the center aisle and into the jury box.

We didn't look at anyone. We didn't smile or frown. We were a stony-faced group of twelve. We hadn't made any agreement beforehand—it was just that we were overwhelmed with the solemnity of the occasion. And besides, if any of us had given any kind of sign as to which way the verdict went, we knew that it would be front page news. Having the world's press looking at your every move puts a damper on your exuberance.

I had folded the sheets of paper lengthwise so there would be no possibility that anyone would catch a glimpse of the signature on the front sheet and guess the verdict. I sat in my chair (Juror Number 7) with the folded sheets in my right hand. Never having been on a jury or having attended a trial, I had no idea what would happen.

Judge Arnason came swooping into the room from the door behind his bench. He looked around the room, made his formal opening statements, then turned to the jury, smiled at us and said, "From the communications that I have received, I assume that you have selected your foreman, or forewoman, or foreperson—however you wish to be called—and that is you, Mrs. Timothy?"

"Yes, Your Honor!"

"Has the jury reached a verdict?"

"Yes, Your Honor!"

"On all three counts?"

"Yes, Your Honor!"

"Will you hand the verdicts to the bailiff, please."

"Yes, Your Honor."

The bailiff came down from his chair to the left and a little below Judge Arnason, walked across the court and took the sheets of paper, still folded. I leaned back in my chair and took a deep breath. I looked down at my right hand resting on the arm of the chair. It was clenched in a tight fist—with the thumb pointing straight up—the old Roman gesture of acquittal!

Embarrassed, I glanced around the room. No one was looking at me. Every eye in the courtroom was on the sheaf of papers in the bailiff's hand. He walked back and handed them to the judge.

Judge Arnason laid the verdicts on his table, out of sight of everyone, removed the staples, shuffled through the stack of papers, looked at each sheet carefully, shuffled them back and forth again, picked out three sheets and handed them over the top of his table to Mr. Vanick, the clerk of the court.

The expression on Judge Arnason's face had not changed. He had moved those verdicts around and in and out and over and under so deftly, no one could possibly have known in which order he selected the actual signed verdicts.

Now it was Mr. Vanick's turn to play his role. He started with the first count, the charge of Kidnapping. He read through the whole long page of legalese—and finally read the words, "NOT GUILTY."

A wrenching, tearing moan rose from the spectators section. There were sounds of soft sobbing. I looked over at the defense group. The women—Ms. Davis, her companion and her counsel —were seated in the row of chairs along the railing which separated the spectators from the court. They were holding each other.

Howard Moore sat alone at the side table hunched over, his hands in his lap—staring at the clerk.

Leo Branton was in his usual position, half-turned away from the center of the court, right arm on the table. He was perfectly still, his face blank, staring off into space—waiting.

Mr. Vanick read the second count—Murder. The same long reading and the same final words: "NOT GUILTY."

When he started on the third page—the count of Conspiracy —the room again became still. This was the big one! Everything hung on this count! Mr. Vanick read slowly, carefully—he didn't skip a word. He had the attention of the entire court. " . . . We the jury find the defendant Angela Y. Davis NOT GUILTY. Signed, Mary M. Timothy, Foreman, June 4, 1972."

Screams, cries, sobs—of joy! I could hear Angela Davis' deep sobs. Leo Branton jumped to his feet, turned to the spectators and led them in applause—applause for the verdict.

Judge Arnason made no move for a few seconds. No one could have stopped the spontaneous expression of relief by the family and friends of the defendant, or her own deep rasping breaths.

Then he rapped his gavel sharply and said something to the effect that he would not allow demonstrations in his court. He sounded stern, and perhaps he would have cleared the courtroom of spectators. He didn't need to—no one wanted to do anything that would spoil the ending of the trial.

Judge Arnason wanted to wrap it up neatly—and he did. He turned to the jury and thanked us and quoted from G. K. Chesterton:

> Our civilization has decided, and very justly decided,
> that determining the guilt or innocence of men is a thing
> too important to be trusted to trained men.
> If it wishes for light upon that awful matter, it asks
> men who know no more law than I know, but who can
> feel the things I felt in a jury box. When it wants a library
> catalogued or the solar system discovered, or any trifle
> of that kind, it uses its specialists. But when it wishes any-
> thing done that is really serious, it collects twelve of the
> ordinary men standing about. The same thing was done,
> if I remember right, by the founder of Christianity.

He then thanked the attorneys for their conduct during the trial. He called them "barristers" and said that they could all walk down the streets of society with their heads held a little higher.

Mr. Branton answered for the attorneys. He rose and said to Judge Arnason, "The law has made us equal. Man has not. But the manner in which Your Honor has conducted this trial, and the verdict of this jury, go a long way towards man's giving us the equality which the law has decreed."

Judge Arnason said that court would be dismissed, and that when he left, Ms. Davis was free, her bail would be returned to her—and the jurors were free to do as they wished.

He rose and left the court. Then the applause and shouting started, at first spontaneous and ragged—and then with rhythmic clapping and stamping and:

"POWER TO THE PEOPLE!

"POWER TO THE PEOPLE!

"POWER TO THE PEOPLE! . . ."

Howard Moore jumped to his feet, raised both fists and shouted:

"POWER TO THE JURY!

"POWER TO THE JURY!"

The crowd picked it up and the chant became a roar!

Epilogue to the Trial

We sat in the jury box and listened. I wanted to get up and walk over to the defense table and join in their happiness. We weren't allowed to do that, despite Judge Arnason's statement that we were free. As long as the sheriff was in charge, we were not going to be free.

The deputies came toward us, signalling that we were to leave the room. They stationed themselves between us and the people in the court. The spectators, too, were well trained. They remained seated as we filed past with the roar of the clapping, stomping, shouting "POWER TO THE JURY!" ringing in the small room.

We were escorted back up to the jury assembly room and left alone. Michelle was crying; I had put my arm around her as we went up the stairs. Bob came over to us and said, "I want to be the first to kiss our forelady!"

Then we all started hugging and kissing and crying.

Mr. Vanick came into the room and said that the press wanted to interview us—me primarily—but any of the jurors who were willing to come. We decided that we would present a united front—we would all go down to the interview together.

As we emerged from the building, I heard someone call, "Mary! Mary!"

I turned and saw my husband at the gate of the security fence. He had heard the verdict on the radio and had come immediately to the Civic Center. We kissed through the fence (still being controlled by the police) and I hurried to rejoin the others as they filed into a basement hall which had been converted into a press room. It was jammed with people.

We were escorted to the front of the room where a table crowded with microphones and tape recorders was set. I sat in one of the two chairs and, after a momentary confusion, Stef, the jury secretary, sat in the other. The rest of the jurors stood behind us.

We faced a mass of reporters with their pads and pencils, and the battery of TV cameras. After I made the statement that we would have to be very careful about the questions we would answer since another trial was coming up and we would not want to do anything that would jeopardize another's chance for a fair trial, the questions were all very straightforward—with one exception.

"When did you first learn of the highjack?"

"What highjack?" I had no idea what he was talking about. I turned around to the other jurors. They were as confused as I. Obviously from our blank looks none of us knew anything about a highjack.

The reporter explained that while we were deliberating a demand had been reported for Angela Davis' release in connection with a plane highjack.

The reporter who asked us that question was apparently using that means to find out if we really had been isolated from the news. We had!

While we were answering questions, I saw Ms. Davis and her family and attorneys enter the back of the room. We beamed at each other across the heads of the reporters. It didn't take long for the newspeople to finish with us when they realized that Angela Davis was in the room.

As we jurors filed out, Ms. Davis moved over to intercept us and opened her arms to each of us. We exchanged hugs and kisses. It was a beautiful way of saying thank you and allowing us to share her joy.

Out in the security area again, a young woman hurried up to me, pressed a scrap of paper into my hand and said, "You're invited to a family-and-friends' picnic in the back yard at that address. Angela will be there and the attorneys—please come!"

I asked if the other jurors were included (they were) and could I have a phone number, because I didn't know if it would be proper for us to come? (Of course, and there would be a big public celebration tonight.) I'll let you know . . . .

While we were talking, Wes Bolling, the only black deputy around the courthouse, came rushing over to protect me—to protect me from what?

I put my hand on his arm and said, "Relax, Wes, it's all over —we're all friends."

He was too well disciplined to do more than grin and move away a step or two, still watching carefully.

After the last round trip to the motel to collect our gear, we members of the jury split, going off with our families or friends —most of us heading for the celebration picnic.

We found the house and parked the car. We were greeted in the driveway by a large, exuberant young man, Franklin Alexander. He stood there and opened his arms wide and said, "You must have questions! Ask us anything—anything in the world. We will tell you anything you want to know."

We walked through a large modern open house, cool and quiet after the sun of the streets, on through the kitchen—whose table was covered with drinks and mixers—into a patio behind the house.

A large fenced yard with trees and shrubs was filled with people of all shades of black and brown and white, and with conga drums and laughter and shrieks of joy. We found food and drink, music and dancing.

Most of the jurors showed up for the private party and celebration. No reporters had been invited, so we all were free to talk to each other without the restraint engendered by public scrutiny.

I was kissed and hugged by everyone I met. It was embarrassing; I didn't know how to handle it—I didn't know how to respond to that kind of gratitude. It didn't make any difference that I had no way of answering. One woman finally told me that she knew how I felt, but she had to thank somebody and it might as well be me.

I learned a lot that afternoon. I am normally not a very demonstrative person. I seldom touch close friends, let alone strangers. But that afternoon I learned I could respond openly to unfeigned expressions of warmth and love.

One of the questions I wanted to ask was, "How did the jury selection work?" How did *I* end up on that jury? I had been sure that the prosecutor would challenge me, simply because I was the wife of an attorney and the mother of a conscientious objector. What had happened?

I was talking to members of the defense committee. They all started to laugh. "You should have seen the faces on that jury when Angela accepted you. You all looked so amazed! As though you couldn't believe it!"

"Well, it was a shock. I was sure I would be home early that day."

Howard Moore, Jr., had joined the group as I was talking. "You're right," he said. "We had to accept the jury as it stood, because if we had challenged Jim or the woman who left for personal reasons early in the trial, we would have lost you or one of the other jurors that we had decided we really wanted. We couldn't take that chance. We were sure some of those we picked would be fair and honest jurors and we hoped that all of them would."

Of course my next question was, "Why did you think you wanted me on the jury? You didn't ask me any searching questions. I was waiting for you to ask me if I had any black friends, or lived in an integrated neighborhood. Why did you think I would be a fair and honest juror?"

"There were a lot of reasons, but the most important one was —you liked your children!" Kendra Alexander made that statement, and Angela Davis nodded in agreement.

"Yes, that really came through when Howard was questioning you."

Their saying that that was an important reason for their wanting me on the jury was very reassuring to me. It meant that they were looking for a person who would not automatically condemn someone whose lifestyle differed from her own, who would be able to listen to and accept reasons for behavior that did not fit established patterns.

"What was all this about a plane highjacking? The reporter asked us when we had heard about it and I haven't heard about it yet. What is that all about?"

One of the others started to say that, while we were deliberating, a plane enroute from Seattle to San Francisco was highjacked and was supposed to be coming into the airport. Among other things a demand was made for the "release of Angela Davis!"

Then, "Angela, you tell Ms. Timothy about it; you were there."

The story that Angela Davis told me that afternoon was that she was eating dinner at a restaurant just a few blocks from the courthouse when she received a phone call from Judge Arnason. He asked her if anyone was with her. She answered, "Yes. My brother, Ben."

Judge Arnason told her to stay with Ben, that he was sending his own car for her. She was not to leave with anyone else. And she was to bring Ben with her.

She did as Judge Arnason instructed and was brought back to the judge's chambers in the courthouse. It was jammed with FBI men. She, of course, didn't know what was going on. Finally they told her that a highjacking had occurred, with a demand for her release. Then suddenly the door opened and in came a couple more FBI agents.

They announced that the demand was now more specific: $500,000 and Angela Davis were to be waiting at the end of Runway 7—and Angela Davis was to be wearing a white dress.

"When he said that, all I could think was—my mother went shopping yesterday. I wonder if she bought a white dress. If she happened by chance to have bought a white dress, then this whole horrible nightmare could start all over again!"

When she started telling the story, she was laughing and happy. When she reached the incident of the white dress, her eyes were focused on some distant point past my shoulder—and they were full of fear and horror.

Power to the Jury:
A Bill of Rights for Jurors

The jury—a collection of twelve human beings or the concept of the fulcrum of justice—is not fragile. But it is susceptible to manipulation and coercion by powers and circumstances.

Some undermining of the power of the jury is the result of self-protective measures by the prosecutors, defenders and judges as they strive to improve and perpetuate their order; some results merely from changing circumstances as the population and economy of an area shift. Undermining may be done knowingly and unknowingly. But whatever the source or intention, the possibility and actuality of obstruction must inevitably affect justice.

Why has the situation remained unvoiced and unchanged?

The jury system has no vested interest defenders. Because of the transitory role of jurors, they have not become a socio-economic group, have not expressed their needs, have not delineated or exercised their rights.

The jury system has no experts. Only someone who has served on a jury can fully appreciate the problems involved and the very nature of the selection process precludes anyone from serving frequently enough to become aware of the extent of these problems.

The judiciary—the lawyers, judges, court officials—look on jurors as tools to facilitate the purposes of the court (that is, themselves).

Alienated members of our society equate the jury system with the rest of the judicial system, in which they place little trust.

The general citizenry seldom anticipates any personal need for protection by the jury system since they feel no threat of ever being falsely accused of a crime; therefore they consider jury duty an unpleasant obligation, an interruption of their daily lives, something to be avoided.

Yet we who have served on juries have found our service to be an experience which often makes us become strong defenders of this system of jurisprudence which allows a citizen to sit in judgment.

From our unique perspective, we also become its greatest critics, aware that the rights of all jurors can be reduced to a single simple right and need—*the right to insist on an atmosphere in which a person can make a reasoned judgment.* I have the following suggestions which could strengthen the jury system.

1. *Jurors have a right to adequate financial remuneration.* Five dollars a day is totally unrealistic. It is nothing but token payment, and as a token it is insulting.

The self-employed, the nonunion worker, the part-time employee cannot afford to serve on the jury.

A feasible way of making jury service more equitable would be to use a form of "jury insurance" comparable to unemployment or state disability insurance—compulsory for those regularly employed, optional for the self-employed. Such insurance cost would be minimal and both the employee and the employer would be protected from financial loss during jury service.

This plan would relieve the judicial district of the great expense involved in providing every juror with an equitable remuneration. Under such a plan, those not currently employed could be paid a standard amount based on the minimum daily wage of the community. By having to pay only the small percentage of veniremen who are not employed (6 to 10 percent), the district certainly should be able to raise the juror's wage to a realistic level.

2. *Jurors should be fully informed of the "rules of the game" before the trial commences.* We should be informed of our

rights to take notes, to ask questions, to insist on clarification of issues.

In the Davis trial none of us knew or were informed whether we would be allowed to take notes. Some of us tried it; nothing happened. We were not frowned on by the judge. He didn't send his bailiff over to the jury box to snatch the notebooks from our hands. So we decided that notetaking must be all right.

One of the Davis jurors asked for clarification on a bit of evidence. He merely raised his hand and asked, "I don't understand —is that the North Arch, or the South Arch?" (The Marin County Courthouse had two arches.) Judge Arnason abruptly announced that he would not receive questions directly from the jury. If we had any questions we were to write them on a piece of paper and hand it to the bailiff, who would then relay it to the judge, who would read the question to himself and make a decision as to whether or not to allow the question to be asked.

So . . . we decided not to bother with questions.

Jurors should have specific instruction as to what actions on our part could lead to dismissal from the jury or cause a mistrial. No doubt must remain in a juror's mind as to what the limits on personal behavior are.

In 1975, in a San Francisco federal court, the presiding judge expelled two women from the jury after a special agent of the Internal Revenue Service testified that he had been sitting next to them at lunch that day when they had "discussed" the case. One woman was quoted as having said that she felt sorry for one of the defense witnesses, " . . . he's seen better days." The other woman just nodded her head. For this exchange, which they admitted could have taken place, they were fined $25 for contempt of court and their names were ordered removed forever from the federal jury rolls.

True, jurors are routinely instructed that they should not discuss the case with anyone, not even with their fellow jurors until deliberations begin. But the phrase "discuss the case" means different things to different people. What it means to the court should be strictly defined to the jurors and the punishment for not strictly obeying the ruling should be delineated.

U.S. District Judge Luther Youngdahl, the same judge who expelled the two women, at the completion of that trial ordered the jury not to discuss the case with anyone. Apparently no one wishes to challenge such arbitrary rulings by judges in their dealings with jurors. Once the case is over no further interest remains in protecting the jurors' rights to freedom of speech. May a judge impose such restrictions on a jury? Such actions, if left unchallenged by disinterested attorneys and unorganized jurors, will erode the remaining rights of the jury member.

At the present time, the instructions received by jurors are frequently haphazard, varying from county to county and state to state, and are always presented to them by judges or jury commissioners. Jury handbooks, instruction manuals, even published reference books available to the public become a further means of projecting the judicial identity through the jury.

Therefore, a commission of former jurors should prepare a comprehensive handbook which would delineate the rights of the juror as well as their duties.

3. *Jurors have the right to make individual, independent judgments.* A sense of identification with the judge seems to be almost universal among jurors. Uncertain and accustomed to conforming, we accept what is told us by authorities and we are even grateful for the instruction. Suddenly made aware of our own inadequacies, our lack of knowledge and competence, we follow the judge's instructions closely; by reflecting his attitudes and reactions we become more secure in our new role.

For example, a juror has been quoted as saying, " . . . but the way the judge charged us, there was no choice" (*The Trial of Dr. Spock,* by Jessica Mitford, New York: Alfred A. Knopf, Inc., 1969).

Jurors have the duty to ignore any prejudicial statements, rulings or attitudes of the judge. Judges are seldom chosen from the minority peoples, they are seldom women, they are almost always firmly aligned with one of the two major political parties —and they are never young.

Even when a judge conducts a trial faultlessly, his influence on an unsophisticated juror may lead to perversion of the purposes of the jury system. The jury so influenced becomes an extension of the court rather than an extension of the community it represents.

An often-cited example of a jury acting as an extension of their community occurred in Seattle, Washington, in December, 1972. A group of anti-war activists were charged with attempting to halt a munitions train. They readily admitted that they had indeed made such an attempt. Despite this admission the jury acquitted them; even though they had broken the law, they were not guilty in the judgment of the jury.

No absolute set of rules fits all cases. Therefore the wording of the law is replete with phrases such as reasonable doubt, ordinary reasonable man, reasonable time . . . . "Reasonableness" is best defined by community standards, not by the value judgments of one man.

The right, in fact the duty, of the jury to interpret the law in light of the standards of our changing world is seldom if ever made clear to jurors. We are told over and over that we are serving on the jury merely to judge facts. In truth jurors are presented with a series of "facts" as evidence and then given the choice of many conclusions. Seldom is a clear-cut single answer to be drawn from the evidence. It is the value placed on the evidence that allows the jury to reach a decision. The value evolves from community standards and is best represented by a cross section of people with various experiences and knowledge.

4. *Jurors have the right to serve on juries which include people from varied socioeconomic groups.* The list of occupations which allow a person to be exempt from jury duty has grown over the years. For example, in Los Angeles County it includes tollgate keepers, people who work on boats, jail and prison workers, railroad workers, telephone and telegraph employees, policemen and firemen, members of the national guard, those serving in the armed forces, legislators, elected local officials and other government employees, teachers, ministers, druggists, hospital

officials, physicians, Christian Science practitioners and readers, monks and anyone who has already served on a jury within the year (from Howard James' "Crisis in the Courts," from *Hearings before the Subcommittee on Improvements in Judicial Machinery of the Senate Judiciary Committee*, 90th Congress, 1st Session).

Somewhere, sometime, someone has made the decision that these people are more valuable to society in their regular jobs than they would be serving on the jury.

By excusing those who qualify for these exemptions, by excusing those for whom it would be an economic hardship to serve, and all the women with small children who wish not to serve, and all those who have not registered to vote, the residual group from which the selection of jurors is made becomes very homogeneous. This arbitrary exclusion of various groups lessens the representation of the community.

5. *Jurors have a right to have members of minorities included on the jury.*

The common conception is that having minorities on juries is of interest only to a minority defendant. But it is critically important to members of the jury that their group be as heterogeneous as possible in order to add insight and awareness to the problems of judging another human being.

An all-white, middle-class, middle-income jury whose members are employed by the large industries in an area is placed in a difficult position when trying to deal with evidence relating to mores and behavior standards of many of those accused of crimes.

By using peremptory challenges, an attorney can easily eliminate members of any minority group. For example, if the area has as many as 25 percent black people on the list of veniremen, the chance that more than three black jurors would be drawn among the first twelve is slight. Even if four black people were picked, those four could be challenged peremptorily and replaced by a new group of four—only one of whom would be likely to be black. One more challenge and the jury is all white.

The civil rights of those called for jury duty must be protected. The selection process must be conducted in a manner comparable to the affirmative action programs in other areas of our lives during the past few years. Preferential selection of minorities to jury lists must be practiced until it becomes impossible for them to be prevented from serving.

6. *Jurors have a right not to be stereotyped.* Even as the defendant should not be judged because of her or his race, religion, dress, or the like, neither should the prospective juror be thus judged. Being eliminated from the jury by either the judge or one of the attorneys is insulting. One feels somehow demeaned when an individual who knows nothing about you decides that you cannot be a fair unprejudiced person.

For the one being questioned, to reveal one's individuality in court is most difficult. It is frightening to sit in a jury box, the center of attention, while you are being asked about your background, your beliefs, your ability to be fair; most people are concerned with making this public and recorded presentation of themselves as "normal" as possible. In many cases the questioning is done by the judge. No matter what your prejudices, when His Honor the Judge says, "Now M— 'X', you will be able to judge the defendant fairly, won't you?" the answer is most likely to be, "Yes, Your Honor!"

Questioning by the judge limits the attorneys' ability to discover subtle attitudes which could influence a juror's ability to judge fairly. Not being able to fully explore the juror's attitudes leads the attorney into the position of having to select the members by use of stereotypes: construction workers are for "law and order," young people are politically liberal, black people will never convict another black person, women make decisions based on emotions rather than logic . . . . An extended *voir dire* by the attorneys allows for full exploration of biases. Ideally, the defendant, the single person most sensitive to prejudice, should be allowed to participate in this segment of the trial.

7. *Jurors have a right to privacy.* The *voir dire,* the questioning of a juror, should be done privately. Only the basic questions of name, residence in county and citizenship should be asked in public. Neither the press, the public, nor even the other

jurors need to know anything beyond those details unless the information is voluntarily given.

All other questions should be asked in private conference with only the judge, the attorneys, the defendant and the court reporter present. The records should be sealed, not to be opened except by court order.

This method would produce a double advantage: the personal privacy of the individual would be protected and the prospective juror being questioned would feel more free to disclose any problems she or he might have.

In the Davis trial a man was questioned about a drunk driving arrest, a woman was questioned in great length about difficulties she and her husband had had with the police and I was asked about my son's having been a conscientious objector to the war. All these questions were asked of us in front of the rows of national, international and local press as well as the courtroom filled with spectators.

That such questions be asked was important but the answers need not have been public.

The juror is not on trial.

8. *Jurors have a right to be free from threats, both direct and implied.* The laws are explicit in protecting people from direct threats. Jury tampering is a serious offense. However, pressures can be exerted in many subtle ways.

When the police, with the concurrence of the judge, build eight-foot-high cyclone security fences, place armed guards at every entrance to the building, conduct body searches of everyone entering the area (even the jurors themselves), they are displaying the awesome power of law enforcement. While ostensibly done for the protection of the jurors, among others, such security measures create an atmosphere of fear and oppression the effect of which is impossible to measure.

When the defendant or defendants are brought into the courtroom handcuffed, shackled and chained to chairs bolted to the floor, the jury is being told that they should be tremendously afraid of that defendant. When a witness is chained to the witness stand and additional armed deputies are stationed around the courtroom, the jury is again being told they should be afraid. How then can a juror accept the testimony of this witness with the same objectivity as that of other witnesses?

A threat need not relate to physical violence; it can also relate to psychological influences. Thus the sequestering of juries throughout a trial is another example of an implied threat. In my opinion, this action is a very real and direct assault on the jury system. It quickly eliminates many people from the jury— those who will not allow themselves to be so manipulated. It makes a prisoner of the juror.

9. *Jurors have a right to be free from investigation.* In the Angela Davis trial, the panel of veniremen was investigated very thoroughly outside the court as well as during the extensive public *voir dire* questioning in court.

It was readily apparent that the prosecution had available all records of government agencies such as police, courts, Alcoholic Beverage Commission, welfare and relief agencies, and the like. The defense used volunteer investigators who checked the neighborhoods in which we lived, the attitudes of our neighbors and fellow employees toward us. Psychologists advised the attorneys. Even a handwriting expert was used to analyze our suitability to serve.

Similar investigations have been made in other recent trials. The people in the Harrisburg area were surveyed by a team of sociologists using sophisticated polling techniques who then drew up a profile of a "good defense juror" before the Berrigan trial. And for the John Mitchell-Maurice Stans trial a marketing-research analyst was hired to construct a jury profile.

In such cases the defendant has been successful in gaining either an acquittal or, as in the Berrigan case, a hung jury.

The government, losing so many of these politically important cases, will blame the juries rather than acknowledge the inadequacy of its own cases and so will be forced to expand the already formidable investigations of prospective jurors.

Historically, government agencies move slowly; therefore such investigations could not be done immediately before each trial after a jury has been selected, but would be done on all citizens included on the jury lists, so that the government would be properly prepared when any juror was chosen. Thus, an effort toward more sophisticated jury selection would mean that dossiers would be compiled on all citizens and kept up to date.

The jury system, devised as a fortification of democracy, would lead us to a police state!

In addition to the obvious and awful consequences, such erosions of our jury system and encroachments of our liberties would result in the jury becoming merely an extension of the court, instead of a citizen jury that can stand between the accused and the accuser.

Our implementation of justice is on trial now, and we are the jurors—those who have served in the jury boxes and in the jails, those yet to be called and yet to be accused, those who never expect to become involved. Deliberation is needed. We must bring in a verdict.

Power to the jury.